EDUARD HANSLICK'S *ON THE MUSICALLY BEAUTIFUL*

EDUARD HANSLICK'S
ON THE MUSICALLY BEAUTIFUL

A New Translation

Lee Rothfarb

AND

Christoph Landerer

OXFORD
UNIVERSITY PRESS

OXFORD
UNIVERSITY PRESS

Oxford University Press is a department of the University of Oxford. It furthers the University's objective of excellence in research, scholarship, and education by publishing worldwide. Oxford is a registered trade mark of Oxford University Press in the UK and certain other countries.

Published in the United States of America by Oxford University Press
198 Madison Avenue, New York, NY 10016, United States of America.

© Oxford University Press 2018

CIP data is on file at the Library of Congress
ISBN 978-0-19-069818-8

This volume is published with the generous support of the Gustave Reese Endowment of the American Musicological Society, funded in part by the National Endowment for the Humanities and the Andrew W. Mellon Foundation.

9 8 7 6 5 4 3 2 1
Printed by Sheridan Books, Inc., United States of America

CONTENTS

Translators' Preface   *vii*

Introductory Essays

  1. Origins, Publication, and Translation History of the Treatise   *xv*
    Christoph Landerer, Alexander Wilfing, and Lee Rothfarb

  2. Introduction to Hanslick's Central Concepts   *xxxi*
    Christoph Landerer and Lee Rothfarb

  3. Philosophical Background   *liii*
    Christoph Landerer and Lee Rothfarb

Readers' Guide: Alternative Routes Through the Treatise   *lxxiii*
  Lee Rothfarb and Christoph Landerer

Preface   *lxxxiii*

1. The Aesthetics of Feeling   1

2. The "Representation of Feelings"
  Is Not the Content of Music   14

3. The Musically Beautiful   40

4. Analysis of the Subjective Impression of Music   63

5. Aesthetic Compared to Pathological Perception
   of Music   81

6. The Relation of Music to Nature   94

7. The Concepts "Content" and "Form" in Music   107

Appendix   117
Glossary   123
Selected Bibliography in English   127
Index   131

TRANSLATORS' PREFACE

Eduard Hanslick's *Vom Musikalisch-Schönen* (first edition 1854) was translated into English twice, first by Gustav Cohen (*The Beautiful in Music*, 1891), then by Geoffrey Payzant (*On the Musically Beautiful*, 1986). Given the renewed, strong interest in Hanslick's ideas, as well as the increased demands of today's scholarly world compared with those of thirty years ago, we decided that a new translation of Hanslick's watershed treatise was necessary. We determined further that a new translation should be a collaboration between an English speaker and a native German speaker with different academic backgrounds, in musicology/music theory and aesthetics, as well as in intellectual history. Judged by the standards of mid-nineteenth-century academic writing in the German-speaking world, Hanslick's language is remarkably clear. Yet some of his vocabulary and the sentence structure of some of his arguments are not easy to comprehend. Our translation, written with the eyes and the expertise of both an English speaker and a native German speaker, aims to provide a new understanding of the text closer to the original than either of the existing translations.

There are, of course, different approaches to translation. *Formal* equivalence attempts to preserve the lexical and grammatical structure of the text, whereas *functional* equivalence strives to give a more natural, user-friendly rendering, though at the expense of lexical and grammatical details. The former approach yields a text more faithful to the original, the latter a more readable text, but less faithful to some of the characteristic features of the original. Because *On the Musically Beautiful* is both a philosophical treatise, based on philosophical and music-theoretical terminology, and a text aimed at a broader audience, including lay readers, translators of the treatise confront a dilemma. On the one hand, in many instances, a translation that captures the German linguistic characteristics of a passage may sound slightly awkward in English. A more liberal rendering, on the other hand, although enhancing readability, may lack source-language characteristics that are essential for understanding Hanslick's aesthetic theory as he conceived and verbalized it.

It is no surprise that the history of the Hanslick translation begins with a *functional* approach. Gustav Cohen's 1891 translation is beautifully written, but also takes extensive liberties with the text. His translation of *tönend bewegte Formen* as "sound and motion," for instance, omitting altogether the element of form, lucidly illustrates the shortcomings of this approach. Hanslick was, after all, considered a formalist. Payzant, in his translation of 1986, pays close attention to philosophical and music-theoretical detail, thereby enhancing our understanding of Hanslick's philosophical and music-theoretical point of view. However, in many ways Payzant's translation is less readable than Cohen's. The very title of the book—*On the Musically Beautiful*—correctly renders the German original, but is without doubt conceptually more demanding than Cohen's *The Beautiful in Music*. Payzant translates the famous phrase *tönend bewegte Formen* as "tonally moving forms," thus preserving the three-part structure that is central to the German construction. However, although we retain Payzant's translation of the title, we argue for a different solution for this central statement. Here and in many other cases we find Payzant's translation rather free and paraphrased, at times bordering on misinterpretation, at others crossing that border.

Corrections that we have made vis-à-vis the Payzant translation fall into different categories. First, we have endeavored to be more precise regarding concepts central to Hanslick's aesthetic approach. For example, Payzant translates Hanslick's notion of tone as "a sound of determinate, measurable pitch, high or low" (Payzant, p. 71). Our translation follows Hanslick's wording more closely, defining tone as a "sound of a specific, measurable height and depth" (Chapter 6, p. 99; 10th ed., p. 188: "Klang von bestimmter, meßbarer Höhe und Tiefe" ["10th ed." refers to the tenth edition of Hanslick's book]). The aspect of determinate pitch is central to Hanslick's concept of a tone (among the most basic concepts of Hanslick's terminology) and thus demands that we adhere to the German text as closely as possible. Second, we have tried to capture the meaning of some of the words and phrases that Hanslick uses in an idiomatic way. For example, in characterizing musical enthusiasts who listen to music pathologically, Hanslick describes them as "half awake, nestled into their armchairs," allowing themselves to be "carried away and rocked by the vibrations of the tones, instead of contemplating them keenly" (Chapter 5, p. 82; 10th ed., p. 155: "Halbwach in ihren Fauteuil geschmiegt, lassen jene Enthusiasten von den Schwingungen der Töne sich tragen und schaukeln, statt sie scharfen Blickes zu betrachten"). Payzant (p. 59) mistranslates *geschmiegt*, connoting here a cozy nestling in a comfortable chair, as "slouched," connoting poor posture and blasé attitude, which is not at all Hanslick's image. Further, Payzant's slouched listeners "brood" instead of being carried away.[1] Finally, we have corrected translations of passages with complicated sentence structure, some of which are challenging even for a native German speaker. For example, in a sentence about musical style, Payzant (p. 48) confuses subject and object. "The style of a piece

---

1. In an essay titled "Hanslick's Composers," Fred Maus unwittingly builds an argument based on Payzant's mistranslation of *geschmiegt* as "slouched." *Rethinking Hanslick: Music, Formalism, and Expression*, eds. Nicole Grimes, Siobhán Donovan, and Wolfgang Marx (Rochester, NY: University of Rochester Press, 2013), p. 39.

of music will violate a higher principle than that of mere proportion if a single bar, though in itself irreproachable, is out of keeping with the effect of the whole." Our translation corrects the passage to read as follows: "A higher logic than that of mere proportionality, the style of a piece of music is violated by a single measure which, irreproachable in itself, does not accord with the expression of the whole" (Chapter 4, p. 67; 10th ed., 125–26: "Eine höhere Gesetzlichkeit, als die der bloßen Proportion, wird der Stil eines Tonstücks durch einen einzigen Takt verletzt, der, an sich untadelhaft, nicht zum Ausdruck des Ganzen stimmt").

Considering the text's many subtleties, some of them vital to Hanslick's argument and in light of the lively academic debate addressing these subtleties, today's readers of his treatise must rely on a translation that is sensitive to characteristics of the German text. With Cohen's approach resulting, on the one hand, in a translation of high readability in English but at the expense of subtleties and key characteristics, and, on the other hand, with Payzant's translation less readable than Cohen's and with a fair number of inaccuracies, it is difficult to produce a new, improved translation that is as readable as Payzant's and simultaneously faithful to Hanslick's intended arguments.

If readers find some of our solutions less graceful than Cohen's and perhaps also less appealing than Payzant's, it is because we find it impossible to pick up where they left off and at the same time provide what their translations lack. We generally avoid "neutralized" or "transformative" translation, which smooths out characteristic Germanic modes of expression and transforms them into idiomatic English ones. In adhering closely to German patterns of expression, our approach thus differs from that of both Cohen and Payzant. We have used such transformative translation only where it was unavoidable. Overall, we believe we have preserved the tone and characteristics of the German in readable English. Although we strive for optimal flow of the text, we also try to preserve its main characteristics, some of which sound a bit inelegant even in the original.

In addition to adopting a different approach to translation, we also base our work on the current state of research and facilitate readers' access to the text by offering introductory essays that cover the central aspects of Hanslick's book and his thought. The first essay, "Origins, Publication, and Translation History of the Treatise," informs readers about the genesis of Hanslick's book, about changes in the different editions, and about the history of its translations. The second essay, "Introduction to Hanslick's Central Concepts," introduces readers to Hanslick's aesthetic thinking by explaining the theoretical concepts that constitute its core. The third essay, "Philosophical Background," guides readers in historically situating the treatise in the realm of aesthetic and philosophical ideas.

Our translation also offers a Readers' Guide, which maps different routes through the text, allowing readers with limited time to focus attention on the essentials. One of the suggested routes follows the logical and chronological order of the text as we reconstruct it in the first essay. We also provide explanatory annotations and a bilingual glossary, with short explanations of the central terms and notions of the treatise. Our annotations, in translators' footnotes, differ from those of Payzant. His are mainly bibliographic, tracing Hanslick's sources to contemporaneous writings. As such, they are a major contribution to Hanslick scholarship. However, they are of little use to the average reader. We focus instead on additional information that promotes modern readers' understanding of the text. Additionally, we include a select bibliography of sources for those who wish to do follow-up readings on the treatise, its history, and its ideas. Finally, from the first edition we translate the opening of chapter one (the most reworked part of the book in subsequent editions) and the last paragraph of chapter seven (partially, then completely excised in later editions), and provide a brief overview of important changes to the text in later editions. Except for the opening of chapter one in the second edition, changes in later editions are generally minor.

Our choice of edition follows and respects the tradition of reading Hanslick in the Anglophone world. German scholarship always had ready access to the full range of editions that appeared during Hanslick's lifetime, from the first edition, published when Hanslick was twenty-nine, to the tenth of 1902, published two years before his death. Whereas the German-speaking world, particularly twentieth-century scholarship, has relied heavily on the original edition of 1854, English readers have based their understanding of Hanslick on later editions, the seventh in Cohen's translation, the eighth in Payzant's. In 1891, Cohen simply translated the latest edition available. The reason for Payzant's choice is unclear. We decided for the tenth, which was Hanslick's last word on the subject. It does not differ substantially from the seventh and the eighth editions but seemed a more logical choice than any of the others.

The idea of a new translation of Hanslick's treatise originated as part of the project "Contextualizing Hanslick" (Christoph Landerer, Principal Investigator), funded by the Austrian Science Fund (Fonds zur Förderung der wissenschaftlichen Forschung, FWF). A new translation was considered "much needed" by one of the anonymous reviewers of the project's proposal. The FWF generously funded Professor Lee Rothfarb's travels to Vienna in the summers of 2014 and 2015. The Department of Musicology at the Austrian Academy of Sciences, under the direction of Barbara Boisits, made additional funds available for Rothfarb's stay in 2015. We are very grateful to these institutions for making possible the kind of international collaboration that is essential for a project of this scope.

During the summers of 2014 and 2015, Rothfarb translated the main text, with Christoph Landerer serving as a translation consultant. The introductory essay on Hanslick's concepts is the result of many discussions on translation strategies and on shades of meaning in the text that we had in a Vienna apartment (the same one where, coincidentally, Geoffrey Payzant also worked on his translation in the 1980s). Rothfarb also authored the Readers' Guide. Alexander Wilfing, team member of the "Contextualizing Hanslick" project, coauthored the introductory essay on the book and its history. We are also grateful to him for contributing material and ideas to the section on Immanuel Kant in the essay on Hanslick's philosophical background. Wilfing further assisted as a research and bibliography consultant. Finally, we are indebted to Sara Ballance, graduate student in musicology at the University of California, Santa Barbara, who served as an editorial assistant for the three introductory essays.

INTRODUCTORY ESSAY 1:
ORIGINS, PUBLICATION, AND
TRANSLATION HISTORY
OF THE TREATISE

When *On the Musically Beautiful* appeared in 1854, jurist and music critic Eduard Hanslick, not yet thirty years old, was set for a career as a civil servant. Young Eduard was born to an enlightened Bohemian family with maternal Jewish heritage, in which the arts and music, in particular, played a major role in everyday life. Hanslick's father, Joseph Adolph Hanslik (Eduard later added a "c" in his surname to give it a less Czech and more German tone), an academic and librarian, began his career as a piano teacher and later gave courses in aesthetics at Prague's Charles University. His mother, the daughter of a Jewish merchant, was devoted to theater and literature. Eduard received a solid musical upbringing, but, like many musically gifted young men of his time, he decided on a career in the growing bureaucratic sector of the Habsburg Empire. Home-taught by his father for most of his primary and secondary educations, Eduard began legal studies in Prague and finished them in Vienna. His administrative career, however, commenced in the then highly provincial town of Klagenfurt, the capital of Carinthia. Cut off from his musical contacts and ambitions, as well as from his spare-time work as a music critic for a Viennese newspaper, the two years spent in provincial Austria (1850–1852) were not the happiest of his life. Yet it was there, amid the impressive scenery of high mountains and gentle slopes, that

Hanslick began to explore the relationship between music and nature in a public talk given in one of Klagenfurt's culturally interested circles. It seems that this talk forms the nucleus of what later became *On the Musically Beautiful*.[1]

Hanslick's "exile" in Carinthia not only isolated him from the musical metropolis of Vienna, it also allowed him to focus on aesthetic studies. As letters to his friend, Vesque von Püttlingen, show, Hanslick intended to prepare for a professorship in music as early as 1851.[2] The letters also document his readings in aesthetics during the Klagenfurt period, particularly his strong interest in the aesthetics of Friedrich Theodor Vischer. Other than that, we have little evidence of his aesthetic thinking during the Klagenfurt years; Hanslick's few publications from this time focus on folk song—a topic that might also be related to the Klagenfurt talk.

In May 1852, Hanslick returned to Vienna, where he joined the Ministry of Finance. He resumed activities as a music critic and engaged in the rich cultural life of Austria's capital—then one of the leading centers of Western music. During this time, the topics and ideas of the Klagenfurt lecture continued to develop and grow, and in March 1854, Hanslick published an essay on music and its relation to nature in Vienna's *Oesterreichische Blätter für Literatur und Kunst* (a supplement to the *Wiener Zeitung*, for which he served as a critic).[3] The essay was the second of two prepublished articles that provide a substantial portion of the text of *On the Musically Beautiful*. Half a year earlier, in the summer of 1853, Hanslick had published an essay on music's subjective impression that appeared in three installments in the same journal.[4] The articles were incorporated,

1. Dietmar Strauß, *Eduard Hanslick: Vom Musikalisch-Schönen. Teil 2: Eduard Hanslicks Schrift in textkritischer Sicht* (Mainz, Germany: Schott, 1991), p. 66.

2. Strauß, *Eduard Hanslick Teil 2*, p. 394. Hanslick's letter from December 13, 1851, is in the Wienbibliothek in Vienna's Town Hall, N. 31.038 (Handschriftensammlung).

3. Eduard Hanslick, "Die Tonkunst in ihren Beziehungen zur Natur" ["Music in Its Relations to Nature"], *Oesterreichische Blätter für Literatur und Kunst*, March 13, 1854.

4. "Ueber den subjektiven Eindruck in der Musik und seine Stellung in der Aesthetik" ["On Music's Subjective Impression and its Position in Aesthetics"],

with few changes, into *On the Musically Beautiful* as chapter six, chapter four, and chapter five, respectively. Although the 1854 article on music and nature was published as one single chapter (chapter six), Hanslick decided to make two chapters out of the first article from 1853, with different headings (chapters four and five).[5]

The manner in which *On the Musically Beautiful* developed out of these prepublications is not yet well understood. A footnote at the beginning of the first installment indicates that the essay is a "fragment of a larger work."[6] This footnote has led scholars such as Geoffrey Payzant to believe that the prepublications were derived from an already finished book.[7] However, an alternative view holds that the book evolved out of more-or-less independent chapters that Hanslick wrote after publishing the 1853 and 1854 articles in the *Oesterreichische Blätter*. Dietmar Strauß, editor of Hanslick's collected works, considers *On the Musically Beautiful* not a "uniform, cohesive text, but rather a collection of essayistic or aphoristic thoughts, grouped around a polemic core."[8] According to that view, *On the Musically Beautiful* can best be seen as a sequence of chapters, originating in Hanslick's prepublished essays, which were then compiled into a book in chronological rather than logical order. Strauß assumes that chapter seven, the final one of the book, was written immediately after the prepublished essays, whereas chapters one through three, those central to Hanslick's argument, were the last ones added to the text.[9]

Oesterreichische Blätter für Literatur und Kunst, July 25,1853, August 1, 1853, and August 15, 1853.

5. "Analyse des subjektiven Eindruckes der Musik" (chapter four), and "Das ästhetische Aufnehmen der Musik gegenüber dem pathologischen" (chapter five).

6. "Fragment einer größeren Arbeit." A similar footnote is missing from the 1854 article on music and nature.

7. "Both installments and book were typeset from one and the same source— namely the final version of the manuscript." Geoffrey Payzant, *"Vom Musikalisch-Schönen*: A Pre-Publication Excerpt," *The Music Review* 46 (1985): p. 180.

8. "[E]s handle sich bei VMS nicht um eine einheitliche, geschlossene Schrift, sondern eher um eine Ansammlung essayistischer oder aphoristischer Gedanken, die um einen polemischen Hauptkern herum angeordnet worden seien," Strauß, *Eduard Hanslick, Teil 2*, p. 394.

9. Carl Dahlhaus rightly observes that some chapters were already in print before Hanslick finished the book, but confuses the sequence when he states that the

Although this view of the chronological order in which the individual chapters were written—rather than being mere excerpts of an already completed text—is certainly plausible, *On the Musically Beautiful* does in fact have a logical order beyond the "aphoristic" structure that the text displays on its surface. There is a clear line of argument running through the text that does not, however, follow the sequence of the published chapters, but rather the supposed chronological order in which they were written. To establish this logical structure of the text, we must take a closer look at Hanslick's arguments in the individual chapters.

Judged by today's standards, *On the Musically Beautiful* is poorly organized. Following some brief methodological remarks, the book begins with the notion and role of feelings in music, explaining why feelings cannot provide a firm theoretical basis for musical aesthetics (chapters one and two). The text goes on to develop the central idea of the "specifically musical" and of "sonically moved forms" as a "positive" thesis (chapter three), then takes two steps back to elaborate on music's subjective impression and its physiological foundations (chapters four and five). This is followed by reflections on the most basic concept of all musical aesthetics—that is, the concept of a tone and its relation to nature (chapter six). The final chapter recapitulates some of the main points from chapter three and attempts to clarify conceptual issues related to the central notion of form.

This organizational scheme makes little sense to the uninformed reader. Read from chapter one to chapter seven, the sequence in which the individual chapters are presented in the published text, *On the Musically Beautiful* does indeed appear as a "a collection of essayistic or aphoristic thoughts," in which a main theoretical conclusion is drawn somewhere in the middle of the book and subordinate chapters assist in reaching this conclusion in a rather nontransparent way.

Beginning from the prepublished chapters four, five, and six, however, the structure of the argument becomes visible. Hanslick

first chapters were prepublished. *Grundlagen der Musikgeschichte* (Cologne: Hans Gerig 1977), p. 198.

first lays the foundation for his investigation by elaborating on the notion of a tone (chapter six, presumably based on the Klagenfurt talk). The argument then continues by explaining how tones are received by the physiological system (chapters four and five). This is followed by reflections on how the physiological response builds the basis for feelings (chapter one) and what status feelings have in musical aesthetics (chapters one and two). Following a negative assessment of feelings in aesthetic contexts, the reader is then led to the positive thesis (chapter three). Concluding remarks sum up some of the main findings and provide a more elaborate conceptual framework (chapter seven). Because Hanslick's estate papers are lost, we have no indication why Hanslick did not revise this rather unintuitive ordering at some point, either prior to the publication of the text or in the course of subsequent revisions. He was, however, well aware of the many shortcomings of the text, as he confessed in all prefaces of the book from the second edition onward.

Following Hanslick's line of argument, as presented in the treatise, it seems obvious that the prepublished articles that Hanslick incorporated into the book as chapters four through six were followed by chapters one through three in the process of producing *On the Musically Beautiful*, with chapter seven written as a closing section. Dietmar Strauß, who argues for chapter seven as a direct antecedent of chapters one through three, supports his view by pointing to a footnote in Hanslick's 1853 article on music and nature that appears later in the main text of chapter seven, in a slightly modified way.[10] Although the footnote certainly demonstrates Hanslick's willingness to reuse material taken from other contexts, it is still difficult to argue that *On the Musically Beautiful* is a mere "collection of aphorisms."[11] Given that chapter seven presupposes and elaborates on arguments that are worked out in greater detail in chapter three, the central one of the book, it seems safe to assume that Hanslick intended it to be

10. Strauß, *Eduard Hanslick, Teil 2*, p. 76.
11. Strauß, *Eduard Hanslick, Teil 2*, p. 77.

a concluding section and thus wrote it after the rest of the text was already finished.

As we can see, the general line of argument running through Hanslick's treatise emerges only when the chapters are reorganized according to the steps that the overall argument takes. The logical sequence of the chapters (six–four–five–one–two–three–seven) likely also reflects the chronological order in which they were written, as the topics and material presented in each chapter typically presuppose arguments developed (logically) in previous chapters.

Readers often struggle with this rather counterintuitive structure of the text. Our translation therefore also provides a "Readers' Guide" (see pp. lxxiii–lxxxi), which enables a reading of *On the Musically Beautiful* in accordance with its logical organization. As mentioned before, we have no indication as to why Hanslick chose to present the arguments in such an inconvenient way. The first three chapters certainly succeeded in capturing the reader's attention better than the rather dry and academic chapters based on Hanslick's prepublished articles. Hanslick also intended to have *On the Musically Beautiful* accepted as a habilitation thesis and thus might have thought it advisable to hide the prepublished parts in a later section of the text (which might also explain why he altered the headings). However, this is all speculation as Hanslick never explained his motivations for the composition of the text.

Careful readers of chapters four through six will notice a certain shift in the focus of Hanslick's argument in chapters one through three. After the rather academic prepublished chapters, with their generous narration of scientific findings and the contemporary state of research, chapters one through three have a more philosophical tone, with a less prominent empirical angle. This is where Hanslick develops his main aesthetic arguments, counters the "feeling theory" in musical aesthetics, and presents his own aesthetic approach. But he struggles with how to begin the book. Chapter one deals mostly with the concept and theory of feelings and their role in musical aesthetics. However, the first few pages are devoted to questions of objectivity and aesthetic method. Here, Hanslick takes up a thread that first appeared at the beginning of chapter six, the nucleus of the book, where he observes a strong tendency toward the "natural side of all phenomena." In Hanslick's view, this results in an academic situation in which even the most abstract investigations—and therefore including aesthetics—"gravitate noticeably toward the method of the natural sciences."[12] However, although this observation leads Hanslick to reflect on music's relation to nature in a rather severely scientific–naturalistic way in chapter six, the thread is taken up differently at the beginning of chapter one, the start of the book. Again, Hanslick pleads for a scientific orientation, even in aesthetic investigations, but science now refers to a meaningful analogy, not the application of actual natural science in the context of aesthetic inquiry. When Hanslick uses notions derived from (natural) science here, it is not entirely clear what he had in mind—certainly not in our time, but perhaps not in the middle of the nineteenth century either. (For more information on Hanslick's concept of objectivity and the role of science in aesthetic method, see the essay on Hanslick's concepts, pp. li–lii.)

1.1 ON THE MUSICALLY BEAUTIFUL AND ITS DIFFERENT EDITIONS

Apparently, Hanslick was less than satisfied with the beginning of the book, and just four years after the first edition, a second edition appeared in 1858, with the first section of chapter one completely reworked. This revised first section is the biggest change to *On the Musically Beautiful* across all later editions. Although the differences between the first and the later editions are sometimes exaggerated, the first edition does have a more youthful and a little less severely "formalist" tone.

12. In our translation, Chapter 6, p. 94.

Hanslick's troubles in writing chapter one are understandable given the difficulty of the task he faced. In the prepublished article that became chapter 6, he had spoken of the relevance of scientific method for aesthetics in an effort to clarify music's relation to nature. His concern in writing chapter one, by contrast, was the aesthetic method per se, not music and nature. Consequently, Hanslick's usage of scientific vocabulary in chapter one differs from that of chapter six. In chapter one, it is embedded in a philosophical framework with no indication of how such vocabulary might apply in aesthetics. As these first pages are also the main divergence for all later editions, we decided to offer a translation of the opening section of chapter one from the first edition as well (see pp. 117–18).

Some of the changes that Hanslick made in the second edition have been attributed to Robert Zimmermann's review of the book.[13] In an otherwise very favorable review, Zimmermann, at that time one of the leading figures of Austrian philosophy (as well as Hanslick's life-long friend), criticized traces of idealist philosophy that he detected in the book. In Zimmermann's opinion, the author did not distance himself enough from a rather old-fashioned "metaphysical" point of view that contradicted the main idea of his argument. Alarmed by Zimmermann's reproof of a "superfluous concession to a false aesthetic,"[14] Hanslick deleted or altered several passages. These include the closing passage of the book, where music was associated with the "infinite" ("Das Unendliche") in a rather idealist–romanticist manner.[15]

Apart from these "amputations" (Mark Evan Bonds) and the reworked opening section of chapter one, there are few changes in

13. For a critical discussion of Zimmermann's review and its influence on the second edition of *On the Musically Beautiful*, see Mark Evan Bonds, "Aesthetic Amputations: Absolute Music and the Deleted Endings of Hanslick's *Vom Musikalisch-Schönen*," *19th-Century Music* 36, no. 1 (2012): pp. 3–23; and Bonds, *Absolute Music: The History of an Idea* (Oxford: Oxford University Press, 2014), pp. 183–209.

14. "[Ü]berflüssige Concession an eine falsche Ästhetik," "Vom musikalisch-Schönen," in Robert Zimmermann, *Studien und Kritiken zur Philosophie und Aesthetik*, vol. 2 (Vienna: W. Braumüller, 1870), p. 314.

15. See Bonds, "Aesthetic Amputations," p. 4

subsequent editions of *On the Musically Beautiful*. Hanslick added footnotes, updated references, and corrected occasional misspellings, but only very rarely added or altered larger portions of the text. As his interests began to shift and turn away from theoretical aesthetics, it seems that his interest in *On the Musically Beautiful* declined as well. It was not until the fourth edition of 1874, for example—two full decades after the publication of the first edition—that he corrected a reference to a "first article" in chapter five. The reference obviously referred to the first installment of the prepublished article of 1853 on music's subjective impression.

When Hanslick discusses his motivations and reflects on the ways in which *On the Musically Beautiful* was received by contemporary readers, it is not so much in the main text itself, but rather in the various (short) prefaces that he reworked extensively from the first edition of 1854 to the fourth edition of 1874. It is also here that the book reveals Hanslick's growing opposition to Richard Wagner and the "music of the future." Contrary to a widely held belief, *On the Musically Beautiful* is not a "book against Wagner."[16] Wagner appears only a few times in the main text of the book, mostly as a theoretician and writer, and only once in connection with his music.[17] However, in the prefaces the Bayreuth "Meister" figures more prominently. Although Wagner is not mentioned at all in the preface to the first edition, and is mentioned in connection with his writings only in the preface to the second, the picture changes in the third edition of 1865, possibly because of the *Meistersinger* affair of 1862.[18] Hanslick's criticism is harsh: Wagner's "endless melody" is now seen as "formlessness elevated to a principle," "systemized non-music," or

16. Karl Popper, *Unended Quest: An Intellectual Autobiography* (London: Routledge, 2010), p. 249.

17. In a footnote in the second chapter, Hanslick first discusses Wagner's *Lohengrin* (first to third editions), then his "later works" (fourth and fifth editions), until he finally deletes the footnote from the sixth edition onward.

18. On November 23, 1862, Wagner gave a reading of the *Meistersinger* libretto in a private Vienna home. Hanslick might have recognized himself in the figure of Beckmesser ("Veit Hanslich" in an early version of the text).

"melodic fever of the nerves, written out on a five-line staff."[19] In the fourth and all later editions, Hanslick again criticizes formlessness "elevated to a principle, the sung and fiddled opium high for whose cult a temple of its own has been opened in Bayreuth."[20] But again, none of these very critical remarks appear in the main text. To be sure, the reworked opening section of chapter one, together with several "amputations," sets a slightly different tone for the main text of editions after the first. But it would certainly be an exaggeration to consider the first and the later editions to be "different books" in any substantial way.

1.2 THE INTRODUCTION OF *ON THE MUSICALLY BEAUTIFUL* TO THE ENGLISH-SPEAKING WORLD AND THE HISTORY OF THE TRANSLATIONS

When Geoffrey Payzant was about to finish his translation in 1986, it was not incorrect to observe that one could "get the impression that commentators in German are writing about one book and commentators in English are writing about another book."[21] Even in 1986, German commentators did "limit their discussions almost entirely to the first edition," whereas "most of the commentators in English have written only about the seventh edition (1885), of which an English translation appeared in 1891."[22] However, it was not so much that the book itself that had changed from the first to later editions, but rather that the discourse about the book had developed

---

19. "[D]ie zum Prinzip erhobene Formlosigkeit, die systemisirte Nichtmusik, das auf 5 Notenlinien verschriebene melodische Nervenfieber." Strauß, *Vom Musikalisch-Schönen, Teil 1*, p. 11.

20. In our translation, Preface, p. lxxxv.

21. "Tone-Words," in Geoffrey Payzant, *Hanslick on the Musically Beautiful. Sixteen Lectures on the Musical Aesthetics of Eduard Hanslick* (Christchurch, New Zealand: Cybereditions, 2002), p. 44–46.

22. Payzant, "Tone-Words," p. 44.

along different lines. With some of the German discourse focusing on the heavily reworked opening passage of chapter one, it is easy to see how readers could get the impression that German and Anglo-American scholars were discussing two different books.

Anglo-American reception of Hanslick's aesthetics, however, predates the first complete translation by Gustav Cohen (1891) by a considerable amount of time.[23] As James Deaville has recently pointed out, the first English renderings of Hanslick's writings were printed in *Dwight's Journal of Music*,[24] the "leading American periodical of its kind,"[25] which was published in Boston between 1852 and 1881. Dwight, who has been called "this country's first music critic"[26] and "the closest thing to a New World Hanslick,"[27] held particularly conservative opinions on the contemporary state of music, and these views were widely shared by a Boston readership that centered its aesthetic principles on the "classical" German tradition.[28] He used his journal to tirelessly promote an "ever-stiffening resistance to Wagner and other new music,"[29] and therefore invoked Hanslick's writings as authoritative evidence for a different kind of musical culture that aligned with his own aesthetic preferences. Dwight's translation activity, which "represents the first point of contact with Hanslick for Americans,"[30] began sparsely in the mid-1860s, increased over

23. Hanslick's book had been previously translated into Spanish (1865), French (1877), Italian (1883), Danish (1885), and Russian (1885). See Bonds, *Absolute Music*, p. 7.

24. James Deaville, "Negotiating the 'Absolute': Hanslick's Path Through Musical History," in *Rethinking Hanslick: Music, Formalism, and Expression*, ed. Nicole Grimes, Siobhán Donovan, and Wolfgang Marx (Rochester, NY: University of Rochester Press, 2013), pp. 15–37, 23.

25. Joseph Horowitz, *Wagner Nights: An American History* (Berkeley: University of California Press, 1994), p. 24.

26. Ora Frishberg Saloman, "American Writers on Beethoven, 1838–1849: Dwight, Fuller, Cranch, Story," *American Music* 8, no. 1 (1990): pp. 12–28, 13.

27. Horowitz, *Wagner Nights*, p. 141.

28. Gilbert Chase, *American Music From the Pilgrims to the Present*, 3rd ed., ed. Richard Crawford (Urbana: University of Illinois Press, 1987), pp. 312–14.

29. Walter Fertig, "Dwight, John Sullivan," in *The New Grove Dictionary of Music and Musicians*, vol. 5, ed. Stanley Sadie (London: Macmillan, 1980), p. 792.

30. Deaville, "Hanslick's Path Through Musical History," p. 23.

the course of the early 1870s, and reached a high point in the years 1878–1880, during which he published roughly twenty reviews by Eduard Hanslick.

Additionally, Hanslick's aesthetic treatise was reviewed favorably in *Dwight's Journal* as a "sensational and epoch-making pamphlet [. . .] which like a flash of lightning pierced the mists which had gathered around the scientific treatment of musical aesthetics, without however fully scattering them."[31] A particularly evocative promotion of *On the Musically Beautiful* appears in Blidge's review of Walter Lawson's translation of *Aesthetics of Musical Art* by the German philologist Ferdinand Hand, which Dwight reprinted from the *Pall Mall Gazette*.[32] Blidge sharply criticizes Lawson for his seemingly ignorant opinion that since the appearance of Hand's book, "but few works on the aesthetics of music have been given to the world," and insists that there would have been far more rewarding candidates for an English translation—namely, Hanslick's aesthetic treatise: "If Mr. Lawson had given us a readable translation of Hanslick he would have done useful and agreeable work."[33] Even though a complete translation did not exist until 1891, *Dwight´s Journal* and the politics behind its selection of reviews can thus be regarded as the main source for Hanslick's early reputation in English discourse. Another important reference work may have been Eustace Breakspeare's paper, "Musical Aesthetics."[34] Although Breakspeare does not translate specific passages from *On the Musically Beautiful*, he outlines Hanslick's position in considerable detail with reference to the French version (pp. 64–67). Even though he ultimately concludes that Hanslick's aesthetic viewpoint,

31. John Sullivan Dwight, "Dr. Edward Hanslick," *Dwight's Journal of Music* 38, no. 8 (July 20, 1878): p. 270.

32. Ferdinand Hand, *Aesthetics of Musical Art or The Beautiful in Music*, trans. Walter Lawson (London: William Reeves, 1880).

33. Blidge, "Aesthetics of Musical Art," *Dwight's Journal of Music* 40, no. 21 (October 9, 1880): pp. 162–63, 163.

34. Eustace Breakspeare, "Musical Aesthetics," *Proceedings of the Royal Musical Association* 6 (1880): pp. 59–77.

which "aims at a thorough subversion of the popularly held tenets of musical philosophy," is "very unsatisfactory" because it diminishes the aesthetic relevance of musical expression, his paper illustrates Hanslick's stance in some depth.[35]

According to Deaville, the first directly translated excerpts of Hanslick's aesthetic treatise can again be found in *Dwight's Journal*.[36] The short essay "Music the Exponent of Emotion," by an anonymous author who critically examines the expressive means of pure music, contains two separate paragraphs from the German original.[37] As far as we know, besides this isolated reference, only William Pole's *Philosophy of Music* included translated passages of *On the Musically Beautiful* prior to Cohen's edition.[38] Pole's book is extremely important in this regard, not only because of its early date, but also because of the specific segments he chose for translation. Whereas Dwight used Hanslick's writings for his own critical agenda, which was closely tied to the musical–political debate on the "New German School," Pole introduced Hanslick's treatise in a philosophical context. Pole rejects an ahistorical conception of the Western tonal system, which is not determined by any law of nature, and argues for its cultural relativity and historical contingency, basing his progressive standpoint on "one of the most celebrated modern works on musical aesthetics, 'Vom Musikalisch-Schönen.'"[39] In support of this view, he quotes three separate passages from *On the Musically Beautiful* that deal with the historical condition of musical beauty, thereby implicitly resisting the prevalent misconception of

35. Breakspeare, "Musical Aesthetics," pp. 64, 72.

36. See Deaville, "Hanslick's Path Through Musical History," p. 32. Although Deaville does not give the exact issue, we are fairly certain that he is referring to the article previously explicated.

37. Anonymous, "Music the Exponent of Emotion," *Dwight's Journal of Music* 7, no. 16 (July 21, 1855): pp. 123–24, 123. The first passage refers to Hanslick's analogy between music and a moving, intelligently constructed kaleidoscope (Chapter 3, pp. 41–42), and the second one deals with the necessarily metaphorical character of musical discourse (Chapter 3, p. 43).

38. William Pole, *The Philosophy of Music* (London: Trübner & Company, 1879).

39. Pole, *The Philosophy of Music*, p. 202.

Hanslick's approach as an aesthetics of timeless, unchanging beauty (see essay on Hanslick´s concepts).[40]

In summary, there was already considerable knowledge about Hanslick's aesthetics in the English-speaking world when Gustav Cohen's first complete English translation appeared in 1891. Cohen's translation is based on the seventh edition of *On the Musically Beautiful* (1885), the most recent edition available when he began translating the book. Almost a century later (1986), Geoffrey Payzant opted for the eighth edition, but gives no reason for that choice. In using one of the later editions, he followed the general path of Anglo-American Hanslick reception; it was only later in the century that *On the Musically Beautiful* was introduced to a wider audience. We see no reason to depart from the preference for later editions in the English-speaking world. Our translation is based on the tenth edition of 1902, the last one published during Hanslick's lifetime. It is, in a way, Hanslick's last word on the matter, though it differs little from the seventh and eighth editions used by Cohen and Payzant.

Produced at the end of the nineteenth century, Cohen's translation reads well, but at many places is not grammatically and rhetorically faithful to the German original. Although Cohen simplified the somewhat eccentric German title of the book, *Vom Musikalisch-Schönen*, to *The Beautiful in Music*, Payzant's title is more literal and captures more closely the German original. As Andy Hamilton has observed, "Hanslick's *Vom Musikalisch-Schonen* has been translated misleadingly as *On the Beautiful in Music*. More accurately, it should be *On the Musically Beautiful*, since for Hanslick the beauty

---

40. Pole, *The Philosophy of Music*, 310–12. In our translation, Chapter 3, p. 51 ("There is no art that exhausts . . . through an invisible fine thread"), and pp. 57, 59 ("that musical beauty has nothing to do with *the mathematical aspect*. . . . Mathematics has as small or as large a part in a musical artwork as in the products of the other arts"), and in Chapter 6, pp. 96, 97 ("that humankind did not learn to make music from the natural world surrounding him . . . a consequence of the endlessly disseminated musical culture").

of music is 'specifically musical.'"[41] Payzant also carefully avoided mistranslations of the German *Ton* [tone] as "sound" or "note" (still present in the Cohen translation), and provided a new translation of Hanslick's central phrase, "Tönend bewegte Formen" (*tonally moving forms* in Payzant´s translation). Although our translation adopts Payzant's version of the title, it differs from Payzant's translation in many details, including the translation of Hanslick's famous central phrase. The following essay on Hanslick's concepts explains our treatment of the central concepts in *On the Musically Beautiful* and informs readers about Hanslick's basic vocabulary.

41. Andy Hamilton, *Aesthetics of Music* (London: Continuum Books, 2007), p. 81. Hamilton got both titles slightly wrong ("Vom Musikalisch-Schönen," "The Beautiful in Music").

INTRODUCTORY ESSAY 2:
INTRODUCTION TO HANSLICK'S
CENTRAL CONCEPTS

When Alexander Baumgarten introduced the term aesthetics [*Aesthetica*] into philosophical discourse in 1750, the newly founded discipline was conceived as the "science of sensual cognition" [*scientia cognitionis sensitivae*]. A century later, when Hanslick wrote his treatise, the focus of attention had shifted considerably, with a more abstract notion of beauty moving toward the center of a philosophical discipline that had already transcended the limitations of Baumgarten's sensual approach. Contrary to Baumgarten's original conception of the discipline, nineteenth-century aesthetics was seen more as a general philosophy of art, encompassing a broad range of subjects that increasingly called for a specialized treatment of specific philosophical questions in each of the particular arts. However, with this broader outlook of a general theory of art, the problem arose of how the sensual, subjective component of aesthetic experience could be reconciled with the philosophical treatment of works of art and their objective, sometimes even highly nonsensual properties. The issue was particularly pressing in music, in which an abstract notational language confronted the rich sensual experience of the listener. Philosophical awareness of this sensual component focused on music's emotional effect, which dominated the discourse in the eighteenth century (and before). However, it was not until Hanslick that the more abstract, intellectual side of (Western classical) music became the subject of a study that considered *beauty* a purely objective, formal property of the artwork, while entirely dismissing the subjective reaction of its recipients.

Beauty is the most essential term of Hanslick's aesthetics. It figures prominently in the title of the treatise and guides Hanslick's analysis throughout the book. For a language (German) that even designates fine arts as "beautiful arts" [*schöne Künste*], such an emphasis on beauty is surprising in aesthetic discourse. But the focus of Hanslick's booklet is unusual even for an aesthetic treatise of the nineteenth century, when the concept of beauty was seen as much less problematic than in later studies on the subject. By the mid-nineteenth century, aesthetics in the Hegelian tradition had already started to undermine the traditional classicist–rationalistic approaches typical of eighteenth-century enlightenment and early bourgeois concert culture. Karl Rosenkranz's *Aesthetics of the Ugly* [*Ästhetik des Häßlichen*], published one year before *On the Musically Beautiful*, paved the way for a broader understanding of aesthetic concepts. Richard Wagner's conception of the sublime as antithetic to aesthetic approaches that aligned music with the fine arts was explicitly directed against Hanslick's treatise, as was Arthur Seidl's 1887 *On the Musically Sublime* [*Vom Musikalisch-Erhabenen*], which regarded Wagner's music as the ultimate refutation of Hanslick's narrower concept. In this philosophical and cultural atmosphere, Hanslick's insistence on a rather traditional notion of beauty, with strong links to the fine arts and their vivid, shaping activity, must indeed have appeared outdated, if not antiquated.

If Hanslick succeeded in reestablishing beauty as the main focal point of musical aesthetics, it was mainly because of his curious combination of a decidedly conservative outlook on music, deeply rooted in the classical tradition, with a radical approach to aesthetic method, anticipating early modernist modes of thought. Central to Hanslick's argument is a conception of beauty as *autonomous*—moreover, as autonomous beauty specific to music. Such autonomous beauty specific to music resists definition, as Hanslick readily admits:

It is extraordinarily difficult to delineate this autonomous beauty in music, this specifically musical aspect. . . . Music demands simply to be understood as music and can only be understood from within itself, be enjoyed in itself.

Hanslick's plea for autonomous beauty in music makes him one of the leading figures of *aesthetic autonomy*. Whereas *aesthetic heteronomy* considers properties or relations that are external to the specific work of art to be relevant for aesthetic analysis, aesthetic autonomy accepts only *internal* properties or relations, that is, properties or relations that inhere in the work of art itself.[1] The key concept of Hanslick's analysis is the *specifically musical* nature of musical beauty, a concept that he explains in one of the most consequential passages of his book—one that is unchanged in all editions:

It is a specifically musical beauty. By that we understand beauty that is independent and not in need of an external content, something that resides solely in the tones and their artistic connection. (Chapter 3, p. 40)

Defining the specifically musical is also "extraordinarily difficult," Hanslick concedes. However, he does give an approximation *ex negativo*. The musically beautiful is not a merely acoustical phenomenon (Chapter 3, p. 43), nor can it be reduced to merely structural

---

1. In recent years, there has been a heated debate over these seemingly evident categories. Postmodernist approaches eroded any strict difference between "internal" and "external" aspects of the musical "work," which—according to Richard Leppert and Susan McClary—are solely constituted by an "ideology of autonomy": *Music and Society: The Politics of Composition, Performance, and Reception* (Cambridge: Cambridge University Press, 1987), p. 9. For a particularly incisive use of postmodern methodology, see Lawrence Kramer, *Music as Cultural Practice 1800–1900* (Berkeley: University of California Press, 1990) and *Classical Music and Postmodern Knowledge* (Berkeley: University of California Press, 1995). For a philosophical exploration of this increasingly problematic demarcation, see also Lydia Goehr, *The Quest for Voice: On Music, Politics, and the Limits of Philosophy: The 1997 Ernest Bloch Lectures* (Oxford: Oxford University Press, 1998), chapter 1; or Aaron Ridley, *The Philosophy of Music: Theme and Variations* (Edinburgh: Edinburgh University Press, 2004), chapter 3.

components without specifically musical significance, as in the case of popular comparisons with architecture (Chapter 3, p. 57), symmetry (Chapter 3, p. 57), or mathematics (Chapter 3, pp. 57–59). Language and its grammar are equally inapt in defining what is specific about *musical* beauty. Both the acoustical and the structural components are relevant and constitute indispensable conditions of musical beauty, as we will see, but neither provides a sufficient basis for aesthetic theory in Hanslick's sense. It is important to note that Hanslick's approach is essentially *nonreductionist*. Given that the concept of the specifically musical is at the heart of his aesthetic conception, this comes as no surprise. However, the image of Hanslick as a strict "formalist" has long obscured some of the most characteristic features of his aesthetic thinking. In the Herbart–Zimmermann tradition, *formalist* conceptions of music usually consider aesthetic properties to be a subclass of formal properties that inhere in a musical work, regardless of its time and place (see the third introductory essay on philosophical background). By contrast, Hanslick's view is historically contextualized (see subsequent discussion). He could, of course, still be regarded a formalist because form is one of the most basic concepts of his aesthetic approach. However, we should be aware that his "formalism" differs strongly from the orthodox conceptions in the Herbartian tradition.

A second and more general line of argument, which reinforces Hanslick's strong focus on the specificity of musical beauty, arises from his conception of aesthetics and the way in which aesthetic investigation should be carried out. For Hanslick, aesthetics should take a bottom-up approach, so to speak, as opposed to the top-down method of traditional metaphysics. Aesthetics thus deals with specific phenomena in specific areas of aesthetic experience and art, not with aesthetic experience and art in general. Hanslick strongly advocates for what in German is called *Spezialästhetik* [servile dependence of genre-specific aesthetics]:

The servile dependence of genre-specific aesthetics on the uppermost metaphysical principle of a general aesthetics is yielding increasingly to the persuasion that every art must be known on its own technical terms, grasped in and of itself. (Chapter 1, p. 2)

Instead of deducing what is beautiful in music from a general and abstract notion of beauty, Hanslick's starting point is the beautiful object itself, with its inherent properties and relations. However, these properties and relations cannot be defined in general terms. They are relative to the specific artistic sphere to which the beautiful object belongs (music, architecture, literature, etc.). It is in this sense that Hanslick emphasizes "that the laws of beauty of each art are inseparable from the characteristics of its material, of its technique" (Chapter 1, p. 2). The title of Hanslick's booklet, odd as it might sound to English ears, reflects the methodological route that he intends to follow: It is not *beauty* as an abstract entity, expressed in works of music, that interests Hanslick, but rather *the beautiful* (the beautiful object), seen as an object with certain specifically musical properties or relations that make the object beautiful. This explains the title, *On the Musically Beautiful*—a correct rendering of the German title, *Vom Musikalisch-Schönen*—that Geoffrey Payzant also used in his translation. By inserting a hyphen between *Musikalisch* [musically] and *Schönen* [beautiful], Hanslick in fact creates a noun.[2] He thus suggests that the "Musically Beautiful" should be seen as an aesthetic category in its own right, just like the *naturally beautiful* (*Das Naturschöne*, the beautiful specific to nature) and the *artifactually beautiful* (*Das Kunstschöne*, the beautiful specific to art).[3] Hanslick's program is in a way distorted by Cohen's translation of the title (*The Beautiful in Music*), as it was not Hanslick's intent to demonstrate how something

2. This neologism was a conscious decision: in the prepublication excerpts of *On the Musically Beautiful* (see the previous essay), Hanslick always uses the more common term "musically beautiful" [*musikalisch Schönes*], substituting these very passages with the unique term "musically beautiful" [*Musikalisch-Schöne*] for the first regular edition.

3. In our translation, we use the word "artifactual" where Hanslick uses adjectival or nominal constructions relating to "art." Alternatives such as "artistic" or "artificial" do not capture the German meaning of the word. Artifactual, however, captures the aspect of art being an artifact, unlike nature.

that is beautiful manifests itself *in* music. Other translations, like that of Henry Pleasants (*Beauty in Music*),[4] Theodore Gracyk (*On Beauty in Music*),[5] or Peter Kivy (*On Musical Beauty*)[6] are even more distortive. It is important to note that it is not beauty per se that interests Hanslick, but rather beautiful musical objects and their specific properties and relations. It is this beautiful musical object that Hanslick has in mind when he claims that aesthetics primarily has to investigate "the beautiful object, and not the perceiving subject" (Chapter 1, p. 3).[7]

Hanslick's strong focus on *objective*, timeless properties, and relations has led many commentators to regard his approach as an aesthetics of timeless, unchanging beauty that precludes the history of musical taste or ideals. In fact, Hanslick clearly states, "Beauty is and remains beauty even if it arouses no feelings, indeed even if it is neither viewed nor contemplated" (Chapter 1, p. 4). Again, recall that Hanslick does not mean beauty per se when he refers to "the beautiful." His insistence on timeless aspects of a beautiful object ("Beauty is and remains beauty") is *not* intended to declare beauty itself timeless and unchanging.[8] Instead, Hanslick focuses his attention on objective, timeless properties of beautiful musical objects. Contrary to a widespread misconception of Hanslick's aesthetics, he accepted, indeed

4. Henry Pleasants, *Eduard Hanslick: Music Criticisms 1846–1899* (London: Penguin Books, 1963), p. 10.

5. http://web.mnstate.edu/gracyk/courses/phil%20of%20art/printer-friendly/Hanslick%20TEXTBOOK%20version%20chpts%201%20and%202.pdf

6. Peter Kivy, *Introduction to a Philosophy of Music* (Oxford: Clarendon, 2002), p. 22.

7. Payzant gives a rather misleading translation of the passage, as he translates *empfindendes Subjekt* not as "perceiving subject," but as "feelings of the subject" (*On the Musically Beautiful*, p. 2).

8. On this point, see, for example, Andrew Edgar, "Adorno and Musical Analysis," *Journal of Aesthetics and Art Criticism* 57, no. 4 (1999): pp. 443–44; Barbara Titus, "The Quest for Spiritualized Form: (Re)positioning Eduard Hanslick," *Acta Musicologica* 80, no. 1 (2008): pp. 80–84; or Thomas Grey, "Hanslick," *The Routledge Companion to Philosophy and Music*, ed. Theodore Gracyk and Andrew Kania (London: Routledge, 2011), pp. 367–68.

embraced the fact that musical ideals and conceptions of beauty continuously change over the course of musical history:

> There is no art that exhausts so many forms and as quickly as does music. Modulations, cadential progressions, intervallic and harmonic progressions wear out in fifty, even thirty years such that the intellectually stimulating composer can no longer employ them, and will be constantly pressured to invent new, purely musical features. Without inaccuracy, we can say of a host of compositions that rank high above the norm of their time that they *were* once beautiful. (Chapter 3, p. 51)

It is here that the progressive element of Hanslick's musical aesthetics manifests itself fully. The very principles of aesthetics must change, he explains, if someday the tonal system itself undergoes change. Writing in 1854, Hanslick was a visionary to hold this relativistic viewpoint, even though he considered such a "change in the *nature* of the system . . . very remote" (Chapter 6, p. 98). By the time Hanslick revised the text for the tenth edition of 1902, Arnold Schönberg's break with the traditional tonal system was in fact not "very remote," but only a few years away. However, it is highly doubtful that Hanslick would have approved of a compositional technique so removed from the musical ideals that he cherished his entire life.

As a critic, but also in *On the Musically Beautiful,* Hanslick was rather outspoken about these musical ideals. A conservative at heart, he cleaved to the classical–romantic tradition, that is, mainly Germanic music from the late eighteenth century up until the more academic music of his time—roughly Mozart to Brahms, but also including French operetta and German *Singspiel.*[9] Despite a clear bias in

9. On Hanslick as a critic, see, for example, Sandra McColl, *Music Criticism in Vienna 1896–1897: Critically Moving Forms* (Oxford: Clarendon, 1996); David Brodbeck, *Defining Deutschtum: Political Ideology, German Identity, and Music-Critical Discourse in Liberal Vienna* (Oxford: Oxford University Press, 2014); and several papers in Nicole Grimes, Siobhán Donovan, and Wolfgang Marx (eds.), *Rethinking Hanslick: Music, Formalism, and Expression* (Rochester, NY: University of Rochester Press, 2013).

his own musical taste and judgments, Hanslick held that his theory of the musically beautiful was itself neutral and open to a variety of styles and musical tastes.

> The "musically beautiful" . . . is not limited to the "classical" style, nor does it include a preference for that style over the "romantic." It pertains to the one as well as to the other orientation, rules over Bach as well as Beethoven, Mozart as well as Schumann. Our thesis thus also does not contain an indication of partisanship. The entire course of the present investigation does not declare any Should Be but rather considers only What Is. No particular musical ideal may be deduced from that standpoint as authentic beauty; rather, it may merely be demonstrated what beauty is in every style in the same way, even the most opposed ones. (Chapter 3, pp. 54–55)

It is difficult to uphold Hanslick's claim that his theory was merely *descriptive*, not *normative*. His usage of "beautiful" is essentially twofold: In one sense, it is a term designating properties and relations that inhere in an object of musical aesthetics, but it is also a term that defines an aesthetic ideal (as the opposite of "ugly"). It is hard to see how the second usage can be purely descriptive if aesthetic ideals change, as Hanslick readily concedes. Hanslick's theory thus oscillates between a proto-phenomenology of music, on the one hand, and a traditional normative approach to aesthetic judgments on the other. The latter promotes a specific point of view relative to a specific historical taste and to a specific historical musical ideal.

These specificities become obvious when we examine closely how Hanslick constructs his theory of the musically beautiful. At its center, he places a very traditional understanding of melody (theme–motive) as a "the fundamental form of musical beauty" (Chapter 3, p. 40). Once created, the melody–theme undergoes "development." It is easy to see that Hanslick is thinking here of the classical model of the sonata form, which features such organic development not only in the development section, but throughout (Beethoven, Brahms).

However, that historical model applies fully only to music from the late eighteenth century up until the more conservative composers of Hanslick's time. Neither Bach's *Fortspinnung* [spinning forth] nor Wagner's "endless melody" follow the classical–romantic scheme that Hanslick has in mind. It thus comes as no surprise that Hanslick's attitude toward Bach is reserved. He never fully appreciated music from the preclassical era, though his assessment of the "delicately fashioned saltshakers and silver candlesticks of the venerable Sebastian Bach" diplomatically evolved into "delicately fashioned shapes in the suites and concertos" by the ninth edition of 1896, when the "Bach renaissance" was long underway. Wagner, on the other hand, was unwilling to limit himself to the traditional model of melody—that is, initially sharply defined, then neatly developed—that underlies Hanslick's aesthetics. It is obvious that this conception of melody-theme as "the fundamental form of musical beauty" dramatically narrows the scope of his theory.[10]

The specifically musical is "beauty that . . . resides solely in the tones and their artistic connection," as we quoted earlier (Chapter 3, p. 40). Hanslick's conception of tone [*Ton*] is crucial for a full understanding of his aesthetic approach. The German language is highly versatile when it comes to using *Ton* as a root word for collocations

---

10. For greater detail on Hanslick's organic model of musical composition, see Geoffrey Payzant, *Hanslick on the Musically Beautiful: Sixteen Lectures on the Musical Aesthetics of Eduard Hanslick* (Christchurch, New Zealand: Cybereditions, 2002), pp. 88–91, 96–98, 117–19; or Nina Noeske, "Body and Soul, Content and Form: On Hanslick's Use of the Organism Metaphor," in *Rethinking Hanslick: Music, Formalism, and Expression*, ed. Nicole Grimes, Siobhán Donovan, and Wolfgang Marx (Rochester, NY: University of Rochester Press, 2013), pp. 236–58. For the historical relevance and the normative implications of this model, also see Ruth Solie, "The Living Work: Organicism and Musical Analysis," *19th-Century Music* 4, no. 2 (1980): pp. 147–56; and several papers in Leo Treitler, *Music and the Historical Imagination* (Cambridge, MA: Harvard University Press, 1989). Today, the organic model is considered more critically in music theory since Joseph Kerman's classical paper, "How We Got Into Analysis, and How to Get Out," *Critical Inquiry* 7, no. 2 (1980): pp. 311–31; and his much-debated reflection on the ideological preconceptions of musicological discourse: *Contemplating Music: Challenges to Musicology* (Cambridge, MA: Harvard University Press, 1985).

and word combinations. Hanslick makes free use of the many possibilities this linguistic flexibility offers. He defines music as consisting of *Tonreihen, Tonformen* [tone successions, tone forms, Chapter 7, p. 109], its ideal content as *tonlich* (Chapter 3, p. 46), or as residing in *Tonbildungen* (tone formations, Chapter 3, p. 46). In German, and also in Hanslick's treatise, *Ton* refers to "a sound of a specific, measurable height and depth" (Chapter 6, p. 99). *Tones* in that sense are "the foundational conditions of all music" (Chapter 6, p. 99); they are "the material from which the composer [literally, tone poet] creates" (Chapter 3, p. 40).

Ton is thus a sound of a specific nature, but Hanslick's usage of the term is nuanced and not entirely consistent. When he defines the concept of tone (Chapter 6), and elsewhere when he speaks of tones as music's raw material, he has in mind sounds with "measurable" [*meßbar*], "specific" [*bestimmt*] vibration rates ("height and depth") that can be mathematically precisely determined (10th ed., p. 188; Chapter 6, p. 99). However, in cases in which Hanslick refers to tones as material of a composer's creative process and as agents in musical works, they are elements that have "secret alliances and elective affinities grounded in natural laws" (10th ed., p. 80; Chapter 3, p. 45), that is, are elements in an "organized tone system" (10th ed., p. 191; Chapter 6, p. 101), such as a diatonic major or minor scale, each step of which has a distinguishable identity.[11]

As *Ton* is a key concept within Hanslick's aesthetics, it is of central importance for any meaningful interpretation of his ideas to have a contextually accurate translation of the many *Ton*-related words that he uses throughout his book. This is particularly true for the pivotal sentence of the treatise, where Hanslick characterizes the musically beautiful as "*tönend bewegte Formen.*" The phrase is virtually

---

11. Payzant mistakenly explains Hanslick's statement about tones being sounds "of a specific, measurable height and depth" as referring to location within a diatonic scale, i.e. to scale-step identity (Payzant, *On the Musically Beautiful*, "Essay: Towards a Revised Reading of Hanslick," 95–96). However, several passages in Chapter 6 make clear that Hanslick's reference to measurable height and depth refers to the uniform frequency of air vibrations necessary to produce musical tones.

untranslatable, and neither Gustav Cohen's nor Geoffrey Payzant's solution to the problem is satisfactory. On the one hand, Cohen's translation ("the essence of music is sound and motion") ignores the aspect of form[12]—and thus omits what can well be considered the most essential element of the phrase. Payzant, on the other hand ("the content of music is tonally moving forms"), limits our understanding of *tönend* to an aspect of the word that does not fully capture Hanslick's intent.

In the German original, the famous motto is as follows:

"Der Inhalt der Musik sind *tönend bewegte Formen*" (Chapter 3, p. 41).

Tönend is the present participle of the verb *tönen*, which in German means "to sound by means of tones."[13] But as Payzant rightly observes, the English language has no means of expressing sound based on what German knows as *Ton*, that is, "a sound of a specific, measurable height and depth." "Sounding," as a verb, lacks the dimension of sound structured in tones, an aspect clearly present in the German verb *tönen*.

Payzant adopts a radical solution to the problem. Because tone words appear so frequently in the treatise, *tönend* must also reflect the sense of tone as (in Payzant's words) a "sound, actual or imagined, perceived as occupying a position in a diatonic musical scale."[14] However, both the generic meaning of *Ton–Tönen* as sound–sounding and the functional diatonic meaning of *Tönen* are

12. As Payzant rightly observed, "Cohen's word *essence* is pure fantasy." *On the Musically Beautiful*, p. 101.
13. On the grammatically difficult construction of *tönend bewegte Formen*, see also Lee Rothfarb, "Nineteenth-Century Fortunes of Musical Formalism," *Journal of Music Theory* 55, no. 2 (2011): p. 169.
14. Payzant, *On the Musically Beautiful*, p. 95. For Payzant's theory of "tone," see also his "Hanslick, Sams, Gay, and 'Tönend Bewegte Formen,'" *Journal of Aesthetics and Art Criticism* 40, no. 1 (1981): pp. 44–47; "Eduard Hanslick and the 'geistreich' Dr. Alfred Julius Becher," *The Music Review* 44 (1983): pp. 107–12; or "Tone-Words," in *Hanslick on the Musically Beautiful*, pp. 44–46.

impossible to capture simultaneously in a one-word English translation. Payzant, for matters of consistency, chose the functional diatonic meaning. Consequently, his translation eradicates altogether the dimension of sound in *tönend* and risks confusion with the idea of tonal music. "Tonally moving forms" are forms moving by means of tones that continually shift their positions in the diatonic tonal system. Theoretically speaking, it is irrelevant whether the tones are actually sounding. They may be "actual or imagined." The only thing that counts is their position in the tonal system.

Although Payzant's translation undeniably gives a highly consistent interpretation of *tönend bewegte Formen*, it is doubtful that Hanslick would have approved of this interpretation. Grammatically, the phrase is structured such that *forms [Formen]* are defined as *moved [bewegt]* and *moved forms [bewegte Formen]* are defined as *tönend*. But how are we to decide what aspect of *tönend* Hanslick intends in this passage, which is arguably the centerpiece of his aesthetic conception?

Previous scholarship has overlooked that the three passages subsequent to the motto explain its meaning by taking up its three components in order. The first of these compares "beautiful form" with the arabesque. Just like the arabesque, "a branch of ornamentation in the visual arts" (Chapter 3, p. 41), musical form also exhibits structural patterns that please without expressing extrastructural meaning or significance. In the second of the passages, Hanslick broadens the definition by comparing music with a kaleidoscope. Both the musically beautiful and the kaleidoscope demonstrate how "the trait of motion, of temporal development" is essential to artistic creations (Chapter 3, p. 42). However, whereas the kaleidoscope is a purely mechanical device, music can only be rightly understood as the "active emanation of an artistic mind" (Chapter 3, p. 41). It is easy to see that Hanslick uses these analogies to illustrate first the element of form, then the element of movement. The third passage should, then, reveal Hanslick's understanding of *tönend*. However, contrary to Payzant's interpretation, Hanslick does not at this point address tones and their structural orderings and relations within the diatonic system. Instead, he discusses the importance of hearing and laments "the *underevaluation of the sensuous*" in musical aesthetics (Chapter 3, p. 42). Thus, if this third passage illustrates the last element of *tönend bewegte Formen*, just as the previous ones illustrate the first and second elements of the motto (forms and movement, respectively), we must conclude that the third passage indeed emphasizes the indispensability of the acoustical component of musical beauty. *Tönend bewegte Formen* thus indicates that *both* the structural and the acoustical components are necessary to fully appreciate and aesthetically evaluate that which the musically beautiful offers.[15] Hanslick later makes a similar point when he explains his nonreductionist approach (see p. xxxiv of this essay). To capture this meaning of *tönend*, absent in the Payzant translation, we decided to render this phrase as "sonically moved forms." Sonically moved forms are thus forms that are moved in a way that can be heard. Although not fully satisfactory, our translation does cover all three elements of the phrase—form, movement, and the acoustical component—whereas Cohen's translation lacks the formal component and Payzant's the acoustical.

If the content of music is sonically moved forms, what, then, makes certain sonically moved forms more beautiful than others? The internal structural relations of a piece of music are crucial, but as we saw, musical tastes and preferences can change over time, and relations once considered beautiful might lose that attribution in the course of history. The key element behind structural relations is what Hanslick calls *Geist*—again, a virtually untranslatable term.[16] *Geist*

15. Although she misses the problematic implications of Payzant's translation, Hanne Appelqvist (formerly Ahonen) particularly emphasizes this aspect in Hanne Ahonen, "Wittgenstein and the Conditions of Musical Communication" (PhD dissertation, Columbia University, 2007), p. 124; and Hanne Appelqvist, "Form and Freedom: The Kantian Ethos of Musical Formalism," *The Nordic Journal of Aesthetics* 40–41 (2011): p. 81.

16. On the terminological nuances of the term *Geist*, see, for example, Geoffrey Payzant, "Hanslick on Music as Product of Feeling," *Journal of Musicological Research* 9, nos. 2–3 (1989): p. 135; Lee Rothfarb, "Nineteenth-Century Fortunes of Musical Formalism," *Journal of Music Theory* 55, no. 2 (2011): p. 194; Mark Evan Bonds, *Absolute Music: The History of an Idea* (Oxford: Oxford University Press, 2014), pp. 48–150.

in German can mean a wide variety of things, all connected to the intellectual sphere in the broadest sense of the word: Intellect, mind, spirit, and wit are the main examples. For a proper understanding of Hanslick's thought, it is important to determine the core meaning of *Geist* and *Geist*-related terms in the treatise.

In fact, the role of *Geist* in Hanslick's aesthetic conception can hardly be overestimated. To constitute beauty, both the acoustical and the structural components must be connected with *Geist*, whereas *Geist* is intimately related to form and to the concept of the specifically musical. To illustrate the problem that can easily arise with a slippery word like *Geist*, we turn to a passage that employs this word several times in different forms.[17]

> In no way is the specifically musically beautiful to be understood as mere acoustical beauty . . . and still less can we talk about an ear-pleasing play of tones and other such images, by which the lack of a mental source of animation tends to become emphasized. . . . For we acknowledge no beauty without its full share of ideality. . . . This already implies that the ideal content of music is in the most intimate relationship with these forms. . . . The forms which construct themselves out of tones are not empty but filled; they are not mere contours of a vacuum but mind giving shape to itself from within.

In translating the passage, Payzant uses a whole range of terms and phrases that in some way refer to the intellectual sphere: "mental source of animation," "ideality," "ideal content," and finally, "mind." In each of those instances, our translation uses "intellect" as a root word ("intellectual animation," "intellectuality," "intellectual content," and "intellect"). This corresponds to Hanslick's use of *Geist* and *Geist*-related terms in the German original (*geistige Beseelung, Geist, geistiger Gehalt*, and again, *Geist*).

---

17. In Payzant's translation, p. 30, in ours, Chapter 3, p. 43.

Geist defies a uniform translation. As with *tönend*, there is no straightforward English rendering for *Geist*. However, in Hanslick's treatise, *Geist* has a core meaning that clearly centers around intellect or mind. Hanslick's theory is as follows: Tones are not the material basis for music in the same way that stone is the material basis for sculpture. Music created by a (skilled) composer is thus the result of an intellectual operation based on the diatonic system and the numerous combinations the diatonic system offers. It is in this sense that Hanslick defines composing as "an operation of the intellect in material of intellectual capacity" (Chapter 3, p. 45). However, as there is no fixed, ahistorical relation between musical beauty and the internal structure of a musical piece, composing is also an act of free creation, limited only by the general laws of musical composition. The mental faculty that enables the composer to select combinations of tones that constitute musically beautiful works of art, as well as the mental faculty that allows a listener to perceive them, is *imagination*: "A musical piece emerges from the imagination of the artist for the imagination of the listener" (Chapter 1, p. 5). If overused, however, certain tone combinations are no longer intellectually stimulating and must yield to new intellectual products created by the imaginative composer. It is this talent of imagination that distinguishes the composer gifted with *Geist* from the one that lacks such gifts. As Hanslick explains, only such *Geist*-gifted composers will be able to select those intellectually stimulating tone combinations and build them into a work of music that we call *geistreich* ("intellectually stimulating"; Chapter 3, p. 51).

Hanslick's theory of *Geist* is thus not about music's "ideal" or "spiritual" content in any way, but rather about the inventiveness of composers and their ability to choose and construct tone combinations that appeal to the intellect of cultured listeners—a skilled and gifted mind creating for other cultured minds. It is problematic, then, to translate *Geist* in variable ways, and with words that are not directly relatable to its core meaning. Such renderings obscure the original meaning of the term, which is a central concept of

On the Musically Beautiful. Thus Hanslick's theory is not about spiritual substance (Payzant, p. 82), but about intellectual substance. The musical intellect creates and stimulates, and its creations have intellectual significance.

Because music is created by, and appeals to, a musical mind or intellect, the mental operation responsible for such creations is also at its core distinctly cognitive. It is a form of "thinking" [*Denken*], Hanslick claims, though the thoughts of the composer are of a specifically musical kind. With his aesthetics centered around the musical theme–melody, Hanslick also conceives of the theme as a "thought" [*Gedanke*], or an "idea" [*Idee*].[18] Melody, for Hanslick, is a "formed idea" [*geformter Gedanke*; Chapter 7, p. 112]. As an idea, the theme–melody can be seen as a cognitive element of some sort—that is, the result of a thought process. But the thought process is a specifically musical one, and the musical idea is an idea without concepts in the semantic sense of the word. Thus, when Hanslick refers to "autonomous musical ideas" (Chapter 7, p. 10), these ideas must be understood as musical ideas that are *durch sich geistvoll*, as Hanslick writes [intellectually stimulating in itself; Chapter 3, p. 47], and not as references to anything extramusical. Translating *selbstständige musikalische Gedanken* as "autonomous musical concepts" (Payzant, p. 82) is misleading because it invokes the notion of a concept as a verbal construct. Idea, *Geist*, and imagination all have a cognitive implication, though one that is specific to music. Our translation strives, as much as possible, to remain true to this cognitive— and at the same time specifically musical—concept of *Geist* and *Geist*-related terms.

With such a decidedly *cognitivist* approach to musical aesthetics, it comes as no surprise that Hanslick refused to assign a leading role to emotive elements. His staunch opposition to the "degenerate

18. Hanslick uses *Idee* and *Gedanke* interchangeably. In our translation, we use the term "idea." In a similar sense, and following a similar theoretical tradition, translators of Schönberg's *musikalischer Gedanke* usually give preference to "musical idea." Similarly, Hanslick does not distinguish between theme [*Thema*] and motive [*motive*] and uses both terms interchangeably.

aesthetics of feeling" (*VMS*, 1st ed., V)[19] that prevailed in his time is still seen by many as his main theoretic feat. However, Hanslick did not devalue emotive qualities and experiences altogether—a point in which he was often misunderstood. In prefaces to later editions of the treatise (including the one translated here), Hanslick tried to clarify his position:

> I fully agree that the ultimate value of the beautiful will always be based on direct evidence of feeling. However, I maintain equally firmly that we cannot deduce a single musical law from all of the usual appeals to feeling. (p. V).

In a way, Hanslick's emotive vocabulary has contributed to some of the misunderstandings. The German word *Gefühl* (rendered as feeling in our translation) is used in a specific way throughout the treatise, again reflecting Hanslick's generally cognitivist point of view. *Gefühl* is in some sense rooted in *Gemüt*, another virtually untranslatable German term that we render as "psychic disposition."

> What is it, then, that makes a feeling into a particular feeling, into yearning, hope, love? Perhaps the mere strength or weakness, the undulating of interior movement? Surely not. These can be the same in the case of different feelings, as well as different in the case of the same feeling in various individuals at different times. Our psychic state can coalesce into a particular feeling only based on a number of mental images and judgments (perhaps unconsciously in a moment of strong feelings). The feeling of hope is inseparable from the mental image of an expected, happier condition, and is compared with the present one. Melancholy compares past good fortune with the present. These are very specific mental images and concepts. Without them, without this cognitive mechanism, "we cannot call the present

---

19. Dietmar Strauß, *Vom Musikalisch-Schönen. Teil 1: Historisch-Kritische Ausgabe* (Mainz, Germany: Schott, 1990), p. 9.

feeling 'hope,' not 'melancholy'" [Chapter 2, p. 16]. That cognitive mechanism transforms them into hope and melancholy.

Hanslick's highly modern cognitive approach to feelings limits his aesthetic theory to those emotive states that are considered feelings according to his own criteria. This is an important point to note, and it is a feature of his aesthetics that has caused a fair amount of confusion. By contrast, the English analytic tradition is inclined to address cognitive feelings as "emotions."[20] Emotions, however, lack other qualities that the German term *Gefühl* possesses. As understood in the analytic tradition, "emotion" can approximate Hanslick's sense of the word only within the specific context in which he discusses feelings. As Geoffrey Payzant has observed, "compared to the 'feelings' of which Hanslick and his contemporaries wrote, the 'emotions' of our analytic philosopher are slab-sided, lacking the dimension of depth, that is, introspection."[21] Whereas Gustav Cohen paid little attention to the specificity of Hanslick's terminology, translating *Gefühl* as "feeling" and "emotion" interchangeably, Payzant pointed to the need for translational precision. To avoid misconceptions that the English term "emotion" might evoke, our translation also renders *Gefühl* as "feeling."

Hanslick uses other complicated emotive terms as well, and one of the most difficult is *Empfindung*. In the treatise, *Empfindung* has two distinctly different meanings: In one sense, it is a less cognition-laden word for feeling; in the other, it carries the meaning of "sensation." Hanslick uses the term in both ways, though in different contexts. He discusses *Empfindung* as sensation when the reference is to the sensory input that underlies all feeling: "*Sensation* is the

20. For the most extensive treatment of this subject in the analytical tradition in regard to Hanslick's treatise, see Malcolm Budd, *Music and the Emotions: The Philosophical Theories* (London: Routledge, 1985), pp. 16–36. See also the detailed analysis in Robert Sharpe, *Philosophy of Music: An Introduction* (Chesam, UK: Acumen Publishing, 2004), pp. 16–22, or Nick Zangwill, "Against Emotion: Hanslick Was Right About Music," *British Journal of Aesthetics* 44, no. 1 (2004): pp. 29–43.

21. Payzant, *Hanslick on the Musically Beautiful*, p. 114.

perception of a specific sensory quality, of a tone, a color. *Feeling* is the awareness of a furthering or an inhibiting of our psychic state" (Chapter 1, p. 4). Because the beautiful object must first affect the senses, *Empfindung* in this sense of the word is "the beginning and precondition of aesthetic pleasure" (Chapter 1, p. 5). It is the precondition of any higher arousal, though it has itself no specifically aesthetic relevance, let alone specifically musical relevance. *Empfindung* in the second sense of the word designates schematic emotional states or moods that eighteenth-century music theorists linked to specific musical modes or musical–rhetorical figures. *Empfindung* in that sense is close to "affect" [*Affekt*], a term typically associated with the eighteenth-century doctrine of affects [*Affektenlehre*]. Payzant also translates this second, music-theoretical use of the term as "feeling." However, this is clearly not the cognitive, psychological meaning of the term that Hanslick uses for his main arguments. We use "sentiment" for this second, music-theoretical meaning of the term, and "sensation" for the first one. The word sentiment is commonly used in similar contexts in translations of the writings of eighteenth-century theorists such as Sulzer (1720–1779).[22] That translation avoids imposing a modern, nineteenth-century psychological term onto an eighteenth-century music-theoretical mindset.

Although Hanslick denied psychological factors any foundational role in musical aesthetics, he did pay considerable attention to recent developments in science, particularly in the field of physiology. Chapters four and five of the treatise give a detailed account of the state of knowledge in Hanslick's time. Hanslick emphasizes that musical aesthetics must be informed about music's bodily roots and its physiological requirements, but he also draws a clear line between

22. On Sulzer's position, see, for example, Nancy Baker and Thomas Christensen, *Aesthetics and the Art of Musical Composition in the German Enlightenment: Selected Writings of Johann Georg Sulzer and Heinrich Christoph Koch* (Cambridge: Cambridge University Press, 1995); or Matthew Riley, *Musical Listening in the German Enlightenment: Attention, Wonder and Astonishment* (Aldershot, UK: Ashgate, 2004), chapter 3.

physiological and *aesthetic* arguments. In aesthetic contexts, physiology can have only an ancillary function:

> What physiology offers to the science of music is of utmost importance for our understanding of auditory impressions as such. In that regard, some progress can still occur by way of physiology. In the main musical issue, that will scarcely ever be the case. (Chapter 4, p. 78)

Although the acoustical component, communicated through hearing, is a necessary prerequisite for musical beauty, its aesthetic evaluation follows rules that belong to a different sphere. Physiological laws build the basis of musical experience. On this lower level, the way in which music is received by the ear and subsequently affects the nerves can only lead to impressions that Hanslick calls *elementarisch* [elemental]. Hanslick uses the term *pathologisch* [pathological] to designate musical hearing that focuses on these bodily sensations. *Pathologisch* in this sense of the word has a twofold meaning, for it not only refers to music's bodily roots, but also has allusions to an "abnormal" mode of hearing. Indeed, judged from an aesthetic perspective, this form of musical hearing misses the element of *Geist* that is central to Hanslick's aesthetic conception.

Aesthetic hearing and pathological hearing are two possible modes of receiving music, or even two distinct poles. The more the aesthetic component outweighs and dominates, the less of an impact the pathological–elemental component can have: "The more significant the aesthetic aspect in the listener (just as in the artwork), the more levelled out is the merely elemental." (Chapter 5, p. 90). In aesthetic contexts, it is only this aesthetic moment, the more complex and more highly developed "contemplative" aspect, that counts:

> We contrast being seized pathologically with deliberate, pure contemplation of a musical work. This contemplative manner of hearing is the sole artistic, true form. . . . An enjoying, not a submitting, correlates with beauty. (Chapter 5, p. 88)

Here at the end of chapter five, Hanslick begins to elaborate on the notion of *Anschauung*. This idea appears in chapter one, where he attempts to lay a methodological foundation for his later positive thesis, and is fully developed in chapter three. *Anschauung* is a difficult concept that might be best explained as a quasi-phenomenological act of apprehending musical beauty (Hanslick also uses the term *Betrachtung*; we translate both as *contemplation*). Hanslick describes it is an "act of attentive listening, which in fact consists in regarding a succession of tone configurations" (Chapter 1, p. 6). *Anschauung* is genuinely aesthetic, and it is confined neither to reason nor (even worse) to feeling (Chapter 1, p. 6). The term is also central to a proper understanding of Hanslick's notion of a scientific, objective aesthetic.

As we saw in the first essay, Hanslick struggled with the task of reconciling a concept of science, in the sense of the lower, physiological–acoustical level, with the higher aesthetic–contemplative one. If Hanslick now refers to "scientific method," the term "science" is used by analogy and aims at characterizing a spirit of aesthetic investigation that is opposed to idealist system-building. It is in this sense that Hanslick writes, "The 'system' is gradually giving way to 'research,' which holds firmly to the maxim that the laws of beauty of each art are inseparable from the characteristics of its material, of its technique" (Chapter 1, p. 2).

Earlier in this essay, we characterized Hanslick's aesthetic as a bottom-up approach vis-à-vis the idealist tradition—a top-down approach that considers the aesthetics of music to be merely a specific branch of general aesthetics. We can now see how Hanslick's bottom-up concept is related to his notion of science and of *Forschung* [research]. The sort of research that Hanslick has is mind is certainly not that of later empirical aesthetics, with its scientific–statistical method, as this approach would contradict Hanslick's ideals of objectivity and exactitude, as well as his concept of *Geist*. Instead, Hanslick's *Forschung* is oriented toward the aesthetic object, with its inherent properties and qualities apprehended in an act of *Anschauung*. It is in this sense that Hanslick calls for an aesthetics of music that would have to "approach the natural–scientific method at least as far as trying to penetrate to the things themselves, and to probe what in those things may be enduring, objective, detached from the thousandfold fluctuating impressions" (Chapter 1, p. 1).

With this concept of objectivity as a guiding principle, focused on the object itself, it is perfectly understandable that Hanslick's aesthetics of music anticipates insights and methodological convictions of later phenomenology of music. However, at the same time his aesthetics is also clearly indebted to traditional normative thinking about music that was typical of the German classic–romanticist tradition. Writing in 1854, Hanslick was both a forerunner of analytical and phenomenological perspectives and a defender of conventional modes of thought that were deeply rooted in his time and place. It thus comes as no surprise that *On the Musically Beautiful* constitutes a meeting place of highly diverse and heterogeneous threads of philosophical thought, as we see in the third essay.

INTRODUCTORY ESSAY 3:
PHILOSOPHICAL BACKGROUND

"It is probably not too much of an exaggeration to say that the terms of this inquiry in modern times were set by Eduard Hanslick's polemical *On the Musically Beautiful*, published in 1854."[1] The "inquiry" in this quotation is the nature of musical meaning, or, more broadly speaking, Western philosophy of music in general. There is no doubt about Hanslick's role and importance in the history of the aesthetics of music. His rather small 1854 publication is generally regarded as "one of the most important (or to some, infamous) treatises on the nature and value of music ever written,"[2] as "a watershed moment in the history of music aesthetics,"[3] or "the inaugural text in the founding of musical formalism as a position in the philosophy of art."[4]

1. James Alperson, introduction to *Musical Worlds: New Directions in the Philosophy of Music*, ed. James Alperson (University Park: Pennsylvania State University Press, 1998), p. 1.

2. Wayne D. Bowman, *Philosophical Perspectives on Music* (Oxford: Oxford University Press, 1998) p. 140.

3. Lee Rothfarb, "Nineteenth-Century Fortunes of Musical Formalism," *Journal of Music Theory* 55, no. 2 (2011): p. 195 .

4. Peter Kivy, *Antithetical Arts: On the Ancient Quarrel Between Literature and Music* (Oxford: Oxford University Press, 2009), p. 53.

This strong awareness of Hanslick's significance is especially wide-spread in Anglo-American scholarship, in which Hanslick's ideas continue to serve as a starting point for aesthetic theorizing, even beyond the boundaries of philosophical and musicological discourse. In an entry in the *Oxford Handbook of Music Psychology*, David Huron underlined the ongoing relevance of Hanslick's aesthetic approach: "Until recently, Hanslick's views have defined the principal parameters in debates concerning musical aesthetics. All major philosophers in the aesthetics of music have started by engaging with Hanslick's ideas."[5]

Given Hanslick's importance and the longevity of the debate, however, there is surprisingly little consensus on Hanslick's place in the history of ideas. During the past century of debate, Hanslick's aesthetic has been seen as founded in German Idealism; in anti-idealist philosophy; as a document of early positivism, as well as documenting a proto-phenomenological approach directed against positivist reductionism; as a plea for the scientization of aesthetics along the lines of natural science, as well as a plea for a more hermeneutical understanding of music that opposes such a scientization; as an expression of "formalism" and of spiritual values transcending a purely formalist perspective; as based on a classicist as well as a romanticist outlook; and as an expression of a reactionary, "bourgeois" approach, as well as an approach sympathetic with musical progress. Even the introductory remarks alone of *On the Musically Beautiful* have provoked interpretations of Hanslick that plead for an "alignment of aesthetics with natural science"[6] and of Hanslick "distancing himself from the methods of natural science."[7]

It is certainly difficult to place Hanslick's ideas in the context of Western aesthetic traditions, despite various efforts to uncover a

---

5. David Huron, "Aesthetics," in *The Oxford Handbook of Music Psychology*, ed. Susan Hallam, Ian Cross, and Michael Thaut (Oxford: Oxford University Press, 2008), p. 234. Huron mentions Langer, Kivy, Scruton, Levinson, and Davies.

6. Dietmar Strauß, *Eduard Hanslick. Vom Musikalisch-Schönen. Ein Beitrag zur Revision der Ästhetik in der Tonkunst. Teil 2: Eduard Hanslicks Schrift in textkritischer Sicht* (Mainz, Germany: Schott, 1990), p. 78.

7. Werner Abegg, *Musikästhetik und Musikkritik bei Eduard Hanslick* (Regensburg, Germany: G. Bosse, 1974), p. 19.

consistent philosophical framework in which his aesthetic approach can be embedded and that can then serve as a key for its understanding. Although the scope of scholarship on the intellectual background of Hanslick's aesthetics has widened considerably in the past thirty years, Rudolf Schäfke's observation of "perplexing and apparently irreconcilable contradictions, historically as well as factually"[8] is almost as appropriate today as it was in 1922. In the discussion that follows, we outline some of the main philosophical streams of thought that form the background of *On the Musically Beautiful*.

3.1 KANT

If we wish to trace the philosophical influences upon Hanslick, we must from this point proceed with caution. . . . Of course there are interesting comparisons to be made between specific passages in Hanslick, and specific passages in the writings of Kant, but we have neither internal nor collateral evidence upon which to make a positive claim for an influence from the one to the other, except perhaps indirectly by way of C. F. Michaelis. Schopenhauer is not mentioned in Hanslick's book by name; there are two apparent allusions to him, both trivial. Hegel is named, quoted and alluded to, not on trivial matters, but there is no argument in Hanslick, no point of doctrine, to which we can confidently point and declare that it is of Hegelian origin.[9]

The caution that Geoffrey Payzant advises in the introductory essay to his translation of *On the Musically Beautiful* is especially appropriate with regard to Hanslick's relation to Kant. In Anglo-American scholarship, the prevailing view today of Hanslick's aesthetics is that, with regard to his general philosophical outlook, its roots lie in Kant.

---

8. Rudolf Schäfke, *Eduard Hanslick und die Musikästhetik* (Leipzig: Breitkopf und Härtel, 1922), p. 377.

9. Geoffrey Payzant, "Translator's Preface," in *Eduard Hanslick. On the Musically Beautiful: A Contribution Towards the Revision of the Aesthetics of Music* (Indianapolis, Indiana: Hackett, 1986) pp. XV–XVI.

The issue is often presented as if the privileged role of Kantian aesthetics for *On the Musically Beautiful* were a matter beyond doubt. Hanslick's aesthetics certainly exhibits several important features of aesthetics typically associated with the Kantian tradition: "From Kant, we see the foundations, if not the details of Hanslick's formalist viewpoint: nonconceptual, subjective purposiveness of form, arising from a harmonious correlation between the faculties of imagination and understanding, accessible only as phenomenon."[10]

It is problematic to ascribe more specific ideas to the influence of Kant, for various reasons. First, Hanslick was not trained as a philosopher. Privately educated by his philosophically interested father, his philosophical upbringing was oriented more toward realist approaches to philosophy than toward the ideas of Kant and his followers.[11] Although certainly discussed and, to a certain extent, also taught, Kant did not exert a dominating influence in the Habsburg Empire as he did in Germany, at least not before the advent of neo-Kantianism and its alliance with more realist streams of philosophical thought in the second half of the nineteenth century. Second, some of the aesthetic ideas usually linked to Kant and Kantianism were either considered common sense in Hanslick's time or were also associated with and popularized by thinkers outside the philosophical sphere—including music aestheticians such as Ferdinand Hand, whom Hanslick knew and valued. Consequently, ideas central to Hanslick's argument that are often seen as essentially Kantian might well have been shaped by traditions as diverse as German Romanticism or the English Enlightenment. Examples include the doctrine of aesthetic disinterestedness or the idea of music as a purpose in its own right.

Aesthetic formalism, on the other hand, a philosophical position often seen as originating with Kant, is a rather complicated theoretical point of view (see essay on basic concepts). Although similarities exist between Hanslick's and Kant's focus on formal properties,

---

10. Rothfarb, "Nineteenth-Century Fortunes of Musical Formalism," pp. 194–95.
11. Hanslick's father admired the philosophy of Eduard Beneke, who belonged to one of the realist schools.

Kant's aesthetic approach lacks the dimension of "musical logic" that is central to Hanslick's position.

Given that both Hanslick's and Kant's positions can in a sense be called "formalist," it comes as no surprise that Kant has long been considered one of the most promising candidates for providing a consistent philosophical framework for the aesthetics of *On the Musically Beautiful*. Less attention has been given to arguments and passages that run counter to the Kantian program of a "subjectivization of aesthetics." Central to Hanslick's methodology is the apparently non-Kantian claim that "in aesthetic investigations primarily the beautiful object, and not the perceiving subject, is to be researched" (Chapter 1, p. 3). The Payzant translation, however, obscures Hanslick's objectivist approach by translating "perceiving subject" as "feelings of the subject." As we saw in the essay on Hanslick's central concepts, *Empfindung* has two distinct meanings in the book: first as sensation, then as feeling. The term *empfindend* used by Hanslick in this quotation is not to be confused with "feeling" as in "aesthetics of feeling." Hanslick refers here to the sensory input, not to the more complex psychological phenomenon he later calls "feeling." This objectivist stance, which privileges the "beautiful object" at the expense of the "perceiving subject," constitutes the main theoretical divide between approaches shaped by Kant's subject-centered "Copernican Revolution" and the object-centered point of view that is central to Hanslick's methodological approach. Thus, although Kant remains an important figure for the theoretical context that informs the contemporary aesthetical debate, it is difficult to consider *On the Musically Beautiful* a work in the Kantian tradition in any strict and meaningful sense of the word.

3.2 GERMAN IDEALISM: HEGEL AND VISCHER

Defining Hanslick's relation to Kant's idealist followers—namely, Hegel and philosophers and aestheticians of the Hegelian school—is no less difficult. There is no doubt that young Hanslick had strong sympathies for Hegelianism. In a newspaper article from 1848, the year of the Austrian revolution (in which he played a very minor role),[12] Hanslick expresses enthusiasm for Hegel's philosophy of art: "Contemporary philosophy of art," he writes, "does not (mainly thanks to Hegel's efforts) consider art a mere tool for sensual enjoyment anymore." Rather, art can now be seen as "a manifestation of the goddess, coequal sister of religion, of philosophy." Hanslick goes on to declare that "the works of our great composers are . . . more than music," they "mirror the philosophical, religious, and political world view of their time."[13]

It is revealing to compare this article with *On the Musically Beautiful*, published just six years later. In the latter work, Hanslick turns against his position of 1848. The opposition to the idea of music as a mere "tool for sensual enjoyment" is unaltered. However, the conception of music's connection with the intellectual world has changed dramatically. The intellectual component is now seen as something intramusical, not as a means of connecting with the extramusical world in any sense. Music is not the manifestation of extramusical ideas, and parallels between music and the composer's contemporary culture are therefore meaningless from an aesthetic point of view: "While the historian, interpreting an artistic phenomenon by and large, may envisage in *Spontini* the 'expression of the

12. For Hanslick's involvement in the Austrian "revolution" see Geoffrey Payzant, "Eduard Hanslick and Robert Zimmermann," in Geoffry Payzant, *Hanslick on the Musically Beautiful: Sixteen Lectures on the Musical Aesthetics of Eduard Hanslick* (Christchurch, New Zealand: Cybereditions 2002), pp. 134–35.

13. "Die Kunst-Philosophie unserer Zeit steht [recte: sieht] in der Kunst (Dank sei es vor Allem *Hegel's* Bemühungen) nicht mehr ein bloßes Spielzeug zu sinnreichem Ergötzen, sie erkennt sie als eine Manifestation der Gottheit, als eine ebenbürtige Schwester der Religion, der Philosophie. . . . Die Werke der großen Tondichter sind mehr als Musik, sie sind Spiegelbilder der *philosophischen, religiösen* und *politischen* Weltanschauung ihrer Zeit." The article "Censur und Kunst-Kritik," appeared on March 24, 1848: http://anno.onb.ac.at/cgi-content/anno?aid=wrz&datum=18480324&seite =1&zoom=33. Cf. Dietmar Strauß, ed., *Eduard Hanslick. Sämtliche Schriften. Historisch-kritische Ausgabe Band I/1: Aufsätze und Rezensionen 1844–1848* (Vienna: Böhlau, 1993), pp. 156–58.

French Empire,' in *Rossini* the 'political restoration,' the aesthetician must stick solely to the works of those men in order to investigate what is beautiful about them, and why" (Chapter 3 p. 55).

This reversal of Hanslick's position illustrates that his new conception of music's intellectual component clearly differs from Hegelian aesthetics. *Geist*, that is, intellect expressed and manifested in music, cannot be conceived as spirituality or ideality in any Hegelian sense of the word. Its meaning in *On the Musically Beautiful*, as we saw in the essay on Hanslick's central concepts, is purely intramusical, having solely to do with the musical idea, its innovative character, logic, and development.

Given this strong disagreement on a central conviction, Geoffrey Payzant's skepticism that there is "no point of doctrine, to which we can confidently point and declare that it is of Hegelian origin" is certainly well founded. Hanslick's main connection with German Idealism, however, was not through Hegel but through Friedrich Theodor Vischer, a famous contemporaneous aesthetician whom Hanslick held in high regard throughout his life. Vischer is mentioned favorably, if only sporadically, in *On the Musically Beautiful*, and is an important source of Hanslick's notion of imagination. However, when Hanslick defines imagination as "activity of pure viewing" in chapter one (Chapter 1, p. 5), he acknowledges Vischer as a source in only the first three editions. The reference is missing in all later editions, including the one we translated.

Vischer's influence on the aesthetics of *On the Musically Beautiful* is complex. Curiously, Vischer has not received much scholarly attention, although he is mentioned more often than Kant in the treatise[14] and is a well-known source of inspiration.[15] Vischer's main

14. Hanslick mentions Kant only once when listing philosophers who plead for music's lack of content (Chapter 7, p. 107).

15. To our knowledge, only Barbara Titus has presented a more exhaustive study of the subject. See "Conceptualizing Music: Friedrich Theodor Vischer and Hegelian Currents in German Music Criticism, 1848–1887" (PhD dissertation, Oxford, 2005), pp. 89–103, and "The Quest for Spiritualized Form: (Re)positioning Eduard Hanslick," *Acta Musicologica* 80, no. 1 (2008): pp. 67–97.

relevance for the aesthetics of *On the Musically Beautiful* is probably rooted in his progressive view of the material aspect of art and the way in which this material aspect is shaped by history.

Contrary to an ahistorical, severely formalist point of view that focuses only on formal relations, regardless of their place in history, Hanslick draws considerable attention to the historical conditions of musical compositions. This even leads him to conclude that "we can say of a host of compositions that rank high above the norm of their time that they *were* once beautiful" (Chapter 3, p. 51). "Modulations, cadential progressions, intervallic and harmonic progressions," Hanslick writes, "wear out in fifty, even thirty years"[16] (Chapter 3, p. 51). Consequently, a piece of music composed on the basis of such "worn-out" features is no longer intellectually stimulating. The creative composer must thus constantly search for new tone combinations, constantly creating new means of expressing and developing intramusical ideas. This conception of a "historicity of the material"—a material that, as Hanslick writes, is "material of intellectual capacity" (Chapter 3, p. 45)—was already present in Vischer's aesthetics, though Vischer was rather ignorant about music and mainly interested in poetry and fine arts.

3.3 *ON THE MUSICALLY BEAUTIFUL* AND ITS PLACE IN CONTEMPORARY AUSTRIAN CULTURE: HERBARTIANISM AS AN AUSTRIAN STATE PHILOSOPHY AND ITS ROLE FOR HANSLICK'S CAREER

Most of the debate about Hanslick's intellectual background has focused on the general intellectual context of contemporary German culture and philosophy, and very little attention has been given to Hanslick's immediate intellectual context—that is, the actual

---

16. See our essay on Hanslick's central concepts for a discussion of Hanslick's treatment of beauty and history.

environment of his time and place. Without doubt, Kant and German Idealism still figured prominently in German aesthetic debates around 1850. However, it is important to note that Hanslick did not develop his aesthetic ideas in Berlin, Heidelberg, or Göttingen, but rather in Vienna, Prague, and Klagenfurt.[17] His intellectual background as well as his aesthetic thinking were thus shaped by the ways in which philosophy and aesthetics were conceived and taught in the Habsburg Empire shortly before and after the revolution of 1848. Recent scholarship points to Hanslick's role as a civil servant in the Ministry of Education, where he was assigned a post in early 1854, just months before the completion of *On the Musically Beautiful*.[18] There Hanslick came into close contact with Education Minister Leopold Thun-Hohenstein's main agenda: the reorganization of Austria's educational system.[19]

17. A lively discussion of Hanslick's Austrian background has developed in recent years. See, for example, Ines Grimm, *Eduard Hanslicks Prager Zeit: Frühe Wurzeln seiner Schrift* Vom Musikalisch-Schönen (Saarbrücken, Germany: Pfau, 2003); Christoph Landerer, *Eduard Hanslick und Bernard Bolzano: Ästhetisches Denken in Österreich in der Mitte des 19. Jahrhunderts* (Sankt Augustin, Germany: Academia, 2004), and "Eduard Hanslick und die österreichische Geistesgeschichte," in *Eduard Hanslick zum Gedenken: Bericht des Symposiums zum Anlass seines 100. Todestages*, ed. Theophil Antonicek, Gernot Gruber, and Christoph Landerer (Tutzing, Germany: Hans Schneider, 2010), pp. 55–64; Mark Evan Bonds, "Aesthetic Amputations: Absolute Music and the Deleted Endings of Hanslick's *Vom Musikalisch-Schönen*," *19th-Century Music* 36, no. 1 (2012): pp. 1–23; and Kevin Karnes, *Music, Criticism, and the Challenge of History: Shaping Modern Musical Thought in Late Nineteenth-Century Vienna* (Oxford: Oxford University Press, 2008). An earlier account can be found in Christoph Khittl, "Eduard Hanslicks Verhältnis zur Ästhetik," in *Biographische Beiträge zum Musikleben Wiens im 19. und frühen 20. Jahrhundert*, ed. Friedrich C. Heller (Vienna: Verband der wissenschaftlichen Gesellschaften Österreichs, 1992), pp. 81–109.

18. Kurt Blaukopf, *Pioniere empiristischer Musikforschung. Österreich und Böhmen als Wiege der modernen Kunstsoziologie* (Vienna: Hölder-Pichler-Tempsky, 1995); Ines Grimm, *Eduard Hanslicks Prager Zeit. Frühe Wurzeln seiner Schrift "Vom Musikalisch-Schönen"* (Saarbrücken, Germany: Pfau, 2003); Landerer, *Eduard Hanslick und Bernard Bolzano*; Karnes, *Music, Criticism, and the Challenge of History*; Bonds, *Absolute Music: The History of an Idea*.

19. See Peter Stachel, "Das österreichische Bildungssystem zwischen 1749 und 1918," in *Geschichte der österreichischen Humanwissenschaften*, vol. 1: *Historischer*

Soon after 1848, Herbartianism, the philosophical system of German philosopher Johann Friedrich Herbart (1776–1841), advanced to become a semiofficial Austrian "state philosophy,"[20] and Hanslick was expected to contribute to the "Herbartization"[21] of the nascent discipline of musicology. The main document that links Hanslick's aesthetics to the politico-ideological background of the Thun reform is Hanslick's habilitation petition, in which he distances himself from metaphysics and declares himself to be closest to Herbart's philosophy.[22] As Kevin Karnes remarks, "Hanslick . . . knew that his proposal would not be approved if it did not appear to be in accord with the broader plans of Exner and Thun-Hohenstein."[23] However, to fully understand the relationship between Hanslick's aesthetics and his less-than-wholehearted Herbartian conviction, as well as his confessed distance from metaphysics, we must draw a broader and, in a way, more complex picture of both the philosophical sources of *On the Musically Beautiful* and the interrelation between philosophy and politics in post-1848 Austria.

Kontext, wissensoziologische Befunde und methodologische Voraussetzungen, ed. Karl Acham (Vienna: Passagen, 2000), pp. 115–46; and Rainer Leitner, "Das Reformwerk von Exner, Bonitz und Thun. Das österreichische Gymnasium in der zweiten Hälfte des 19. Jahrhunderts. Kaderschmiede der Wiener Moderne," in, *Zwischen Orientierung und Krise. Zum Umgang mit Wissen in der Moderne,* ed. Sonja Rienofner-Kreidl (Vienna: Böhlau, 1998), pp. 17–69.

20. Cf. Andreas Hoeschen and Lothar Schneider, eds., *Herbarts Kultursystem. Perspektiven der Transdisziplinarität im 19. Jahrhundert* (Würzburg, Germany: Königshausen & Neumann, 2001); Georg Jäger, "Die Herbartianische Ästhetik. Ein österreichischer Weg in die Moderne," in, *Die Österreichische Literatur. Ihr Profil im 19. Jahrhundert (1830–1880),* ed. Herbert Zeman (Graz, Austria: Akademische Druck- und Verlagsanstalt, 1982), pp. 195–219.

21. Karnes, *Music, Criticism, and the Challenge of History,* p. 31

22. The petition is reprinted in Dietmar Strauß, *Eduard Hanslick. Vom Musikalisch-Schönen. Ein Beitrag zur Revision der Ästhetik in der Tonkunst. Teil 2: Eduard Hanslicks Schrift in textkritischer Sicht* (Mainz, Germany: Schott, 1990), pp. 136–45 (There is a page missing in Strauß's transcription); for an English translation, see Karnes, *Music, Criticism, and the Challenge of History,* p. 32.

23. Karnes, *Music, Criticism, and the Challenge of History,* p. 32. See also Landerer, *Eduard Hanslick und Bernard Bolzano,* pp. 83–86; Payzant, *Hanslick On the Musically Beautiful,* p. 131; Bonds, "Aesthetic Amputations," p. 7.

Like many young intellectuals of the Vormärz era, Hanslick had sympathies not only for the revolution but also for what Austrian authorities considered its philosophical basis: German Idealism. As we saw in the section on Hanslick and Hegelianism, Hanslick changed his positions considerably in the years before 1854, sometimes even completely reversing them.[24] Shocked by the execution of fellow music critic Alfred Julius Becher in 1848, Hanslick also distanced himself from Hegelianism while still retaining some of the idealist elements that are present in Vischer's aesthetics.

The rationale of the Thun agenda is the key to understanding the political and institutional context in which Hanslick's aesthetic ideas are embedded. As early as the late eighteenth century, Austrian authorities dismissed metaphysics, then seen as the core of Kantian philosophy and its revolutionary teachings, and promoted the study of "physical and mathematical" disciplines.[25] However, it was not until the Thun reform that these ideas were fully implemented in the grand scheme of reorganizing the Austrian educational system. As part of the Thun agenda, the organizational framework for Austrian high schools was completely reworked, reflecting a new and prominent, though restricted, role for philosophy. Philosophy was now integrated into the high school curriculum, and Robert Zimmermann was commissioned to write the first textbooks for "philosophical propaeduetics." The state strictly regulated the philosophical

---

24. The development of his views is complex, with some aesthetic convictions changing even before 1848. For Hanslick's "volte-face," see Geoffrey Payzant, *Eduard Hanslick and Ritter Berlioz in Prague: A Documentary Narrative* (Calgary: University of Calgary Press, 1991).

25. See also Werner Sauer, "Von der 'Kritik' zur 'Positivität'. Die Geisteswissenschaften in Österreich zwischen josephinischer Aufklärung und franziszeischer Restauration," in, *Vormärz. Wendepunkt und Herausforderung. Beiträge zur Literaturwissenschaft und Kulturpolitik in Österreich*, ed. Hanna Schnedl-Bubeniček (Vienna, Salzburg: Geyer-Edition, 1983), pp. 17–46; Harald Haslmayr, "Geistige Hintergründe des Biedermeier," in *The Other Vienna: The Culture of Biedermeier Austria. Österreichisches Biedermeier in Literatur, Musik, Kunst und Kulturgeschichte*, ed. Clifford A. Berlin, Robert Pichl, and Margarete Wagner (Vienna: Lehner, 2002), pp. 285–96. See also William Johnston, *The Austrian Mind. An Intellectual and Social History, 1848–1938* (Berkeley: University of California Press, 1972), chapter 19.

content taught in these courses. Philosophy at Austrian high schools comprised only two subjects: formal logic and empirical psychology.[26] To align himself with the profile that the Thun ministry expected for work in disciplines relating to philosophy, Hanslick had to focus on either formal or empirical aspects, at the expense of metaphysics.

From July 1853 to March 1854, he published the articles that later became chapters four through six of *On the Musically Beautiful*.[27] The articles prepare the main arguments of *On the Musically Beautiful*, while citing a great deal of empirical work, thus contributing to the empirical discourse on art that the Austrian authorities wanted to see. The most important chapters, one through three, were written later, when Hanslick had already transferred to the Thun ministry and was thus in closer contact with its agenda. It is within those first chapters that Hanslick fully develops his argument by focusing much more sharply on formal discourse in musical aesthetics. In chapter three, in which he develops his notion of "sonically moved forms," he gives a more phenomenologically oriented analysis, in which empirical discourse plays a subordinate role. We still lack a full understanding of how the Thun ministry and Hanslick's personal contacts within it influenced this shift of emphasis.

26. In an 1855 address to the minister, Rudolf von Eitelberger, founding father of the Austrian school of art history and an advisor to Thun, once again stressed the role Herbartianism could play, as it conflicted with neither the state nor the church and was a perfect philosophical vehicle for fostering the "positive and exact sciences" (Eitelberger as cited in Taras Borodajkewycz, "Aus der Frühzeit der Wiener Schule der Kunstgeschichte," in *Festschrift für Hans Seldmayr*, ed. Karl Oettinger and Mohammed Rassem (Munich: C.H. Beck, 1962), p. 335. See also Christoph Landerer, "1848 und die Wissenschaften. Staatliche Bildungsplanung und der österreichische Weg in die Moderne," in *Die Revolution 1848 und die Musik*, ed. Barbara Boisits (Vienna: Hollitzer, 2013), pp. 617–32. Just two years before the publication of *On the Musically Beautiful*, Eitelberger himself was awarded the first Austrian professorship in art history. Thun, in his promotion speech, stressed the importance of academic work that effectively based the study of art on empirical work instead of simply deducting from abstract systems. In addition, Eitelberger did not fail to align himself with Herbartian philosophy, despite early sympathies for Hegelianism.

27. See the essay in this volume on the book and its history.

However, the empirical and formal discourses, together with the (older) idealist undercurrent that is also present in *On the Musically Beautiful*, created a tension that Hanslick might have later found impossible to resolve. As Karnes observes, Hanslick abandoned his aesthetic ambitions soon after he secured a salaried professorship, thus disappointing hopes that he would produce an aesthetics of music in a Herbartian spirit.[28]

On the Musically Beautiful also reflects a historicist discourse on music that Hanslick develops along the lines of Vischer's aesthetics. Although he eliminated passages in the second edition of *On the Musically Beautiful* (1858) that Zimmermann, in a review of the work, had dismissed as metaphysical,[29] Hanslick left unaltered claims about the historical relativity of beauty, even though those claims were clearly in conflict with Zimmermann's static, and therefore with the orthodox Herbartian concept of beauty.[30] Apparently those claims were seen as less of a risk for his academic ambitions, although they were certainly not in line with the Herbartian view of art. For Hanslick, the critical point was to eradicate what could be seen as a metaphysical line of argument.

3.4 AGAINST IDEALISM: HERBART, BOLZANO, ZIMMERMANN

Herbart himself was by no means an anti-metaphysical thinker in a modern understanding of the term, but his philosophy was clearly opposed to lofty idealist system-building and committed to a realist position that meshed well with the desired focus on formal and empirical knowledge. Even in Hanslick's lifetime and shortly after, it was common to consider *On the Musically Beautiful* a work

28. See Karnes, *Music, Criticism, and the Challenge of History*, p. 32.
29. See Bonds, "Aesthetic Amputations" and *Absolute Music*.
30. Of interest in this regard is Andrew Edgar, "Adorno and Musical Analysis," *Journal of Aesthetics and Art Criticism* 57, no. 4 (1999): pp. 439–49.

in the Herbartian tradition. Indeed, early scholarship pointed out important similarities between Hanslick and Herbart's aesthetic approaches, such as the general focus on formal properties and the strict exclusion of feelings from aesthetic theory.

For the sake of aesthetic theory, and very much like Hanslick, Herbart dismisses the psychological dimension of music altogether.[31] Although aesthetic objects evoke such effects, he argues that they must be abstracted from the work to allow for aesthetic principles that transcend such contingent psychological variations.[32] When focusing on those objective properties in which Herbart's aesthetics is exclusively interested, we must concede that the beautiful in music consists in formal relations—that is, the formal relations specific to music that constitute a musical composition.

Although these elements of Herbartian aesthetics indeed sound very Hanslickian, we must also be aware of important differences between Herbart's and Hanslick's aesthetic approaches that highlight the peculiarity of Hanslick's musical aesthetics. First, the sonic element of Hanslick's "sonically moved forms" is not present in Herbart's aesthetics of music: "The tones," Herbart writes, "should merely be heard, or even . . . merely read, yet they please anyway."[33] Hanslick never went so far as to declare the sonic element of music, the actual performing of music, a coincidentally, and—strictly speaking—aesthetically irrelevant dimension of a musical composition. Unlike Herbart's notion of musical relationships, Hanslick's forms are sounding [tönend].

A second element of Hanslick's aesthetics that is lacking in Herbart's approach is the historical dimension of musical beauty that aligns Hanslick's aesthetics with the historicist position of Vischer. Herbart's concept of objective beauty does not allow for compositions

---

31. For Hanslick's relation to Herbart see also Bonds, *Absolute Music*, pp. 158–62.

32. See Rothfarb, "Nineteenth-Century Fortunes of Musical Formalism," pp. 177–78.

33. Johann Friedrich Herbart, *Kurze Enzyklopädie der Philosophie aus praktischen Gesichtspunkten entworfen*, ed. G. Hartenstein, vol. 2 of *J. F. Herbarts Sämmtliche Werke* (Leipzig: Leopold Voss, 1850), p. 111 (§ 71), translation by Lee Rothfarb.

that "*were* once beautiful." If combinations of tones—or even just notes—are beautiful, their beauty is founded in the timeless, formal relations that constitute the specific piece of music. For Herbart, those relations do not get "worn out," as Hanslick claims. Whereas Hanslick's forms are "moved" [*bewegt*] also in a historical sense of the word, Herbart's relations remain static.

Other similarities are less problematic. Hanslick aligns with Herbart when he declares, in his habilitation petition, "my principle of gaining the aesthetical foundations of an art from their peculiar, specific nature keeps me at a distance from purely metaphysical considerations."[34] As Geoffrey Payzant observed, "this contradicts the Hegelian doctrine that all arts form one great system under a unifying principle, namely the idea."[35] As we saw in the second essay, on Hanslick's central concepts, Hanslick advocates for a bottom-up approach, as opposed to the top-down approach of Hegel's aesthetics.[36] The idea of such an approach is not typically, or even exclusively, Herbartian, as Payzant rightly observes. In this point as in many others, Hanslick agrees not only with Herbart, but also with the philosophical views of Bernard Bolzano (1781–1848), a Prague priest, philosopher, and mathematician who was also the teacher of Hanslick's lifelong friend Robert Zimmermann. Bolzano's philosophy, like Herbart's approach, can be considered realist, and has a strong, even polemic, anti-idealist orientation. Bolzano shares many aesthetic convictions with Hanslick and has been considered

---

34. "Mein Princip, die aesthetischen Grundsätze einer Kunst aus deren eigenster, specifischer Natur zu gewinnen, hält mich von rein metaphysischen Erörterungen fern" (see Dietmar Strauß, *Eduard Hanslick. Vom Musikalisch-Schönen. Ein Beitrag zur Revision der Ästhetik in der Tonkunst. Teil 2: Eduard Hanslicks Schrift in textkritischer Sicht* (Mainz, Germany: Schott, 1990), p. 145 (translation by Christoph Landerer).

35. Geoffrey Payzant, "Eduard Hanslick and Robert Zimmermann," in *Hanslick on the Musically Beautiful: Sixteen Lectures on the Aesthetics of Eduard Hanslick* (Christchurch, New Zealand: Cybereditions, 2002), p. 137.

36. "The 'system' is gradually giving way to 'research,' which holds firmly to the maxim that the laws of beauty of each art are inseparable from the characteristics of its material, of its technique" (Chapter 1, p. 2).

one of the candidates for a philosophical basis of *On the Musically Beautiful*.[37]

It is, however, difficult to point to elements of Hanslick's thinking that could be considered Bolzanist, and that contrast with others that we can regard as Herbartian. As Kurt Blaukopf has observed, Bolzano's and Herbart's aesthetic views form an "amalgam of thoughts" [*Gedankenamalgam*][38] that becomes readily apparent only in the reception of their ideas. Blaukopf names Hanslick and Robert Zimmermann as theoretical executors of this dual intellectual heritage. To be sure, the similarities between Herbart's and Bolzano's aesthetics are far reaching: Herbart's and Bolzano's anti-idealist orientation, their exclusion of feelings from aesthetic judgment, their opposition to a generalized aesthetics, and plea for specialized aesthetic theories for individual artistic domains. However, important differences remain, some of which are particularly interesting with regard to Hanslick's little book.

As we have seen, Herbart's conception of objective beauty is static and does not allow for any meaningful role of history. If relations are beautiful, they remain beautiful even if aesthetic preferences, as an effect of fashion, may change. Their beauty is founded on timeless formal relations. By contrast, Hanslick's aesthetic conception strongly emphasizes the element of change, of progress and historical development. For him, all features and properties of the musically beautiful are products of an ever-changing mind—the mind of the composer as well as that of the listener.

Although "relation" is at the hub of Herbart's conception of aesthetics, Bolzano's approach is based on the concept of a "rule," and rules are much more closely bound to history. Rules are cultural phenomena. Bolzano scholars have stressed that this approach also allows Bolzano to assign the aspect of reception a more prominent

---

37. See Landerer, *Eduard Hanslick und Bernard Bolzano*; Karnes, *Music, Criticism and the Challenge of History*, p. 31; Bonds, *Absolute Music: The History of an Idea* (New York: Oxford University Press, 2014), p. 162.

38. Kurt Blaukopf, *Die Ästhetik Bernard Bolzanos* (Stankt Augustin, Germany: Academia, 1996), p. 68.

role. As Dietfried Gerhardus, editor of Bolzano´s aesthetic writings, has put it, "So far as actions of reception in general, and aesthetic actions in particular, cannot be conceived solely as phenomena designed by nature, . . . , these actions have to be called 'historical' "[39]—historical in the sense that this activity was "discovered, developed and interpreted at a given time and continues to do so."[40] Although he did not draw the conclusions that Hanslick drew in his little book, there is less of a theoretical gap between his approach to aesthetics and that of Hanslick than between Hanslick's aesthetics and any aesthetics in the Herbartian tradition.

We might gain a better understanding of Bolzano's rule- and reception-centered approach and its possible relevance for Hanslick if we return to Hanslick's central concept of *Geist*. If a composition possesses *Geist*, it is because of the inventive, specifically musically beautiful tone forms that the composer chose in his day. However, the forms he created are beautiful not only for him. His musical ideas are laid down in an abstract notation and exist in a special ontological sphere that forms the basis for a full musical realization in a performance of the piece. The approach is similar to Bolzano's Platonist conception of *An-Sich* [per se] that links his aesthetic ideas to his general logical point of view.

Bolzano developed a notion of *An-Sich* in his logic and theory of science, though not in his aesthetics. Nevertheless, Karl Popper's theory of "objective knowledge"—a modern version of Bolzano— reveals similarities with Hanslick's aesthetics. For Popper, our knowledge of the world falls into three categories, or "worlds." Physical objects and events occupy world 1, mental objects and events world

---

39. Dietrich Gerhardus, "Bolzanos methodische Grundlegung einer rezeptionstheoretisch ausgerichteten Ästhetik," in *Untersuchungen zur Grundlegung der Ästhetik*, ed. Bernard Bolzano (Frankfurt: Athenäum, 1972), p. XXX: "Insoweit Rezeptionshandlungen allgemein und ästhetische Handlungen im besonderen nicht allein als von der Natur vorgezeichnete Phänomene verstanden werden können . . . sind diese Handlungen 'geschichtlich' zu nennen."

40. Gerhardus, "Bolzanos Grundlegung," p. XXXI ("zu bestimmten Zeiten entdeckt, entwickelt und gedeutet wurde und zukünftig weiterhin noch wird").

2, and world 3 constitutes "objective knowledge," which Popper identifies in science as well as in art. The "feeling-theory" regards music as an object in world 2, but for Hanslick it clearly resides in world 3. Although inhabiting the abstract, objective sphere of world 3, like theories, music has a history. However, its existence is confined to neither historical performances nor to individual mental events. A product of the human mind, of *Geist* in Hanslick's sense of the word, music is as much abstract and objective as a scientific theory. In their strong emphasis on the cognitive dimension of music, Hanslick, Bolzano, and Popper thus develop similar lines of thought.[41]

Compared with Herbart's metaphysical realism, with its conception of fixed beautiful relations, Bolzano's logical realism, with its openness to inventiveness and historical change, might be better suited to the Platonic but at the same time to historically open forms of Hanslick's aesthetics. In this regard, Bolzano is also closer to Hanslick's conception than to Zimmermann's orthodox elaboration in his seminal *Allgemeine Ästhetik als Formwissenschaft* of Herbart's static, ahistoric formalism.[42]

If there is one single important outcome of research into the intellectual background of Hanslick's aesthetics, it might be that there is no consistent philosophical basis for *On the Musically Beautiful*. We thus need to understand how various and rather heterogeneous philosophical discourses are intertwined in the treatise. Hanslick's textual techniques are at times close to a collage, as demonstrated by a central paragraph from the heavily reworked first chapter in the second edition. The passage reads, "Beauty is and remains beauty even if it arouses no feelings, indeed even if it is neither viewed nor contemplated. Beauty is thus namely merely *for* the pleasure of the

41. It certainly comes as no surprise that Popper, in his autobiography, confesses that "my attitude towards music resembles the theories of Eduard Hanslick." Popper, *Unended Quest. An Intellectual Autobiography* (London, New York: Routledge, 1994), p. 249.

42. For Hanslick's relation to Zimmermann, see Geoffrey Payzant, "Eduard Hanslick and Robert Zimmermann."

viewing subject, but not *by means of* the subject" (Chapter 1, p. 4). A closer analysis of this passage reveals that Hanslick took the first sentence from Zimmermann's review of *On the Musically Beautiful*.[43] It might have a textual basis in Bolzano, Zimmermann's teacher in Prague.[44] However, the first part of the second sentence has a textual basis in Vischer.[45] Apparently, Hanslick's goal was to adopt Zimmermann's claim while retaining a central argument of Vischer's aesthetics.[46]

It is this fusion of different and, at times, even contradictory streams of philosophical thought that undergirds Hanslick's aesthetics. His originality thus lies in how elements of heterogeneous philosophical frameworks are combined and form the background of his arguments. This rather eclectic textual strategy also allowed Hanslick to stay clear of orthodox schools. His indebtedness to Vischer and Zimmermann, two strongly opposed poles in contemporary discussion, might best illustrate how Hanslick´s more open— and more open-minded—conception of beauty, and of aesthetic method, keeps one-dimensional and narrow theoretical approaches

43. Rudolf Schäfke was the first to make this observation, in *Eduard Hanslick und die Musikästhetik* (Leipzig: Breitkopf & Härtel, 1922), p. 30.

44. Consider Bernard Bolzano, "Über den Begriff des Schönen," in *Untersuchungen zur Grundlegung der Ästhetik*, ed. Dietfried Gerhardus (Frankfurt: Athenäum, 1972), p. 81: "Auch wenn es auf dem ganzen Erdenrunde nur einen einzigen Menschen, oder auch gar keinen gäbe, also auch wenn gar keine Mittelbarkeit stattfände, bliebe doch das Schöne schön und das Garstige garstig." Zimmermann is more aligned here with Bolzano's objectivism, which is stricter than that of Herbart.

45. Friedrich Theodor Vischer, *Ästhetik oder Wissenschaft des Schönen*, vol. 3,1 (Reutlingen, Germany: Mäcken, 1851), p. 13: "Das Schöne ist . . . wesentlich Erscheinung, also für ein anschauendes Subjekt." The context of the passage is Hanslick's introduction of the concept of *Anschauung*, which Zimmermann, in his review, regarded as rooted in Vischer.

46. The sentence is from Zimmermann's review of *On the Musically Beautiful*. As Grimm (1982) has noticed, Hanslick did not adopt the following remarks: "Denn das Schöne beruht auf sich gleichbleibenden Verhältnissen." Hanslick did not support Zimmermann's claim of timeless beauty, founded in timeless relations. Instead, he continued with the (unquoted) reference to Vischer, already present in the first edition. The Payzant translation does not include the final sentence, on the grounds of it being "vestigial" (Payzant, *OMB*, p. 105). It is, however, a typical case of Hanslick trying to make use of a variety of sources that are not easy to reconcile.

at a distance. Vischer as well as Zimmermann are perfect examples for the sort of "system-building" that Hanslick, in the first chapter of his book, attempted to replace with "research." Vischer´s and Zimmermann´s aesthetics are dependent on, and applications of, the great philosophical schools of their time: Hegel and Herbart. Compared with their approach, Hanslick´s conception is modern and open for continued development and new perspectives that enhance our view of music and its beauty. It is for this reason that, philosophically speaking, Hanslick continues to fascinate and perplex readers even in the light of recent theoretical conceptions of aesthetics. After all, Hanslick is still widely read and continues to be relevant, whereas Zimmermann and Vischer are largely forgotten.

READERS' GUIDE: ALTERNATIVE ROUTES THROUGH THE TREATISE

The sequence of topics covered in the seven chapters of Hanslick's *On the Musically Beautiful*, read consecutively, might well confuse readers. After beginning with two chapters that discuss what the content and purpose of music is *not*—neither the arousal nor the representation of feelings (Hanslick's negative theses)—readers at last encounter the centrally important (best-known) third chapter, where Hanslick proposes and argues forcefully for what music's content and purpose *is* (Hanslick's positive thesis): the presentation of intrinsically musical ideas in beautiful tone forms. Returning, then, to ideas from the book's opening, the subsequent two chapters (4, 5) interrupt the thread of continuity with analyses of music's psychological impressions and pathological impact on listeners, followed by a seemingly unmotivated discussion of the relationship between music and nature (Chapter 6). Finally, picking up the abandoned thread from Chapter 3, the book closes by focusing on the notions of content and form in music (Chapter 7). It is easy to see why readers might become disoriented.

We address this problem by proposing four strategically designed alternative routes through the treatise. Three of them are abbreviated paths for expedited tours through the book: Route 1 is a single-chapter reading (the quintessentials of the treatise, Chapter 3); Route

2 is a two-chapter reading (expanded quintessentials, Chapters 3 and 7); and Route 3 is a four-chapter reading (rhetorical arc, Chapters 1–3, 7). These three routes, intended as *separate* tours, are subsequently explained. To fill in gaps left by reading only certain chapters in full and not others, each route calls for the reading of accessory passages excerpted from other chapters, thus allowing readers with limited time to engage with the essentials of Hanslick's work without reading the entire treatise. The fourth route takes readers through all chapters but reorders them according to the logic of their unfolding arguments and according to the probable chronology in which they were written. The following paragraphs outline and explain the four routes and their linked accessory passages.

ROUTE 1. QUINTESSENTIALS: SINGLE-CHAPTER READING

(Chapter 3 plus accessory passages from Chapters 1, 2, and 6)

This is the most abbreviated route, suggesting that Chapter 3 be read in full as a stand-alone unit. The signal ideas of the "specifically musical," of music's true content ("sonically moved forms"), of its unique "sense and logic," of its origin in a "thinking and feeling mind," and other key ideas all appear in this chapter. Several accessory passages excerpted from Chapters 1, 2, and 6 round out this route.

ROUTE 2. EXPANDED QUINTESSENTIALS: TWO-CHAPTER READING

(Chapters 3 and 7 plus accessory passages from Chapters 1, 2, and 6)

Route 2 calls for reading Chapter 3 as well as its elaboration in Chapter 7, which distinguishes content [*Inhalt*] from subject [*Gegenstand*] and material [*Stoff*]—distinctions vital to Hanslick's understanding of what music is and is *not*, and what it *can* and *cannot* do—and asserts the inseparability of content and form in music. Further, we learn that, for Hanslick, musical form evolves organically from a work's theme [*Thema*], analogous to a "logical chain of reasoning" or to the growth of a crystal (Chapter 3). The aforementioned accessory passages excerpted from Chapters 1, 2, and 6 round out this route as well.

ROUTE 3. RHETORICAL ARC: FOUR-CHAPTER READING

(Chapters 1, 2, 3, and 7 plus accessory passages from Chapter 6)

In Route 3, we read Chapters 1–3 in full. They constitute a rhetorical arc, with Chapters 1 and 2 (negative theses) leading climactically to Chapter 3 (positive thesis), coupled in this route, again, with its elaboration in Chapter 7. We learn at length here about Hanslick's arguments against making feelings the foundation of music aesthetics, whether they are aroused in the listener or contained in or represented by music. Accessory passages are limited here to excerpts from Chapter 6.

ROUTE 4. LOGICAL-CHRONOLOGICAL ROUTE: REORDERED READING

(Chapters 6, 4, 5, 1, 2, 3, and 7)

This route, which involves reading the entire treatise, strategically reorders its chapters so that they present a logically unfolding line of argument. We begin with Chapter 6, on the relationship of music to nature, a common starting point for authors on music aesthetics, and learn about Hanslick's conception of tones in music as opposed to sounds in nature. Route 4 continues, then, with Chapters 4 and 5 on, respectively, the psychology and physiology of hearing based on the latest research available in Hanslick's day. Equipped with the knowledge of material in Chapters 6, 4, and 5, *read in that order*, we continue by reading the chapters prescribed in Route 3, traversing the rhetorical arc through Chapters 1–3, and ending with Chapter 7 as a summation. In addition to representing a logical path through the treatise, Route 4 also represents the chronology in which Hanslick wrote it. Chapters 4–6 were prepublished up to a year earlier than the treatise in the *Österreichische Blätter für Literatur und Kunst.*

ACCESSORY PASSAGES

Chapter 1

[1] The way musical aesthetics has been handled up to now has suffered almost entirely from the serious blunder of concerning itself, not with exploring what is beautiful in music, but rather with describing the feelings that take hold of us. Those investigations align fully with the standpoint of the older aesthetic systems that viewed the beautiful only with regard to elicited sensations, and reared the philosophy of *beauty* as the offspring of sensation [αἰσθησις].

Unphilosophical in themselves, in their application to the most ethereal of all arts, such aesthetic systems acquire something almost sentimental [2] that, while utterly invigorating for gushers, offers the studious a minimum of elucidation. Whoever seeks instruction about the nature of music wishes to escape the obscure hegemony of feeling and not to be constantly referred to feeling, as occurs in most guidebooks.

[4] Addressing its subject matter clearly and distinctly as an autonomous type of beauty was up to now an insuperable struggle for music aesthetics. [5] Instead, "sensations" perpetuate the old phantom in broad daylight. The musically beautiful is still viewed only from the perspective of its subjective impression, and in books, reviews, and conversations it is affirmed daily that *affects* are the sole aesthetic foundation of music and are alone qualified for staking out the boundaries of judgment about music.

[6] First, as the *aim* and *purpose* of music, it is proposed that music should arouse feelings or "beautiful feelings." Second, feelings are designated as the *content* that music represents in its works.

Both propositions are similar in that the one is just as false as the other.

[7] To investigate that relationship (between music and feelings) more closely, we must first differentiate rigorously here between the concepts of feeling and sensation, whose confounding in ordinary usage raises no objection.

Sensation is the perception of a specific sensory quality, of a tone, a color. Feeling is the awareness of a furthering or an inhibiting of our psychic state, thus of a state of well-being or of displeasure.

[8] The beautiful first affects our senses. That route is not unique to the beautiful, which shares it with all phenomena in general. Sensation is the beginning and precondition of aesthetic pleasure and initially forms the basis of feeling, which always presupposes a relationship and often the most complicated relationships. Arousing sensations does not require art. A single tone, a single color can do that. As mentioned, the two terms are randomly interchanged, what we designate as feelings mostly being called sensations in older writings. Thus music, those authors say, is supposed to arouse our feelings and to fill us alternatingly with reverence, love, joy, melancholy.

However, in truth, [9] neither music nor any other art has such a purpose. Art is primarily for representing something *beautiful*. The agency by which the beautiful is received is not feeling but rather *imagination*, as the activity of pure viewing.

[12] But we could no more acknowledge that effect as the purpose of the arts in general than we can view the specific essence of *music* in that effect. Once it is established that imagination is the actual agency of beauty, a secondary effect on feelings would occur in *every* art.

[13] *Every* true work of art will enter into some kind of relationship with our feelings, but *none* in an exclusive relationship. We thus say nothing at all decisive about the aesthetic principle of music if we characterize it only very generally based on its effect on feeling, just as little, say, if we wanted to grasp the nature of wine by getting drunk. It depends solely on the *specific* manner how such [14] affects

are evoked *through music*. Thus instead of getting stuck on the secondary and vague effects of feeling brought on by musical phenomena, we should penetrate to the interior of works and explain the specific power of their impression based on the laws of their internal organization.

[17] The strong feelings that music awakens from their slumber, and all of the sweet as well as painful moods into which it lulls us half-dreaming listeners: We certainly do not wish to underestimate them. Surely among the most beautiful and beneficial mysteries is that, by the grace of God, art is capable of evoking such stirrings without earthly cause. It is only against the unscientific assessment of these facts for *aesthetic principles* that we register our protest.

Chapter 2

[26] The representation of a specific feeling or affect does not at all lie within music's own capabilities.

This is because feelings do not reside in the mind in isolation such that they can be, so to speak, called up from the mind by an art to which the [27] representation of other mental activities is sealed off. On the contrary, they are dependent on physiological and pathological conditions, are conditioned by mental images, judgments, in short by the entire range of intelligible and rational thought to which people so willingly juxtapose feeling as something opposite.

[32] *What* can music portray of feelings, then, if not their content?

Only their *dynamic properties*. It is capable of simulating the motion of a physical process according to the aspects fast, slow, strong, weak, ascending, descending. However, motion is but one trait, one aspect of feeling, not feeling itself. It is commonly believed that the representational capability of music is sufficiently limited when it is asserted that it can in no way signify the *object* of a feeling, but surely the feeling itself, cannot signify the object of a particular love, for example, but surely "love." In truth, it can do that just as little. It can depict, not love, but only a motion that can occur with love or also with another affect, but is always the nonessential aspect of its character. Love is an abstract concept, like "virtue" and "immortality." The [33] assurance of theorists that music is not supposed to represent abstract concepts is superfluous, because *no* art can do that. It is self-evident that only *ideas*, that is, concepts brought alive, are the content of artistic embodiment.[1] But instrumental works cannot portray the *ideas* of love, anger, or fear either, because no necessary link exists between those ideas and beautiful tone connections. So, which aspect of these ideas is it then that music can appropriate so effectively? It is *motion* (naturally in the broader sense that also regards as motion the intensification and deintensification of a single tone or a chord). It is the element that music shares with states of feeling and that it is capable of creatively shaping in a thousand gradations and contrasts.

The concept of *motion* has to date been conspicuously neglected in [34] investigations of the nature and effect of music. To us, it seems the most important and fruitful concept.

What otherwise seems to us to portray specific psychic states in music is *symbolic*.

This is because tones, like colors, possess symbolic significance, inherently and individually, which operates apart from and before all artistic intention.

[36] Other than the analogy with motion and symbolism of tones, music does not possess another means for this ostensible purpose (portraying feelings).

[54] Music is perhaps not supposed to evoke and represent definite feelings but possibly "indefinite feelings." On rational grounds, that can only mean that music should contain the motion of [55] feeling, abstracted from its content, from that which is felt, thus what we have called the *dynamics* of the affects and have fully granted to music. However, that aspect of music is not a "representing of indefinite feelings." For "representing" "indefinite content" is a

---

1. Vischer (*Ästhetik*, §11, Note) defines specific ideas as the realms of life, provided that their reality can be thought of as corresponding to their concept. For *idea* always indicates the concept present to the mind, pure and unblemished in its reality.

contradiction. Psychic motions as motions in themselves, without content, are not an object of artistic embodiment because it is not possible to address artistic embodiment without the question of what moves or is moved.

[56] From here, the small step is very simple to the recognition that music cannot depict any feelings *at all*, neither definite nor indefinite.

[57] But even more decisively than we contested the possibility of the musical representation of feeling do we have to fend off the opinion that it could ever yield the *aesthetic principle* of music.

CHAPTER 6

[180] If we investigate the extent to which nature might provide *material* [*Stoff*] for music, the outcome is that nature does so only in the sense of raw material, which humankind compels to resound in tones. The silent ore of the mountains, the wood of the forest, the skin and gut of animals are all that we find for preparing the actual building material [181] for music, *pure* tone. We thus initially receive (raw) material for (musical) material, the latter of which is pure tone, determined in height and depth, that is, measurable tone. It is the primary and inescapable prerequisite of all music, which fashions tone into *melody* and *harmony*, the two chief factors in music. Neither occurs in nature; they are creations of human intellect.

[188] People will object to our claim that there is no music in nature by pointing out the wealth of manifold voices that so wonderfully animate nature. Should the babbling of the brook, the splash of ocean waves, the thunder of avalanches, the raging of a cyclone, not have been the occasion and model for human music? Did all of the whispering, whistling, crashing sounds have nothing to do with our musical life? We must in fact answer in the negative. All of these manifestations of nature are just *noise* and *sound*, that is, successive irregular vibrations of air. Very seldom, and then only in isolated instances, does nature produce a *tone*, that is, a sound of a specific,

measurable height and depth.[2] However, tones are the foundational conditions of all music.

[189] Even the purest manifestation in the sonorous world of nature, birdsong, has no relation to human music as it cannot be aligned with our scale. The phenomenon of the harmony of nature [*Naturharmonie*, i.e. overtone series]—in any case the sole and incontrovertible natural foundation on which the chief relationships of our music are based—must be traced to its proper significance. The harmonic series arises of its own accord on the unison-tuned Aeolian harp and is thus founded on a natural law. But we do not hear the phenomenon itself directly produced anywhere by nature. When no specific, measurable fundamental tone is played on a musical instrument, no sympathetically vibrating subsidiary tones appear, no harmonic series.[3]

[191] The measurable tone and the organized tone system [192] are initially those *with which* the composer creates, not *what* he creates.

CHAPTER 7

[216] The content of a musical work can therefore never be understood concretely but rather only musically, namely as that which actually resounds in each piece of music.

---

2. *Translators' note*: In the German original, this passage reads "Klang von bestimmter, meßbarer Höhe and Tiefe." Payzant's translation, "sound of determinate, measurable pitch, high or low," is a bit imprecise as it lacks the idea of a continuity central to Hanslick's definition. "Measurable" refers to determinable vibration rates. See our essay on Hanslick's central concepts, p. xl.

3. *Translators' note*: See also Chapter 3, note 6. Although the "primordial law of the harmonic series" is essentially a mathematical concept, Hanslick here appears to have the overtone series in mind, as a musical manifestation of the abstract mathematical relation.

PREFACE

[iii] In the eighth edition (1891) of this book, which first appeared in the year 1854, there was nothing new other than the more fitting format and the more tasteful layout. The same goes for the present *new* edition. For it, I also would like to adapt the words with which *Friedrich Theodor Vischer* prefaced the reprint of an earlier essay ("The Dream"). "I include this study in the present collection," says Vischer, "without defending it against the attacks it encountered. I also refrained from improvements, except for small, minor helpful hints. I would perhaps formulate some things differently today, would deal with the subject more extensively, would present it more mutedly, more cautiously. [iv] Who is fully pleased with a work when reading it years later? However, one knows, too, how easily more is spoiled than improved with retrospective tampering."[1]

If I wanted to engage in polemics, answering all criticisms that my text elicited, this little booklet would grow to an alarmingly thick volume. My convictions have remained the same, as have the standpoints and the sharply opposing musical parties of the present. Perhaps the reader will therefore permit me to repeat some remarks that I included at the

---

1. Friedrich Theodor Vischer, *Altes und Neues* (Stuttgart, Germany: Bonz, 1881), p. 187. *Translators' note*: Numbers in square brackets indicate the pages in Hanslick's 10th edition of the treatise.

appearance of the third edition. I am very well aware of the shortcomings of this essay. Nevertheless, the favorable lot of the earlier editions, which far exceeded expectations, and the highly gratifying consideration with which eminent specialists in philosophy and music have taken notice, has convinced me that my ideas have fallen on good ground, even in the somewhat sharp and rhapsodic manner of their original appearance. To happiest surprise, I found a remarkable agreement with those views [v] in *Grillparzer's* brief essays and aphorisms on music that appeared after the poet's death. In this new edition, I could not resist citing a few of the most valuable of those accounts. My essay "Grillparzer and Music" covers them in greater depth.[2]

Impassioned opponents have occasionally attributed to me an all-out polemic against everything called feeling, while every unbiased and attentive reader can easily see that I am only protesting against the mistaken intrusion of feelings in the domain of *science*, i.e. fighting against those aesthetic enthusiasts who with pretensions of lecturing musicians merely convey their sonic opium dreams. I fully agree that the ultimate value of the beautiful will always be based on direct evidence of feeling. However, I maintain equally firmly that we cannot deduce a single musical law from all of the usual appeals to feeling.

[vi] That conviction constitutes the one *main negative thesis* of this study. First and foremost, it counters the prevalent view that music is supposed to "represent feelings." It is incomprehensible how, from that view, people wish to derive the "requirement of a total absence of feeling in music." A rose is fragrant, but its "content" is surely not "the representation of fragrance." A forest spreads shady coolness, but it certainly does not *represent* "the feeling of shady coolness." It is not an idle battle of words if we argue expressly against the concept of "representation," for the biggest errors in musical aesthetics have arisen from it. "Representing" something always involves the idea of two separate, different things, one of which is referred to by the other through a particular [mental] act.

---

2. Eduard Hanslick, *Musikalische Stationen*, 5th ed. (Berlin, Verein für deutsche Litteratur, 1885).

Through an apposite image, *Emanuel Geibel* expressed this relationship more vividly and satisfyingly than philosophical analysis was capable of doing, indeed in the following couplet:[3]

> [vii] Why do you never succeed in describing music with words?
> Because music, a pure element, spurns images and thoughts.
> Even feeling is merely a vaguely visible riverbed
> upon which music's resounding flow unfolds, swelling and subsiding.

Further, if this beautiful epigram arose under the reverberating impression of this book, as I have reason to believe, then my view, mostly branded as heretical by the poetically minded, must surely also be reasonably compatible with true poetry.

Opposite the *negative* thesis stands, correspondingly, the *positive* one: the beauty of a piece of music is *specifically musical*, i.e. inheres in the tone connections without reference to a foreign, extramusical sphere of thought. It was the author's sincere intention to fully illuminate the "specifically musical" as the vital issue of our art and chief standard of its aesthetic. If nonetheless the polemical, negating element gains the upper hand in carrying out that intention, it will hopefully be excused considering the special circumstances of the time. When I was writing this essay, the advocates of the music of the future were just at their loudest [viii] and surely had to provoke a reaction from people of my convictions. While arranging for the second edition, along came Liszt's program symphonies, which succeeded more completely than anything before in dismissing the independent significance of music and in presenting music to the listener merely as a means for conjuring up figures. Since then, we now also possess Richard Wagner's *Tristan, Ring of the Nibelungs*, and his theory of *"endless melody,"* i.e. formlessness elevated to a principle, the sung and fiddled opium high for whose cult a temple of its own has in fact been opened in Bayreuth.

3. *Neue Gedichte.*

Readers may count it in my favor that I felt no inclination to curtail or temper the polemical aspects of my book when confronted with such signs, but on the contrary pointed even more emphatically to the unique and imperishable in music, to *musical beauty*, as our great masters embodied it, and genuinely musical innovators will cultivate it throughout the future.

ON THE MUSICALLY BEAUTIFUL

A Contribution To the Revision of the
Aesthetics of Music

Chapter 1

The Aesthetics of Feeling

[1] The way musical aesthetics has been handled up to now has suffered almost entirely from the serious blunder of concerning itself, not with exploring what is beautiful in music, but rather with describing the feelings that take hold of us. Those investigations align fully with the standpoint of the older aesthetic systems that viewed the beautiful only with regard to elicited sensations and also reared the philosophy of *beauty* as the offspring of sensation [ἀισθησις].

Unphilosophical in themselves, in their application to the most ethereal of all arts, such aesthetic systems acquire something almost sentimental [2] that, although utterly invigorating for gushers, offers the studious a bare minimum of elucidation. Whoever seeks instruction about the nature of music wishes to escape the obscure hegemony of feeling and not to be constantly referred to feeling, as occurs in most guidebooks.

The urgency for as objective a knowledge of things as possible, as it motivates all areas of knowledge in our day, must necessarily also engage the investigation of the *beautiful*. That investigation will be adequate only insofar as it breaks with a method that starts from subjective feeling in order to return to feeling after a poetic stroll across the entire fringe of the subject. If the investigation is not to become completely illusory, it will have to approach the natural-scientific method at least as far as trying to penetrate to the things themselves and to probe what in those things may be enduring, objective, detached from the thousandfold fluctuating impressions.

Poetry and the visual arts are in their aesthetic research and theoretical foundation far ahead of [3] similar attainments of music. Their scholars have for the most part discarded the delusion that the aesthetics of a particular art could be achieved by merely adapting the general, metaphysical concept of beauty (which of course in every art engages a series of new variations). The servile dependence of genre-specific aesthetics[1] upon the uppermost metaphysical principle of a general aesthetics is yielding increasingly to the conviction that every art must be known on its own technical terms, grasped in and of itself. The "system" is gradually giving way to "research," which holds firmly to the maxim that the laws of beauty of each art are inseparable from the characteristics of its material, of its technique.[2]

[4] Accordingly, the aesthetics of literary and visual arts, as well as their practical offshoots, art criticism, tends to stick to the rule

---

1. *Translators' note*: We use the term "genre-specific aesthetics" for what Hanslick calls *Spezial-Ästhetiken*. The term is difficult to translate. Payzant adopts "various special aesthetics," but "various" is not in the text, and "special aesthetics" seemed insufficiently clear to us. *Spezial-Ästhetiken*, as Hanslick uses the term, are aesthetic doctrines specific or relative to artistic genres (music, literature, visual arts, etc.). Hanslick gives a bit more detail about his understanding of the term in the first edition of chapter one (see our Appendix, p. 118): "Those genre-specific aesthetics are of course to be substantiated in a wholly different manner than through a mere adaptation of the general concept of beauty because that concept involves a series of new differentiations in each art."

2. Robert Schumann stirred up a lot of trouble with his statement, "the aesthetics of one art is [the same as] that of the others, only the material is different" (*Collected Works*, vol. 1, p. 43). Franz Grillparzer judges totally differently and gets it right with the following quotation. "In Germany, the greatest disservice that could have been done to the arts was probably lumping them together under the name of art. As many commonalities as they may have with one another, just as infinitely different are they in their means, indeed in the basic conditions of their practice. If we wanted to tellingly characterize the fundamental difference between music and the art of poetry, we would have to point out how the effect of music begins from sensation, from activity of the nervous system and, after the arousal of feelings, reaches the intellect only in the final analysis. By contrast, poetic art first evokes concepts and only through them acts on feelings, and permits the sensuous to participate only at the highest level of consummation or of degradation. The path of each is therefore exactly the opposite. The one, an intellectualizing of the corporeal, the other, a corporealizing of the intellectual" (*Collected Works*, vol. 9, p. 142).

that in aesthetic investigations primarily the beautiful object, and not the perceiving subject, is to be researched.[3]

Music alone still seems not to be capable of achieving that objective standpoint. Music strictly separates its theoretic-grammatical rules from aesthetic investigations, and prefers to keep the former as dryly rational, the latter as lyrically sentimental as possible. Addressing its subject matter clearly and distinctly as an autonomous type of beauty was up to now an insuperable struggle for music aesthetics. [5] Instead, "sensations" perpetuate the old phantom in broad daylight. The musically beautiful is still viewed only from the perspective of its subjective impression, and in books, reviews, and conversations it is affirmed daily that the *affects* are the sole aesthetic foundation of music and are alone qualified for staking out the boundaries of judgment about music.

Music, so we are taught, cannot entertain the intellect through concepts, as in poetry, as little as it can the eye through visible forms, as in visual arts. Thus the job of music must be to act on *feelings*. "Music has to do with feelings." This phrase "having to do" is one of the typical expressions of previous music aesthetics. Those who had "to do" with it left us completely in the dark on *what* the connection is between music and feelings, between specific musical pieces and specific feelings, according to which laws of nature the connection is to act, according to what laws of art it is to be fashioned. Only when we have adjusted our eyes a bit to the dark do we come to discover [6] that in the prevailing musical view feelings play a dual role.

First, as the *aim* and *purpose* of music it is proposed that music should arouse feelings or "beautiful feelings." Second, feelings are designated as the *content* that music represents in its works.

Both propositions are similar in that the one is just as false as the other.

---

3. *Translators' note*: Payzant gives a rather misleading rendering of the passage. He translates *empfindendes Subjekt* as "feelings of the subject" (*On the Musically Beautiful* [hereafter *OMB*], p. 2) rather than as "perceiving subject." See p. xxxvi of our essay on Hanslick's central concepts for the philosophical implications of the statement.

Refuting the first one, which introduces most musical manuals, need not detain us long. The beautiful has no *purpose* at all, for it is mere *form*, which can be used, of course, for the most diverse purposes according to the *content* with which it is filled, but that has no content of its own other than itself. When pleasant feelings arise for the viewer as a result of contemplating something beautiful, they do not at all concern beauty as such. I can certainly present something beautiful to observers with the specific intention that they find enjoyment in it. But that intention has nothing to do with the beauty of the presented thing itself. The beautiful is and remains beautiful even if it arouses no [7] feelings, indeed even if it is neither viewed nor contemplated. The beautiful is thus namely merely *for* the pleasure of the viewing subject, but not *by means of* the subject.[4]

We thus cannot speak of a *purpose* in this sense with regard to music either, and the fact that this art exhibits a dynamic connection with our feelings does not at all justify the assertion that its aesthetic significance resides in that connection.

To investigate that relationship more closely, we must first differentiate rigorously here between the concepts "feeling" and "sensation," whose confounding in ordinary usage raises no objection.

Sensation is the perception of a specific sensory quality, of a tone, of a color. *Feeling* is the awareness of a furthering or an inhibiting of our psychic state, thus of a state of well-being or of displeasure.[5] When with my senses I simply discern (perceive) the odor or taste of

4. *Translators' note*: Payzant omits the sentence "The beautiful is thus namely merely *for* the pleasure of the viewing subject, but not *by means of* the subject" because he considers it "vestigial" (*OMB*, p. 105). The omission strikes us as odd. Read together with the preceding sentence ("The beautiful is and remains beautiful . . ."), it is a typical example of Hanslick's occasionally collage-like writing style. He adopted the preceding sentence from Robert Zimmermann's review, but decided not to continue in Zimmermann's purely formalist manner. The sentence missing in Payzant's translation marks precisely the theoretical line that Hanslick was not willing to cross. See also our essay of Hanslick's philosophical background, pp. lxx-lxxi.

5. *Translators' note*: Hanslick's term for sensation is *Empfindung*. For a discussion of the concept and its fundamental ambiguity, see our essay on Hanslick's central concepts, pp. xlviii–xlix.

something, of its form, color, or tone, I *perceive* those qualities. When melancholy, hope, happiness, or [8] hate noticeably uplift me above the usual psychic state or depress me below it, *then I am feeling*.[6]

The beautiful first affects our senses. That route is not unique to the beautiful, which shares it with all phenomena in general. Sensation is the beginning and precondition of aesthetic pleasure and initially forms the basis of *feeling*, which always presupposes a relationship and often the most complicated relationships. Arousing *sensations* does not require art. A single tone, a single color can do that. As mentioned, the two terms are randomly interchanged, what we designate as "feelings" mostly being called "sensations" in older writings. Music, those authors say, is thus supposed to arouse our *feelings* and to fill us alternatingly with reverence, love, joy, melancholy.

However, in truth [9] neither music nor any other art has such a purpose. Art is primarily for representing something *beautiful*. The agency by which the beautiful is received is not feeling but rather *imagination*, as the activity of pure viewing.[7]

It is curious how musicians and older aestheticians deal only with the contrast of "feeling" and "understanding," as though the main thing were not situated directly *amid* this supposed dilemma. A musical piece emerges from the imagination of the artist for the imagination of the listener. The [activity of] imagination, confronted with the beautiful, is of course not merely a *viewing*, but rather a viewing

6. The older philosophers agree with the newer physiologists in this terminological designation, and we absolutely had to choose that terminology over the terms of the Hegelian school, which, as generally known, distinguishes between inner and outer perception.

7. Hegel showed how the investigation of "sensations" (in our terminology, feelings) that an art arouses remains wholly indefinite and disregards actual concrete content. "What is perceived," he says, "remains enclosed in the form of the most abstract, individual subjectivity, and therefore the perceptual differences are also wholly abstract, not differences in the thing itself" (*Aesthetics*, vol. 1, p. 42). *Translators' note*: "Imagination" is our rendering of *Phantasie*. The term is explained in broader detail in Chapter 3. For a discussion of imagination and its relation to Hanslick's concept of *Geist* [mind/intellect], see our essay on Hanslick's central concepts, pp. xliv–xlvi.

with *understanding*, that is, mental representation and judgment. The latter of course occurs with such speed that the individual processes do not even rise to consciousness, and the deception arises that something [10] *unmediated* happens, which in reality depends on intellectual processes mediating in various ways. The word "contemplation," long since extended from the visual to all sensory phenomena, accords fittingly, moreover, with the act of attentive listening, which in fact consists in a successive observing of tone configurations. Imagination is here by no means an isolated domain. Just as it drew its vitality from sensory perceptions, in turn it rapidly transmits its radial waves to the activity of understanding and feeling. However, for the genuine comprehension of beauty, these measures are merely peripheral.

In pure contemplation, the listener enjoys the sounding piece of music; all material interest must be kept at a distance. However, one such interest is the tendency to allow affects to be aroused. The exclusive activation of *understanding* through the beautiful operates *logically* instead of aesthetically. A predominating effect on *feeling* is more dubious, indeed even *pathological*.

All of this, long since developed by general aesthetics, is equally valid for the beauty of all fine arts. Thus if *music* is to be treated *as art*, [11] imagination, not feeling, must be recognized as its aesthetic agency. The modest first premise therefore seems advisable to us because, given the prominent emphasis placed untiringly on the desired soothing of human passions through music, we in fact often do not know whether with music we are talking about a police, pedagogical, or medical regulation.

Musicians, however, are less prone to the error of wanting *all* of the arts to stake a claim on feelings to the same degree. In this matter, they see, rather, something specifically unique to *music*. It is [for them] precisely the power and tendency to evoke any type of affect in the listener that characterizes *music* among the other arts.[8]

---

8. Where "feeling" was not even separated from "sensation," there can be no talk of a deeper probing into the differentiations of the (subspecies of the) former.

[12] But we could no more acknowledge that effect as the purpose of the arts in general than we can view the specific essence of *music* in that effect. Once it is established that *imagination* is the actual agency of beauty, a secondary effect on feelings would occur in *every* art. Does not a great historical painting move us with the power of a personal experience? Do not Raphael's Madonnas attune us to reverence, Poussin's landscapes to a yearning wanderlust? Does the sight of the Strasbourg Cathedral remain without effect on our psyche? The answer cannot be in doubt. It is likewise valid for poetry and indeed for some nonaesthetic activity, for example religious uplifting or rhetorical eloquence, among others. We see that the other arts likewise affect feelings strongly enough. We would therefore have to base the supposed fundamental difference between those arts and music on the greater or lesser strength of that effect. Completely unscientific in itself, this dodge would in addition rightly leave to each individual the decision whether one has stronger or deeper feelings in the case of a Mozart symphony or a tragedy by [13] Shakespeare, in the case of a poem by Uhland or a Hummel rondo. However, if we say that music acts "directly" on feelings—the other arts only through mediatory concepts—then we err but with different words because, as we saw, with the musically beautiful, feelings are to be engaged only secondarily, only imagination *directly*. In musical studies, the analogy that doubtlessly exists between music and *architecture* is invoked innumerable times. But did it ever occur to a rational architect that the *purpose* of architecture is to arouse feelings or that feelings were the *contents* of architecture?

Every true work of art will enter into some kind of relationship with our feelings, but *none* in an exclusive relationship. We thus say nothing at all decisive about the aesthetic principle of music if we characterize it only very generally based on its effect on feeling, just as

Sensuous and intellectual feelings, the chronic form of *mood*, the acute form of *affect*, preference, and passion, as well as the typical shades of those as "pathos" of the Greeks and *passio* of the more modern Latins were equated in a potpourri, and of music simply was declared that it was especially the art of arousing feelings.

little, say, if we wanted to grasp the nature of wine by getting drunk. It depends solely on the *specific* manner how such [14] affects are evoked *through music*. Thus instead of getting stuck on the secondary and vague effects of feeling brought on by musical phenomena, we should penetrate to the interior of works and explain the specific power of their impression based on the laws of their own internal organization. Painters or poets no longer persuade themselves to have accounted for beauty in their art by investigating what "feelings" their landscape or their drama evokes. They will trace the compelling power to understand *why* the work pleases, and for what reasons it does so in exactly this and no other way. As we will see later, the fact that this investigation is much more difficult in music than in other arts, indeed that the researchable aspects in music reach only just so far, by no means entitles its critics to directly intermingle emotional affectations and musical beauty instead of expounding on them scientifically as separately as possible.

If feelings cannot at all be a basis for aesthetic laws, then there are, additionally, some substantial things [15] to note against the reliability of musical feeling. We do not mean here merely the conventional bias that, through texts, titles, and other merely incidental associations, especially in church, military, and theatrical compositions, enables our feelings and mental representation to take a direction that we tend to mistakenly ascribe to the character of music itself. The link between a piece of music and the feelings it evokes is, rather, not necessarily a causal one. The mood changes with the varying perspective of our musical experience and impressions. Today, we often hardly understand how our grandparents could consider a *particular* succession of tones as a corresponding expression of a *particular* affect. Evidence for that, for example, is the extraordinary variety with which many of Mozart's, Beethoven's, and Weber's compositions affected listeners at the time when they were new in contrast to today. How many of Mozart's works were in their time declared to be the most passionate, fiery, and most daring possible in portraying musical moods? Contemporaries contrasted the outbursts of intense passion, of the most severe struggles, of the bitter, poignant anguish in Mozart's music with the leisurely quality and pure [16] wholesomeness of Haydn's symphonies.[9] Twenty to thirty years later, people determined exactly the same between Beethoven and Mozart. Beethoven assumed the position of Mozart as the representative of powerful, captivating passion, and Mozart was advanced to Haydn's Olympian classicism. In the course of an extended life, every attentive composer will experience similar changes in the reception of himself. However, throughout these differences in emotional effect, the *musical* appreciation of many works, once so exciting in effect, the aesthetic enjoyment that their *originality* and *beauty* still give us today, remains essentially unchanged. The connection of musical works with certain [17] moods does not always hold, everywhere, necessarily, as an absolute imperative. It is rather incomparably more mutable than in any other art.

The effect of music on feeling therefore possesses neither the necessity nor the exclusivity nor the consistency that a phenomenon would have to exhibit to be able to establish an aesthetic principle.

The strong feelings that music awakens from their slumber, and all of the sweet as well as painful moods into which it lulls us half-dreaming listeners: We certainly do not wish to underestimate them. Surely among the most beautiful and beneficial mysteries is that, by the grace of God, art is capable of evoking such stirrings without earthly cause. It is only against the unscientific assessment of these facts for *aesthetic principles* that we register our protest. Delight and grief can be evoked to a high degree through music. That is correct. But could it not be true to an even greater degree because of hitting the lottery big or because of the terminal illness of a friend? Accordingly, as long as we take exception to counting a [18] lottery ticket among symphonies or a doctor's report among overtures, we may not treat actually produced affects as an aesthetic specialty of

---

9. There are some, for us today, very astonishing statements about Mozart's instrumental music, particularly from Rochlitz. He calls the charming Menuetto capriccio in Weber's A-flat major sonata an "uninterrupted outpouring of a passionate, violently agitated mind, and yet controlled with admirable stability."

music or of a particular piece of music. The *specific manner* of *how* such affects are evoked *by music* is the only thing that counts. We shall devote closest consideration to the influence of music on feeling in Chapters 4 and 5, and will investigate the *positive* aspects of this peculiar relationship. Here, at the outset of our book, the negative aspect could not be too pointedly emphasized in protest against an unscientific principle.

To my knowledge, the first person who attacked this aesthetics of feeling in music is *Herbart* (in the ninth chapter of his *Encyclopedia*).[10] After declaring himself against the "oversubtle interpretation" of artworks, he says,

For millennia, interpreters of dreams and astrologists have not accepted that people dream because they sleep, and that the stars appear now here, now there because they move. [19] Up to the present day, even good music connoisseurs thus repeat the proposition that music expresses feelings, as though the feelings that are perchance aroused by it—and for whose expression, if we like, it is therefore used—were the basis of the general rules of simple and double counterpoint on which music's true nature rests. What might the old artists who developed the possible forms of the fugue have intended to express? They did not want to *express* anything at all. Their thoughts did not go outward but rather into the inner nature of art. However, those who *commit to* meanings reveal their hesitance vis-à-vis the inner self and their preference for exterior appearances.[11]

10. *Translators' note*: The reference to Herbart was added in the sixth edition [of OMB]. Curiously, Herbart is not mentioned in the treatise until the third edition of 1865, though Hanslick declared himself a Herbartian in his habilitation petition of 1856. For a discussion of Herbart's importance for Hanslick's aesthetics, see our essay on the treatise's philosophical background, pp. lxv–lxvii.

11. Johann Friedrich Herbart, *Kurze Encyklopädie der Philosophie* (Halle, 1831), 124–25; *Werke*, 19 vols. (Langensalza, 1897), vol. 9, 109–10. *Translators' note*: Our translation of the last sentence of the quotation from Herbart's *Kurze Encyklopädie*, about the inner self and exterior appearances, follows the philosopher's original text, quoted correctly in the ninth edition of *OMB*. In Hanslick's tenth edition, translated

Unfortunately, Herbart did not substantiate this casually stated opposition in closer detail, and alongside these brilliant remarks about music, with him we find some outlandish ones as well. In any case, his previously quoted words have not been accorded their deserved attention, as we will presently see.[12]

> **Johann Mattheson**: "In every melody, we must make the *movement of feeling* (if not more than one) the main purpose." (*Vollkommener Kapellmeister*, p. 143)
>
> **Johann Georg Neidhardt**: "The ultimate purpose of music is to arouse *all affects* by means of mere tones and their rhythms, beyond the best orator." (*Vorrede zur Temperatur*)
>
> **Johann Nikolaus Forkel** understands by "figures in music" "the same thing that they are in poetry and rhetoric, namely the expression of the different ways in which *sentiments* and *passions* manifest themselves." (*Über die Theorie der Musik.* Göttingen, Germany, 1777, p. 26)
>
> **Ignaz Franz von Mosel** defines music as "the art of expressing *specific sentiments* through organized tones."
>
> **Christian Friedrich Michaelis**: "Music is the art of expressing *sentiments* by means of modulating the tones. It is the language of affects," etc. (*Über den Geist der Tonkunst*, 2nd ed., 1800, p. 29)
>
> **Friedrich Wilhelm Marpurg**: "The goal that the composer should set for himself in his work is to imitate nature . . . to arouse

in this volume, an error occurred that rendered *Innern* (uppercase, translated as "the inner self" here) as *innern* (lowercase, misleadingly suggesting a grammatical relation to "appearances"). Our translation corrects the error.

12. *Note*: For the present purpose, it seems to us hardly necessary to attach the names of the authors to the views that we seek to impose, as those views are less the result of special convictions [20] than the expression of a mode of thought that has generally become traditional. Just to allow a glimpse into the widespread predominance of these principles, some quotations are included here from older and newer authors on music from the large mass of those available. *Translators' note*: The list of feeling-theorists appears as an appendix in Payzant's translation. In all editions of the treatise, it appears at the end of chapter one. We decided to reproduce the list where Hanslick originally placed it.

the passions according to his will . . . [21] to portray the motions of the soul, the inclinations of the heart according to life." (*Kritischer Musikus*, vol. 1, 1750, section 40)

Wilhelm Heinse: "The main ultimate goal of music is imitating or rather arousing the *passions*." (*Musikalische Dialoge*, 1805, p. 30)

Johann Jakob Engel: "A symphony, a sonata, etc., must contain the realization of a passion, which however mutates into various sentiments." (*Über musikalische Malerei*, 1780, p. 29)

Johann Philipp Kirnberger: "A melodic phrase (theme) is a comprehensible sentence in the language of sentiments, which allows a sensitive listener to feel the emotional state that evoked it." (*Kunst des reinen Satzes*, vol. 2, p. 152)

Heinrich August Pierer: "*Music* is the art of expressing *sentiments* and states of mind by means of beautiful tones. It ranks higher than *poetry*, which is only (!) capable of representing moods recognizable with the intellect, since music expresses wholly inexplicable sentiments and intuitions." (*Universallexikon*, 2nd ed.)

Gustav Schilling's *Universallexikon der Tonkunst* provides the same explanation in the article "Music."

Heinrich Christoph Koch defines music as the "art of expressing a pleasant play of *sentiments* by means of tones." (*Musikalisches Lexikon*, "Musik")

Anton André: "Music is the art of producing tones that portray, arouse, and delight *sentiments* and passions." (*Lehrbuch der Tonkunst*, vol. 1)

[22] **Johann Georg Sulzer**: "Music is the art of expressing our passions by means of tones, as in language by means of words." (*Theorie der schönen Künste*)

Johann Wilhelm Böhm: "Harmonious tones of strings engage, not the intellect, not reason, but rather solely the *faculty of feeling*." (*Analyse des Schönen der Musik*. Vienna, 1830, p. 62)

Gottfried Weber: "Music is the art of expressing *sentiments* by means of tones." (*Theorie der Tonsetzkunst*, 2nd ed., vol. 1, p. 15)

Ferdinand Hand: "Music represents *feelings*. Every feeling and every state of mind has both in itself and thus also in music its particular tone and rhythm." (*Ästhetik der Tonkunst*, vol. 1, 1837, § 24)

Amadeus Autodidaktus: "Music springs from and is rooted only in the world of mental *feelings* and *sentiments*. Musically melodic tones (!) resound, not for the understanding, which only describes and analyses feelings . . . they address *the mind*," etc. (*Aphorismen über Musik*, Leipzig, 1857, p. 329)

Fermo Bellini: Music is art that expresses sentiments and passions by the means of sounds. (*Manuale di Musica*, Milan, Ricordi, 1853)

Friedrich Thiersch: "Music is the art of expressing or arousing feelings and moods of the psyche through the selection and connection of tones." (*Allgemeine Ästhetik*, Berlin, 1846, § 18, p. 101)

[23] **Arrey von Dommer**: "*Purpose of Music*: Music should arouse *feelings* in us and, through feeling, *mental images*." (*Elemente der Musik*, Leipzig, 1862, p. 174)

Richard Wagner, *Das Kunstwerk der Zukunft* (1850, Collected Works, vol. 3, p. 99 and similarly elsewhere): "The voice of the *heart* is *tone*, its artistically conscious language, music." Wagner's definitions become yet vaguer, of course, in the later writings. There, music is for him equivalent to the "art of expression" generally (in *Opera und Drama*, Collected Works, vol. 3, p. 343), which as "the idea of the world" seems to him capable of grasping "the essence of things in its most immediate manifestation," etc. (*Beethoven*, 1870, pp. 6ff)

Chapter 2

The "Representation of Feelings" Is Not the Content of Music

[24] Partly as a consequence of this theory that declares feelings to be the *ultimate goal* of musical effects and partly as a corrective to that theory, the proposition is set forth that *feelings* are the content that music is supposed to represent.

The philosophical investigation of an art pursues the question of the *content* of that art. The diversity of content among the arts and the related fundamental difference in their design follows necessarily from the difference among the *senses* to which they are tied. For every art there is an applicable range of ideas that, with its expressive means, it represents as tones, words, colors, stone. [25] Accordingly, the individual artwork embodies a specific idea as beauty in sensuous appearance. That specific idea, the form that embodies it, and the unity of the two are conditions of the concept of beauty from which no scholarly inquiry of any art can ever diverge.

What the content of a work of poetic or visual art is can be expressed in words and traced back to concepts. We say, this picture represents a flower girl, this statue a gladiator, that poem a feat of Roland. The more-or-less complete absorption of a so-designated content in the artistic manifestation undergirds, then, our judgment on the beauty of the artwork.

With considerable agreement, the entire spectrum of human *feelings* has been considered the *content of music* because people believed to have found in feelings the opposite of conceptual certainty, and thus the appropriate differentiation [from music] of the ideal of visual and poetic art. Accordingly, tones and their artful coherence would be just material, expressive means, through which the [26] composer portrays love, courage, reverence, enchantment. These feelings, in their rich diversity, are considered to be the idea clothed in the worldly body of sound in order to walk the earth as a musical artwork. What delights and elevates us in a charming melody, a suggestive harmony, is considered to be, not these themselves, but rather what they signify: the whisperings of tenderness, storming of combativeness.

To secure firm ground, we must first ruthlessly set aside such stale metaphors. *Whispering*? Yes, but by no means of "yearning." *Storming*? Absolutely, but certainly not of "combativeness." Music indeed possesses one without the other; it can whisper, storm, rustle. But only our own heart imparts to them love and rage.[1]

The representation of a specific feeling or affect does not at all lie within music's own capabilities.

This is because feelings do not reside in the mind in isolation such that they can be, so to speak, called up from the mind by an art to which the [27] representation of other mental activities is sealed off. On the contrary, they are dependent on physiological and pathological conditions, are conditioned by mental images, judgments, in short by the entire range of intelligible and rational thought to which people so willingly juxtapose feeling as something opposite.

What is it, then, that makes a feeling into *a particular* feeling, into yearning, hope, love? Perhaps the mere strength or weakness, the undulating of interior movement? Surely not. These can be the same in the case of different feelings, as well as different in the case of the same feeling in various individuals at different times. Our psychic

---

1. *Translators' note*: Regarding the sentence "Music indeed possesses one without the other," from the sixth edition onward the passage reads "one or the other." In print, the German word for "without" [*ohne*] is easy to confuse with the German word for "or" [*oder*]. Dietmar Strauß, editor of the historical–critical edition of *Vom Musikalisch-Schönen*, assumes a typesetting error that Hanslick failed to correct. Given the context of the passage, "or" is implausible, so we follow Strauß's assumption.

state can coalesce into a particular feeling based on only a number of mental images and judgments (perhaps unconsciously in a moment of strong feelings). The feeling of hope is inseparable from the mental image of an expected, happier condition and is compared with the present one. Melancholy compares past good fortune with the present. These are very specific mental images and concepts. *Without them*, without [28] this *cognitive* mechanism, we cannot call the present feeling "hope," not "melancholy."[2] That cognitive mechanism transforms them into hope and melancholy. If we abstract from that mechanism, there remains indefinite motion, at most the sense of general well-being or discomfort. *Love* cannot be conceived without the thought of a beloved person, without the wish and aspiration for the happiness, glorification, and for the possession of this object. Not the type of mere psychic movement but rather its conceptual core, its genuine, historical content transforms it into *love*. According to *its dynamics*, the movement can be gentle as well as passionate, happy as well as painful, and yet still remains love. This observation alone is sufficient to show that music can express only those various accompanying adjectives, never the substantives, love itself. A specific feeling (a passion, an affect) never exists as such without an actual historical content, which can be presented only in concepts. Granted, music cannot convey concepts as an "indefinite language." Then is [29] not the conclusion psychologically irrefutable that it is also not capable of expressing specific feelings? The *specificity* of feelings resides precisely in their conceptual core.

How it is, nevertheless, that music *can* (not must) *arouse* feelings such as melancholy, mirth, and the like we will explore later, when we speak of music's subjective impression. Here, we wanted merely to establish theoretically whether music is capable of *representing* a specific feeling. That question was to be answered negatively because specificity of feelings cannot be separated from concrete mental images and concepts, which lie outside the sphere

---

2. *Translators' note*: Note that Hanslick's notion of "feeling" is distinctly cognitivist. For further detail, see our essay on Hanslick's central concepts, pp. xlvii–xlviii.

of musical design. By contrast, with its distinctive means, music can most richly represent a certain circle of *ideas*. According to the organ that receives them, these are, to begin with, all those ideas that relate to audible changes in force, motion, and proportion, that is, the idea of intensification, attenuation, of hastening, hesitation, of contrived complexities, of straightforward progressions, and the like. [30] Furthermore, the aesthetic expression of a particular piece of music can be called charming, gentle, vigorous, forceful, graceful, vivacious, all ideas that have a corresponding sensuous manifestation in connections of tones. We can thus use these adjectives with regard to *musical* constructions without thinking about the ethical significance that they have for psychic life and that for music so quickly introduces a common association of ideas, indeed tends to be confounded surreptitiously with purely musical traits.

The ideas that the composer represents are above all and foremost purely *musical* ones. A particular beautiful melody appears in his imagination. It should not be anything other than itself. However, just as every tangible phenomenon refers to its higher generic concept, to the idea that initially fulfills it, and so on, higher and higher, up to the absolute idea, so too with musical ideas. Thus, for example, *this* gentle, harmoniously subsiding adagio produces the beautiful manifestation of the idea of the gentle, the harmonious *in general*. [31] Common imagination, which readily associates the ideas in art with one's own psychic life, will interpret this subsiding on a yet higher plane, for example as the expression of calm resignation of a self-reconciled mind, and *can* perhaps escalate further, similarly, to the notion of eternal otherworldly peace.[3]

---

3. *Translators' note*: Our "further, similarly" appears as "instantly" in the Payzant translation. Given the context of the passage, we again assume a typesetting error. From the third edition onward, *so fort* (two words), with a broad meaning in German of "further, in this way," is mistakenly printed as *sofort* (one word), meaning instantly. The image that Hanslick wanted to convey is clearly that of a step-by-step movement, not that of an abrupt transition. We therefore translate *sofort* in the meaning of *so fort*, as it appears in the first and second editions. Regarding the phrase "notion of

Poetry, too, and visual art portray for the moment something tangible. The picture of a flower girl can only indirectly allude to the more general idea of girlish contentment and unassuming nature, a snowy churchyard to the idea of earthly transience. In the same way, only with an incomparably more uncertain and arbitrary interpretation can a listener hear the idea of youthful satisfaction in one piece of music, the idea of transience in another. But these abstract *ideas* are no more the content of the musical work than in the aforementioned pictures. There can be no talk whatsoever of the representation of the "*feeling* of transience," of the "*feeling* of youthful contentment."

There are ideas that can be [32] fully represented through music and yet not occur as *feeling*, just as, conversely, *feelings* in such mixture can move the mind so that they have no corresponding designation in an *idea* capable of representation by music.

What can music portray of feelings, then, if not their content?

Only their *dynamic properties*. It is capable of simulating the motion of a physical process according to the aspects fast, slow, strong, weak, ascending, descending. However, motion is but one trait, one aspect of feeling, not feeling itself. It is commonly believed that the representational capability of music is sufficiently limited when it is asserted that music can in no way signify the *object* of a feeling, but surely the feeling itself, cannot signify the object of a particular love, for example, but surely "love." In truth, it can do that just as little. It can depict, not love, but only a motion that can occur with love or also with another affect, but is always the nonessential aspect of its character. "Love" is an abstract concept, like "virtue" and "immortality." The [33] assurance of theorists that music is not supposed to represent abstract

---

eternal otherworldly peace," in the first edition, the target of the escalatory movement described was the "intimation of the absolute." In his revisions for the second edition, Hanslick toned down some of his youthful, idealist vocabulary and streamlined the treatise in a more "formalist" manner, particularly in reaction to Robert Zimmermann's review. See our Appendix, pp. 120–21 for details.

concepts is superfluous, because *no* art can do that. It is self-evident that only *ideas*, that is, concepts brought alive, are the content of artistic embodiment.[4] But instrumental works cannot portray the *ideas* of love, anger, fear either, because no necessary link exists between those ideas and beautiful tone connections. So, which aspect of these ideas is it, then, that music actually can appropriate so effectively? It is *motion* (naturally in the broader sense that also regards as "motion" the intensification and deintensification of a single tone or a chord). It is the element that music shares with states of feeling and that it is capable of creatively shaping in a thousand gradations and contrasts.

The concept of *motion* has to date been conspicuously neglected in [34] investigations of the nature and effect of music. To us, it seems the most important and fruitful concept.

What otherwise seems to us to portray specific psychic states in music is *symbolic*.

This is because tones, like colors, possess symbolic significance, inherently and individually, that operates apart from and before all artistic intention. Every color embodies a unique character. It is no mere cipher for us that simply acquires a location from the artist, but rather a force that by nature is already placed in sympathetic relation with certain moods. Who does not know interpretations of colors as they are commonly, in their simplicity, or by sophisticated minds elevated to poetic refinement? We associate green with the feeling of hope, blue with loyalty. *Rosenkranz* recognizes "graceful dignity" in russet, in purple "petty geniality," and so on.[5]

Similarly, the elemental materials of music—keys, chords, and timbres—are in themselves already *characters* for us. We also have

---

4. Vischer (*Ästhetik*, §11, Note) defines specific ideas as the realms of life, provided that their reality can be thought of as corresponding to their concept. For *idea* always indicates the concept present to the mind, pure and unblemished in its reality.

5. *Psychologie*, 2nd ed., p. 102.

[35] an all-too-busy hermeneutics for the interpretation of musical elements. *Schubart*'s symbolism of keys offers in its manner a companion to *Goethe*'s interpretation of colors. However, in their artistic application these elements (tones, timbres) follow completely different laws than the effect of their appearance in isolation. Just as little as every color red in a historical painting means joy to us, every white innocence, as little does all music in A-flat major in a symphony arouse for us an effusive mood, everything in B minor a misanthropic one, or every triad gratification, every diminished-seventh chord despair. In the aesthetic domain, such elemental autonomy is neutralized through the commonality of higher laws. Such a natural relationship is far removed from *expression* or *representation*. We called that relationship "symbolic" because it in no way directly represents the content but rather remains a form substantially different from that content. When we see jealousy in yellow, cheerfulness in G major, grief in the cypress, that interpretation possesses a physiologic–psychological correlation with the specificities of those feelings, but [36] only our interpretation possesses that correlation, not the color, the tone, the plant in themselves. Accordingly, we can neither say of a chord in itself that it represents a particular feeling, nor yet less that it does so in the context of an artwork.

Other than the analogy with motion and symbolism of tones, music does not possess another means for this ostensible purpose.

Thus if music's inability to represent specific feelings can easily be deduced from the nature of tones, it seems almost inconceivable that through experience it has not penetrated even more quickly into general awareness. Let anyone whose affections resonate with an instrumental work try to demonstrate with clear reasoning *which* affect is its content. The experiment is indispensable.

Let us listen to Beethoven's overture to *Prometheus*, for example. What the alert ear of the art lover hears in continuous succession is roughly the following. After a descent of a fourth in the first measure, the notes of the first measure spume upward quickly and softly, and repeat exactly in the second. The third and fourth measures follow the same course in [37] larger compass. The droplets cast upward by the fountain ripple downward in order to execute the same figure and the same pattern in the next four measures. Thus before the mind of the listener a symmetry unfolds in the *melody* between the first and second measures, then between those two and the next two, and finally between the first four measures as one large arch counterposed to the corresponding equally sized arch of the following four measures. The bass, setting out the *rhythm*, marks the beginning of each of the first three measures with one attack, the fourth with two attacks, [repeated] in the same way in the next four measures.[6] Compared with the first three measures, the fourth is thus a variation that, through repetition, will become symmetrical in the next four measures, and delights the ear in a feature of newness in the previous equilibrium. The *harmony* in the theme again shows us the correspondence of one large and two small arches. The four–two chord in the fifth and sixth measures, then the six–five chord in the seventh and eighth, corresponds to the C-major triad in the initial four measures. This [38] reciprocal correspondence among melody, rhythm, and harmony produces a symmetrical yet highly varied image that acquires even richer highlights and shadows through the timbres of the different instruments and the shifts in tone volume.

6. *Translators' note*: Hanslick's example, mm. 17–24 of the Beethoven overture, is incorrect. The two chords shown in the bass clef at m. 4 and the two in m. 8 of the example belong in mm. 3 and 7, respectively. Measures 4 and 8 should contain only one chord, on beat one. Further, in the treble voice the second eighth note in m. 5 of the example should be an A, not a G. The errors appear in many editions (e.g. in the 1st, 2nd, 4th, 5th, 9th, 10th, 11th, 13th, 15th). Hanslick's description of the musical events is correct only if applied to the incorrectly printed example, as it is shown here.

Example 2.1. Beethoven, *The Creatures of Prometheus*, Overture, measures 17–24.

[39] We are not at all capable of recognizing an additional *content* in the theme other than the one just indicated, least of all of specifying a *feeling* that it represents or must arouse in the listener. Such analysis admittedly makes a skeleton out of a flourishing body, suitable for destroying all beauty, but also all false, oversubtle interpretation.

It is the same with every other instrumental theme as it is with this completely randomly chosen subject. A large group of music lovers considers it merely a characteristic of older "classical" music to be averse to affects, and concedes from the outset that no one would be able to verify in any of the forty-eight fugues and preludes of J. S. Bach's *Well-Tempered Clavier* [hereafter *WTC*] a feeling that forms its content. Even as dilettantish and as arbitrary as the distinction is—whose explanation lies in the circumstance that that older music is more unmistakably an end in itself, the interpretability more difficult and less enticing—the proof would be thereby evinced [through the aforementioned example of Bach's *WTC*] that music *need* not awaken feelings and have them as its [40] subject. The entire field of figural music would cease to exist. But if large historically and aesthetically founded genres have to be ignored to maintain a theory by trickery, then that theory is wrong.[7] A ship must sink as soon as it has just *one* leak. Anyone for whom that is not enough can demolish the theory's entire hull. He should play the theme of any Mozart or Haydn symphony, of a Beethoven adagio, a Mendelssohn scherzo, a Schumann or Chopin piano piece, the mainstays of our most substantive music; or even the most popular overture themes by Auber, Donizetti, Flotow. Who will step forward and dare to demonstrate a specific feeling as the content of those themes? One will say "love." Possible. Another says "yearning." Perhaps. A third feels "reverence." No one can [41] refute it. And so on. Now, is that *representing* a specific feeling if no one knows *what* is actually represented? Everyone will probably concur on the beauty and beautiful aspects of this piece of music, yet think differently about the content. However, *representing* [something] means producing a content clearly, vividly, "placing" it before our eyes. How, then, are we to designate something as an art's represented object that, as the most uncertain and ambiguous element of that art, is subject to endless debate?

We have intentionally chosen *instrumental movements* as examples. For only what can be asserted about instrumental music is valid for music as such. If some specific characteristic in music is examined, something that is supposed to characterize its essence and its nature and to establish its boundaries and orientation, there can be talk only of instrumental music. Whatever *instrumental music* cannot do, can never be said that *music* can do it. For only instrumental music is

---

7. Bachians like *Spitta* of course aim at the opposite. Instead of arguing the theory itself to the advantage of their master, they interpret the fugues and suites with equally eloquent and positive outpourings of feelings as only a subtle Beethovenian could do with his master's sonatas.

pure, absolute *music* [*reine, absolute Tonkunst*].[8] Whether we prefer vocal or [42] instrumental music for its value and effect—an unscientific procedure for which mostly dilettantish bias prevails—we will always have to allow that the concept of "music" is not fully exhausted in a piece of music composed to the words of a text. In a composition for voice, the effectiveness of the tones can never be severed so precisely from that of the words, the action, the staging, such that the evaluation of the different arts can be rigorously separated. We even have to reject pieces with specific titles or programs in which it is a matter of the "content" of the music. The unification with poetry extends the power of music, but not its boundaries.[9]

---

8. *Translators' note*: The famous term "absolute music," often associated with Hanslick, does not appear in *OMB*. Wagner, who coined the term, applied it pejoratively. Hanslick, by contrast, gives it a positive spin. However, instead of using the word *Musik* here—and in many other instances when referring to *Musik*—he uses the synthesized compound *Tonkunst*, literally "art of tones." Payzant's translation ("because only instrumental music is music purely and absolutely") slightly distorts the grammar of the sentence and thus also the idea that Wagner and Hanslick wanted to convey, each with different intentions.

9. *Gervinus* took up the dispute over supremacy between vocal and instrumental music in his *Händel and Shakespeare* (1868). But in declaring "vocal art" genuine and true music, "instrumental art" "an art form impoverished in everything interior in favor of everything exterior," a physical means for physiological stimulation, he only proves with all effort of his acumen that one can be a learned Händel fan and still be biased into odd errors on the nature of music. No one has refuted these errors more compellingly than Ferdinand Hiller, from whose review of Gervinus's book we extract the following apposite passages. "The connections of words with tones are of the most manifold types. From the simplest recitative, half spoken in tones, to Bach's choruses or a Mozart operatic finale: what an assortment of combinations! But only in the recitative-style passages, whether they appear independently or interrupt the course of a vocal piece just with an outcry, can a text with music seize the listener with equal power. As soon as music enters in its full-blown essence, it leaves words, the otherwise omnipotent words, far behind. The proof, we *unfortunately* would say, lies all too near. The worst poem can hardly lessen the joy in a well-composed piece of music. But the greatest poetic masterwork cannot shore up boring music. What little interest does the text of an oratorio arouse when read. We can barely grasp that it could provide an inspired composer with material for hours of music that satisfies the ear, heart, and mind. Moreover, in most cases it is not even possible for the listener to simultaneously comprehend words and melody. The conventional sounds out of which a spoken sentence is composed must be rather rapidly connected with one another so that, retained

[43] In a piece of vocal music we have before us an indivisibly fused product in which [44] it is no longer possible to determine the scope of the individual components. When it is a matter of the effect of *poetry*, it will not occur to anyone to cite *opera* as evidence. It requires greater disavowal, but just the same insight, to do the same with the fundamental tenets of *music* aesthetics.

Vocal music illuminates the design of a poem.[10] We recognized in the musical [45] elements colors of the greatest glory and delicacy,

---

intact in memory, they are intellectually understood. However, music seizes the listener with the first tone and guides him onward without leaving time for, or even the possibility of, revisiting what has been heard. . . . We may," Hiller continues, "listen to the most naïve folk song, may encounter Händel's Halleluyah, borne by a thousand voices. In the former case, the charm of a barely opened melodic bud, in the latter the power and glory of the unified elements of an entire world of tones that charms and enchants us. It contributes nothing to that aforementioned, immediate effect that, in the one case, it is a matter of a lady-love, in the other of the heavens. That effect is of a purely musical nature and would not fail to occur even if we neither understood the words, nor could understand them." (From *Tonleben unserer Zeit, Neue Folge*. Leipzig, 1871, p. 40ff.)

10. We can use this familiar figurative expression here as apposite where, disregarding all *aesthetic* requirement, it is merely a matter of the abstract relation of text to music in general, and thus of the decision from which of these two components the autonomous, decisive determination of the *content* (object) emerges. However, as soon as it is no longer a matter of the *what* but rather of the *how* of musical accomplishments, the sentence ceases to be fitting. Only in the *logical* (we almost said "legal") sense is the text the main thing, music an accessory. The *aesthetic* demand on the composer escalates considerably. It requires autonomous (likewise, of course, text-appropriate) *musical beauty*. If we no longer ask abstractly what music does in setting texts but rather what it is *supposed to do* in actual cases, then we may not confine its dependence on the poetry within the same narrow boundaries that the draftsman draws for the colorist. Ever since Gluck, in the grand, necessary reaction against the melodic excesses of the Italians, retreated not to the happy midpoint but beyond (exactly like Richard Wagner in our day), the stated principle in the dedication to *Alceste* that the text is the correct and "well-designed drawing" that music merely has to color has been unceasingly parroted. If music does not treat the poetry in a sense much grander than merely as coloration, if (itself simultaneously drawing and color) it does not introduce something wholly new that, sprouting leaves with primally inherent powers of beauty, refashions the words as a mere trellis, then it has attained the level of a classroom exercise or a dilettante's glee, but never again the heights of art.

and of symbolic significance to boot. They might transform a mediocre poem into [46] the heart's most intimate revelation. Nevertheless, it is not the tones that do the *representing* in a vocal piece but rather the text. The design, not the coloration determines the represented object. We appeal to the listener's capacity for abstraction, which should aim at imagining a dramatically effective melody purely musically, *detached* from all poetic determination. In a very effective dramatic melody that is to express *anger*, we will actually find, for instance, no psychic expression other than one of rapid, impassioned movement. Words of a passionately animated *love*, that is, the exact opposite [of anger], are perhaps rendered equally correctly by means of the same melody. When the aria of Orpheus,

> J'ai perdu mon Euridice,
> Rien n'égale mon malheur,

moved thousands to tears (and among them men like J. J. Rousseau), a contemporary of Gluck, *Boyé*, remarked that one could underlay this melody equally well, indeed far more accurately, with the opposite words: [47]

> J'ai trouvé mon Euridice,
> Rien n'égale mon bonheur.

We provide here the beginning of the aria, with piano accompaniment for brevity's sake, but exactly according to the original Italian score.[11]

---

11. *Translators' note*: The excerpt from Gluck's aria contains two errors in the voice part. In m. 5 of the example, the second eighth note of beat three should be E, not D, and the second eighth note in m. 7 should be G, not A. The errors appear in several editions (e.g. 9th, 10th, 11th, 13th–15th).

Example 2.2. Gluck, *Orfeo ed Euridice*, Act 3, Scene 1, "Che farò senza Euridice," measures 6–16.

[48] In this case, we are, indeed, not entirely of the opinion that the composer is to be fully acquitted insofar as music certainly possesses far more specific tones for the expression of the most poignant sadness. Out of hundreds, we choose this particular example, though, first because it befits the composer to whom the greatest precision in dramatic expression is ascribed, and second because several generations have admired the feeling of consummate anguish in this *melody*, which the associated *words* declare.

But even far more definite and more expressive vocal passages, detached from their text, at best leave us *guessing* which feeling they express. They resemble silhouettes whose original figure we usually recognize only when someone has told us who it is.

[49] What was shown here in individual instances proves to be the case in works of larger and largest scope. Entire vocal pieces have often been underlaid with other texts. When Meyerbeer's *Hugenots* is performed in Vienna with alteration of the setting, the time, characters, the event, and the words as *The Ghibllines in Pisa*, then the clumsy handiwork of such a reworking is no doubt annoying, but the purely musical expression is not offended in the least. And yet the religions feeling, the fanaticism of faith is supposed to be the very motivation of the *Hugenots*, which is dropped entirely in *The Ghibllines*. Luther's chorale may not serve as an objection here; it is a *quotation*. As music, it fits any religious denomination. Has the reader never heard the allegro fugato from the overture to *The Magic Flute* as a vocal quartet of quarreling Jewish merchants? Mozart's music, in which not one note is altered, suits the comically vulgar text startlingly well, and we could not enjoy ourselves at the opera any more heartily at the seriousness of the composition than we have to laugh here at its humor. Such examples for [50] the broad adaptiveness of any musical theme and any human affect can be endlessly presented. The mood of religious reverence is rightly considered one least likely to be mistaken musically. Now there are countless German village and marketplace churches where for the holy consecration Proch's *Alphorn* or the concluding aria from *Sonnambula* (with the coy leap of a tenth at "in my arms") or the like is played on the organ. Every German who travels to Italy will hear with amazement the best-known opera melodies by Rossini, Bellini, Donizetti, and Verdi in churches. Those and even more secular pieces, if they have a gentle sound to some extent, are far from disturbing the congregation in their prayers. On the contrary, everybody tends to be edified to the utmost. If music in itself were able to represent religious reverence as content, then such a *quid pro quo* would be as impossible as the preacher reciting from the pulpit a novel by Tieck or an act of parliament instead of his exhortations. Our greatest masters of sacred music offer abundant examples for [51] our thesis. Especially *Händel* acted in this regard with grand nonchalance. *Winterfeld* has shown that many of the most famous pieces in the *Messiah* most admired for their pious expression

were incorporated from secular, mostly erotic duets that Händel wrote (1711–1712) for Princess-Elect Caroline of Hannover to *madrigals* by *Mauro Ortensio*. The music for the second duet,

> No, di voi non uo' fidarmi,
> Cieco amor, crudel beltà;
> Troppo siete menzognere
> Lusinghiere deità![12]

Händel used, unchanged in key and melody, for the chorus "For unto us a child is born" in Part 1 of the *Messiah*. The third movement of that same duet, "So per prova i vostri inganni," has the same themes as the chorus "All we like sheep have gone astray" in Part 2 of the *Messiah*. Madrigal number 16 (duet for soprano and alto) essentially matches completely [52] the duet "O Death, where is thy sting" in Part 3 of the *Messiah*. The text there reads

> "Si tu non lasci amore
> Mio cor, ti pentirai
> Lo so ben io!"

Of the numerous other examples in Sebastian Bach's music, we only need to recall all of the madrigal-style pieces of the *Christmas Oratorio*, which, as is well known, were innocently incorporated from quite disparate occasional *secular* cantatas. And *Gluck*, of whom we are taught that he achieved the lofty dramatic truth of his music only by adapting every note exactly to the particular situation, indeed by deriving his melodies from the vocal inflections of the verses themselves, incorporated into *Armida* no fewer than five pieces from his older Italian operas. (See my *Moderne Oper*, p. 16.) We see that *vocal music*, whose theory can never determine the nature of music, is in

---

12. "No, I will not trust you, blind love, vicious beauty; you are too deceitful, flattering deity!"

practice incapable of negating the principles derived from the concept of instrumental music.

The proposition that we are contesting has, incidentally, [53] so infiltrated the flesh and blood of the current music-aesthetic view that all of its descendants and distant relatives also enjoy its inviolability. The theory of imitation of visible or nonmusically audible objects through music also belongs to that view. With a special aura of wisdom, on the issue of "tone painting" we are repeatedly assured that music can by no means portray the very *phenomenon* that lies outside of its domain, but rather only the *feeling* that is thereby aroused in us. Exactly the opposite. Music can attempt to imitate only the external phenomenon, but never the specific feeling it induces. I can musically paint the falling of snowflakes, the fluttering of birds, the rising of the sun only by invoking analogous aural impressions related dynamically to those phenomena. In pitch, intensity, speed, rhythm of the tones, a *figure* is presented to the ear whose impression exhibits that [particular] analogy with the specific visual perception that sensory perceptions of various types can reciprocally achieve. Just as physiologically there is [54] a "substituting" of one sense for another up to a certain limit, so too aesthetically there is a certain substituting of one sense impression for another. Because well-founded analogies prevail between motion in space and in time, between color, texture, and size of an object, and the pitch, timbre, and intensity of a tone, we can in fact musically paint an object. But wanting to depict the "feeling" in tones that falling snow, the crowing rooster, the flash of lightening evoke in us is simply ridiculous.

Although to my recollection all music theorists tacitly draw inferences from and build on the principle that music can represent specific feelings, a correct intuition prevented some from outright acknowledging it. The lack of *conceptual* definiteness in music bothered them and led them to modify the principle as follows: Music is perhaps not supposed to evoke and represent definite feelings but possibly "*indefinite feelings*." On rational grounds, that can only mean that music should contain the *motion* of [55] feeling, abstracted from its content, from that which is felt, thus what we have called the *dynamics* of the affects, and have fully granted to music. However, that aspect of music is not a "representing of indefinite feelings." For "representing" "indefinite content" is a contradiction. Psychic motions as motions in themselves, without content, are not an object of artistic embodiment because it is not possible to address artistic embodiment without the question of what moves or is moved. What is correct about the proposition, namely the requirement that music should not depict a *definite* feeling, is solely a negative aspect. However, what is the positive, the creative aspect of a musical artwork? Indefinite feeling as such is not a *content*. If an art is to acquire a content, everything depends on *how* the indefinite feeling is *formed*. All artistic activity consists, however, in *individualization*, in the coining of the definite from the indefinite, the particular from the general. The theory of "indefinite feelings" demands exactly the opposite. The situation in this case is even worse than with [56] the earlier proposition, that we should believe that music represents something, and yet never know what. From here, the small step is very simple to the recognition that music cannot depict any feelings *at all*, neither definite nor indefinite. But what musician would want to surrender this imperial domain of his art, claimed through squatter's rights from time immemorial?[13]

Our conclusion would perhaps yet leave room for the opinion that the representation of definite feelings in music is admittedly an ideal that it can never fully reach, but that it [57] can and should ever more closely approach. The many high-flown phrases about the tendency of music to breach the barriers of its indefiniteness and to become actual language, the popular extolling of those compositions in which

---

13. In the works of brilliant men like *Mattheson*, we see to what absurdities the erroneous principle leads, finding in every piece of music the representation of a definite feeling, and yet more mistaken, dictating a special feeling for each genre of musical art forms. Loyal to his tenet that "we must establish a psychic motion in every melody," he teaches in his *Der vollkommene Kapellmeister* (pp. 230ff) that "The passion that should be expressed in a courante is hope." "The sarabande has no other passion to express than *great respect*." In a concerto grosso, "*voluptuousness* rules." The *chaconne* is to express "satiety," the *overture* "noble mindedness."

that aspiration is perceived, or thought to be perceived, evinces the true prevalence of that view.

But even more decisively than we contested the possibility of musical representation of feeling do we have to fend off the opinion that it could ever yield the *aesthetic principle* of music.

Beauty in music would not amount to the fidelity of the representation of feelings even if such representation were *possible*. Let us for the moment assume that possibility in order to convince ourselves.

We obviously cannot test this fiction with *instrumental music*, which on its own disallows the verification of specific affects, but rather only with *vocal music*, to which the emphasis on prefigured psychic states can be attributed.[14]

[58] Here the *words* before the composer determine the object to be depicted. Music has the power to animate it, to comment, to impart to it the expression of individual interiority in more-or-less high degree. It does that through the most characteristics possible of the motion and through capitalizing on the symbolism inherent in the tones. If music focuses on the text as its main consideration and not its own distinct beauty, then it can achieve a high degree of individualization, indeed can achieve the illusion that it alone is actually representing the feeling, which already lay unalterably in the words, though capable of enhancement. That tendency achieves something similar in its effect to the ostensible "*representation* of an affect as the content of the particular piece of music." Assuming that this actual and that ostensible power of music were to coincide, [59] that the representation of feeling were possible and were the content of music, we would logically deem those compositions the height of perfection that *most definitely achieved* the task. But who does not know works of music of supreme beauty *without* such content (we

---

14. In reviews of vocal music, for brevity and convenience the author (and other critics who agree with his tenets) have innocently used the words "express," "depict," "represent" of tones and the like, and we may surely use them if we remain strictly aware of their impropriety, that is, of their restriction to symbolic and dynamic expression.

remind [readers] of Bach's fugues and preludes)? Conversely, there are vocal compositions that attempt to exactly portray a definite feeling within the boundaries just explained, and for which the *truth* of that depiction supersedes every other principle. On closer examination, our result is that the most uncompromising wedding of such a musical portrayal [to feeling] stands in inverse relationship to its autonomous beauty, thus that the declamatory–dramatic *accuracy* and the *musical perfection* cover only half of the distance together, but then part ways.

The *recitative* best illustrates this point as that form that adheres most directly to the declamatory expression of the individual word, down to the accent, striving no more than to be a faithful replica of specific, [60] usually rapidly changing, psychic states. As a true embodiment of that theory, this must be music at the highest degree of perfection. However, in the recitative, music in fact sinks altogether to the status of a servant and loses all of its autonomous significance. This is proof that the expression of specific psychic processes does not amount to the task of music but rather ultimately is inhibitingly opposed to it. Try playing a lengthier recitative while omitting the words and then ask about its musical value and meaning. However, *any music* to which, *alone*, we should ascribe the elicited effect must withstand that test.

By no means limited to the recitative, with the highest and most developed art forms we can, moreover, likewise confirm how *musical beauty* always tends to yield *specific expression* because musical beauty demands an autonomous course of development, specific expression a servile self-negation.

Let us move on from the recitative's declamatory to opera's dramatic principle. The pieces in *Mozart's* operas [61] fully accord with their text. If we listen to even the most complicated pieces—the finales—without text, the middle sections will perhaps remain unclear, but the principle ones and the whole will in themselves be beautiful music. As is generally known, the balanced fulfillment of musical and dramatic demands is rightly considered to be the ideal of opera. However, to my knowledge it has never been exhaustively argued how the nature of opera is thus a constant *struggle* between the principle of dramatic accuracy and that of musical beauty, an unceasing compromise of the one to the other. It is not the untruthfulness of all involved characters *singing* that makes the principle of opera variable and difficult; the imagination very readily engages in such illusions. However, the constraint that forces music and text into continual transgressing or yielding causes opera, like a constitutional state, to be based on a constant struggle of two legitimate powers. That struggle, in which the artist must allow now one, now the other, principle to prevail, is the point from [62] which all inadequacies of opera emanate, and that all rules of art aimed at saying anything decisive for *opera* must take as point of departure. Pursuing their consequences, the musical and dramatic principles must necessarily intersect with one another. But their two paths are sufficiently lengthy to appear *parallel* to the human eye for a considerable distance.

Something similar holds for *dance*, as we can observe in any ballet. The more it departs from the beautiful rhythmic patterns of its forms in order to become *expressive* [*sprechend*] with gesticulation and mimicking, to express specific thoughts and feelings, the more it approaches the amorphous significance of mere pantomime. The heightening of the dramatic principle in dance ends to the same degree in a breach of its vivid rhythmic beauty. An opera is not capable of existing *wholly* as a spoken drama or a piece of pure instrumental music. Thus the focus of a genuine opera composer will at the least be a constant merging and mediating, never a fundamental relative predominance of one or the other factor. [63] When in doubt, however, he will decide for privileging the *musical* requirements, for opera is foremost music, not drama. We can easily gauge this on our own, very different intentions in attending a drama or an opera of the same story line. The disregard of the musical element will always affect us much more acutely.[15]

---

15. What Mozart says *about the position of music relative to poetry* in opera is exceptionally characteristic. Entirely contrary to Gluck, who would prefer to subordinate

[64] The greatest significance for the history of art of the famous quarrel between the camps of *Gluck* and *Piccini* lies for us in the fact that the internal conflict within *opera* came up for the first time through the antagonism of its two factors, the musical and the dramatic. This occurred, of course, without a scholarly awareness of the vast fundamental significance of the verdict. Whoever will not rue the rewarding effort of tracing this quarrel back to the sources[16] will discern how, on the varied scale between crassness and flattery, the entire facetious sword-fighting skill of French polemics prevails, but also such an immaturity in the understanding of the fundamental element, such a lack of deeper knowledge that no *outcome* for music aesthetics of those extended debates is evident. The foremost figures, *Suard* and [65] *Abbé Arnaud* on Gluck's side, *Marmontel* and *de la Harpe* against him, did repeatedly go beyond Gluck's critique to an illumination of the *dramatic* principle in opera and its relationship to the *musical*. But they treated that relationship as one characteristic of opera among many, and not as opera's innermost animating principle. They had no idea that the entire existence of opera would depend on the decision on that relationship. It is curious how very

music to poetry, Mozart holds that poetry should be the obedient daughter of music. In opera, he decisively assigns sovereignty to music where it is related to the expression of mood. He appeals to the fact that good music causes the most miserable texts to be forgotten. A case in which the converse occurred can scarcely be cited. It follows irrefutably, too, from the essence and *nature of music*. Merely because it seizes and wholly engages the senses directly and more powerfully than any other art, music causes the impression that can be evoked by the poetic representation momentarily to retreat. Further, in a way that, it seems, has not yet been clarified, through the sense of hearing music acts directly on imagination and feeling with a stirring force that momentarily surpasses that of poetry (O. Jahn, *Mozart*, vol. 3, p. 91). *Translators' note*: Curiously, from the sixth edition onward this footnote about Mozart replaces one on Wagner. Apart from the Preface, the original footnote was the only passage in the main text that reported Hanslick's judgment on Wagner as a composer. All other references to Wagner deal with him as a poet and a theoretician. The original footnote was updated in the fourth edition to refer to *Tristan and Isolde* (instead of to *Lohengrin*).

16. The most important of those polemical writings are in the collection "Mémoires pour servir à l'histoire de la Révolution opérée dans la musique par Mr. le chevalier Gluck" (Naples and Paris, 1781).

close Gluck's opponents, in particular, are several times at the point from which the error of the dramatic principle may be perfectly beheld and vanquished. *De la Harpe* wrote the following in the *Journal de Politique et de Littérature*, October 5, 1777:

> One may object that it is not natural to sing a song of this kind in an emotionally excited situation, that to burst into song is to stop the action and to nullify the dramatic effect. I find these objections absolutely illusory. To begin with, if we are going to have singing at all, we must have the most beautiful possible singing, and it is not more natural to sing badly than to sing well. [66] All the arts are founded on conventions, on the given. When I go to the opera, it is to listen to the music. I do not overlook the fact that Alceste did not make her farewell to Admetus while singing an aria, but, since Alceste is in the theatre to sing, if I recognize her sadness and her love in a melodious aria, then I enjoy her song while being interested in her misfortune.[17]

Are we to believe that de la Harpe himself failed to recognize how splendidly he stood on firm ground? For soon after, it almost occurs to him to dispute the duet between Agamemnon and Achilles in *Iphegenia* "because it is definitely not congruous with the dignity of these two heroes to speak simultaneously." He thereby forsook and betrayed that solid ground, the principle of *musical* beauty, tacitly, unwittingly acknowledging the principle of the opponent.

The more systematically we want to keep the *dramatic* principle pure in opera, withdrawing from it the life-breath of musical beauty, the more feebly it fades away, like a bird beneath [67] a vacuum jar.[18] We must necessarily come back to the purely *spoken* drama, whereby we at least have proof that opera is actually *impossible* if we do not

17. *Translators' note*: The translation from French is from Payzant, *On the Musically Beautiful*, p. 24.

18. *Translators' note*: The mention of "a bird beneath a vacuum jar" refers to one of Robert Boyle's air-pump experiments in which a bird is deprived of air, to demonstrate the creation of a vacuum.

accord sovereignty in opera to the *musical* principle (in full awareness of its reality-averse nature). In actual artistic practice, that truth has also never been denied. To be sure, even the most rigorous dramatist, Gluck, postulates the erroneous theory that operatic music is to be nothing more than heightened declamation, but in practice the *musical* nature of the man breaks through often enough, and always to great benefit of his work. The same holds for *Richard Wagner*. For our context, it need only be stressed decisively that *Wagner*'s main tenet, as he articulates it in the first volume of *Opera and Drama*— "The error of opera as a genre of art consists in the means (the music) being made the end, the end (the drama), however, the means"—is a false premise. For an opera in which music is always and actually used *only as a means* for dramatic [68] expression is a musical absurdity.[19]

19. I cannot restrain myself from citing a few apposite statements from Grillparzer and Moritz Hauptmann. "It is nonsense," Grillparzer calls it, "to make music in opera the mere slave of poetry." He continues *"if music in opera were only there to express again what the poet has already expressed, then for me, leave out the tones. . . .* Whoever knows your power, Melody—which you, directly from Heaven, again return through the breast to Heaven without needing the verbal explanation of a concept— whoever knows your power will not make music into the mere follower of poetry. He may give priority to the latter (and I believe poetry deserves it, as does manhood over childhood), but he will also grant music its own autonomous realm, will consider both like siblings, and not like lord and servant, or only like guardian and ward." He wants the tenet upheld that "No opera should be considered from the viewpoint of poetry— every *dramatic* musical composition is nonsense from that perspective—but rather from the viewpoint of music."

Another passage in Grillparzer reads, "For no opera composer will it be easier to precisely set the words of the text to music than for one who assembles his music mechanically. By contrast, the composer whose music has organic life, an internally founded necessity, readily comes into conflict with the words. To wit, every true melodic theme has its internal law of formation and development, which is sacred and inviolable, and which he cannot surrender to please the words. The musical prosaist can begin anywhere and end anywhere because pieces and sections can easily be transferred and can be ordered differently. However, whoever has a sense for a whole can either wholly give, or wholly let it be. That is not intended to endorse the neglect of the text but rather only to excuse, indeed justify it in individual cases. Hence Rossini's childlike trifling is more valuable than Mosel's prosaic learned aping, which shreds the essence of music in order to imitatively stammer after the empty words of the poet. Hence we can rebuke *Mozart* for frequent violations against the text, but never *Gluck*. Hence is the so highly praised

[69] One consequence of *Wagner*'s tenet (about means and end) would be, among others, also that all composers have done a great injustice if [70] they sought to write more than mediocre music to mediocre text and plots, and that we would likewise commit a grave injustice in liking such music.

The connection of poetry with music and opera is a left-handed marriage. The closer we ponder that morganatic marriage, which musical beauty enters into with the content specifically prescribed for it, the more deceptive does their insolubility seem to us.[20]

How is it that we can undertake one or another small modification in any vocal piece [71] that, without weakening in the least the accuracy of the expression of feeling, nevertheless immediately destroys the beauty of the theme? That would be impossible if the beauty of the theme lay in the accuracy of the expression. How is it that some vocal pieces that flawlessly express their text seem to us intolerably

---

characteristic quality of music often a very negative merit, which is mostly limited to expressing happiness by nonsadness, anguish by nonjoyousness, gentleness by nonabrasiveness, anger by nonmildness, love by flutes, and despair by trumpets and kettledrums with double basses. The composer must remain faithful to the *situation*, not to the *words*. If he finds better ones in his music, he may bypass the words of the text." Does not much in these aphorisms, written decades ago, sound like polemics against Wagner's theories and the Valkyrie style? With this statement, Grillparzer takes a piercing look into the nature of the public: "Those who demand from *opera* a *purely dramatic* effect are usually those who, conversely, also seek a *musical* effect from a *dramatic* poem, that is, an effect with blunt force" (vol. 9, pp. 144ff).

Similarly, M. Hauptmann writes to O. Jahn: "To me (on hearing Gluck's operas) it was often as though the intent of the composer was to be true, *but not musically true, only verbally true*, and thereby it not infrequently becomes musically untrue. Words finish off curtly, music fades. Music always remains the vowel to which the word is just the consonant, and here as always only the vowel can ever have the accent, the thing that sounds, not that which accompanies the sound. *We indeed always hear the music for itself, no matter how faithful it is to the words. It must therefore also be heard for itself* (Letters to Spohr, ed. F. Hiller. Leipzig, 1867, p. 106).

20. *Translators' note*: A "left-handed marriage" or "morganatic marriage" is one between a wife and a husband of unequal social rank.

bad? From the standpoint of the feeling principle, there is no getting around this. What remains, then, as the principle of beauty in music after we have rejected feelings as insufficient for the task?

A completely other autonomous element that we will now consider more closely.

Chapter 3

The Musically Beautiful

[72] So far, we have proceeded negatively and sought solely to fend off the mistaken premise that the beautiful in music could consist in the representation of feelings.

We must now add the positive content to that sketch by answering the question of what nature might the beauty of a musical composition be.

It is a specifically musical beauty.[1] By that we understand beauty that is independent and not in need of an external content, something that resides solely in the tones and their artistic connection. The meaningful relationships among intrinsically appealing sounds, their mutual concord and discord, their fleeing [73] and coalescing, their soaring and subsiding—that is what arises in free forms before our intellectual contemplation and pleases as beautiful.

The primal element of music is *harmonious sound*, its essence *rhythm*, large-scale rhythm, as the consistency of a symmetrical structure, and small-scale rhythm, as the changing, patterned motion of individual units in tempo. The material from which the composer creates, and whose wealth cannot be conceived extravagantly enough, is the entire collection of *tones*, with their inherent capacity for different melodies, harmonies, and rhythmic deployment. Unexhausted and inexhaustible, *melody* rules primarily as the fundamental form of musical beauty. *Harmony*, with thousand-fold transformations, reversals, reinforcements, provides ever-new

---

1. *Translators' note*: For Hanslick's notion of the "specifically musically beautiful" and its role in his aesthetics, see our essay on his central concepts, pp. xxxiii–xxxiv.

foundations. *Rhythm*, the artery of musical life, animates the union of both, and the charm of manifold *timbres* colors them.

If the question now is what is to be expressed with this tone material, the answer is *musical ideas*.[2] However, a musical idea brought to full manifestation [74] is already autonomous beauty, is an end unto itself and in no way primarily a means of or material for representing feelings and thoughts.

The content of music is *sonically moved forms*.[3]

A branch of ornamentation in the visual arts, *the arabesque*, shows us roughly how music can present for us *beautiful forms* without the content of a specific affect. We observe contoured lines, here gently sloping, there boldly climbing, converging and diverging, corresponding in small and large arcs, seemingly incommensurate, yet always well structured, everywhere part complementing counterpart, a collection of small details and yet a whole. Now let us imagine an arabesque, not inanimate and static but arising before our eyes in perpetual self-formation. How the heavy and delicate lines pursue one another, ascend from small curves to magnificent heights, and then sink back again, expand, contract, and surprise the eye ever anew with a rational alternation of repose and tension! [75] Now, the image is already becoming more grand and dignified. Let us imagine this animated arabesque altogether as an active emanation of an artistic mind that unceasingly pours the entire wealth of its imagination into the arteries of this movement. Does this impression not approximate somewhat a *musical* one?

As a child, each of us probably delighted in the changing play of colors and shapes of a *kaleidoscope*. Music is such a kaleidoscope, but

---

2. *Translators' note*: Regarding Hanslick's notion of "musical ideas," see our essay on his central concepts, p. xlvi.

3. *Translators' note*: This is arguably the single most important phrase in the treatise. In the first and second editions, Hanslick used an even more pointed formulation when he stated that sonically moved forms are "solely and exclusively the content and subject of music" ("*tönend bewegte Formen* sind einzig und allein Inhalt und Gegenstand der Musik"). For an explanation of the passage, and the motivation for our translation, see our essay on Hanslick's central concepts, pp. xli–xliii.

on a vastly higher, abstract level. In ever-more-developing diversity, music presents beautiful forms and colors, gently evolving, sharply contrasting, always coherent and yet always fresh, self-contained and self-fulfilled. The chief difference is that such a *tone* kaleidoscope presented to our ear is the direct emanation of an artistically creative mind, whereas the visible one is an ingenious mechanical toy. If not merely in thought but in actuality we want to elevate color to [the level of] music and to embed the means of one art into the effects of another, we then end up [76] with the tasteless gimmickry of the "color keyboard" or the "eye-organ," whose invention proves, though, how the formal dimension of both phenomena [music and color] have the same basis.

If some sensitive music lover finds our art demeaned by analogies like the preceding ones, we counter that it is merely a matter of whether or not the analogies are *correct*. Nothing is demeaned by getting to know it better. If we want to forgo the trait of motion, of temporal development through which the example of the kaleidoscope is especially apposite, we can of course identify a loftier analogy for the musically beautiful, as in architecture, the human body, or in a landscape, which also possess a primitive beauty in outline and color (apart from the mind, the intellectual expression).[4]

If people did not understand how to discern the abundance of beauty that subsists in the purely musical, the *underevaluation of the sensuous* bears much of the guilt that we encounter in older aesthetics in favor of morality and mental disposition, [77] in Hegel in favor of the "Idea." Every art begins from the sensuous and is enmeshed in it. The "feeling theory" fails to recognize that. It overlooks *hearing*

---

4. *Translators' note*: This passage was added in the second edition. It is an unacknowledged citation of a passage in a letter by David Friedrich Strauß to Hanslick from 1855. Strauß was a well-known contemporary author whom Hanslick regarded highly. The letter is reprinted in Hanslick's *Musikalisches und Litterarisches* (Berlin, 1889, p. 286). Hanslick often reused material in later revisions of the treatise, mostly his own, but in some cases also material taken from other authors. Not all of these borrowings are acknowledged.

entirely and proceeds directly to *feeling*. Music creates for the heart, they say. The ear is something trivial.

Indeed, what they call the ear, exactly—the "ethmoidal labyrinth" or the "eardrum"—no Beethoven composes for that. But *imagination*, which is organized around aural sensations and for which *sense* means something completely different than a mere funnel to the surface of phenomena, *imagination* enjoys in conscious sensuousness the sounding configurations, the tones arranging themselves, and exists freely and directly in their contemplation.

It is extraordinarily difficult to delineate this autonomous beauty in music, this specifically musical aspect. Because music has no model in nature and communicates no conceptual content, it allows us to speak of it only with dry technical specifications or with poetic fictions. Its realm is truly "not of this world." All of the richly imaginative depictions, characteristics, [78] circumlocutions of a musical work are figurative or fallacious. What in every other art is still description, in music is already metaphor. Music demands simply to be understood as music and can be understood only from within itself, be enjoyed in itself.

The "specifically musical" is in no way to be understood as merely acoustical beauty or proportional symmetry—branches that it includes as subordinate—yet less can there be talk of an "ear-titillating play of tones" or similar designations, for which the lack of an intellectual animation tends to be highlighted. In insisting on musical beauty, we have not excluded intellectual content but rather in fact have required it. For we recognize no beauty without any share of intellectuality. However, our transfer of musical beauty essentially to *forms* indicates that the intellectual content is in the most intimate relationship with those tone forms. In music the concept of "form" experiences a completely unique actualization. The forms [79] constructed from *tones* are not empty but rather filled, not mere borders in a vacuum but rather intellect shaping itself from within. Compared with the arabesque, music is, accordingly, in fact an *image*, but one whose subject we cannot formulate in words and subordinate to our concepts. In music there is sense and logic, but *musical* sense and logic. It is a language that we speak and understand, but are unable to *translate*. There is a profound insight in the fact that we also speak of "thoughts" in musical works, and just as in verbal discourse seasoned judgment readily distinguishes [in music] between genuine thoughts and mere figures of speech. Similarly, we recognize the rationally closed group of tones by calling it a "phrase" [*Satz*]. After all, we feel exactly the same as with every logical periodic sentence [*Periode*], where its sense is at an end, although the truth of both is wholly incommensurable.[5]

The gratifying reasonableness that can exist in itself in musical formations is based on certain primitive fundamental laws that nature has implanted into the organization of human beings, and into external audible phenomena. [80] It is primarily the primordial law of the [numerical] "harmonic series"[6] [*harmonische Progression*] that, in analogy to the circular shape in the visual arts, embodies the seed of the most significant further developments [in music], and the (alas nearly unexplained) explanation of the various musical relationships.

---

5. *Translators' note*: In the preceding sentence, Hanslick uses the word *Satz*, which in musical contexts such as this means "phrase." As Geoffrey Payzant rightly observes, *Satz* is used "in its musical and logical sense" (*On the Musically Beautiful*, p. 107). However, like *Satz*, *Periode* in the subsequent sentence has an additional grammatical meaning common in mid-nineteenth-century terminology that we also consider central here. Our "logical periodic sentence" (*logische Periode*) is in Payzant's translation "logical proposition." However, Hanslick is clearly thinking of a sentence and its hierarchic grammatical clause structure. A periodic sentence is built of mutually dependent parts organized according to rules of grammar. In addition to grammatical correctness, the parts of a sentence also relate to each other syntactically in a logical manner. The core idea in this passage is that a musical phrase, like a periodic sentence in language, consists of components that relate to each other in such a logical, meaningful way.

6. *Translators' note*: A series of numbers is "harmonic" when any number within the series is the harmonic mean between the two neighboring ones—where the harmonic mean between any two numbers, *a* and *b*, is calculated with the formula 2 (*ab*) / *a* + *b*. In mathematical shorthand, the series is symbolized by $\sum_{n=1}^{\infty}(1/n)$, which produces the series 1, 1/2, 1/3, 1/4, 1/5, etc. Three strings whose proportional lengths conform to the harmonic series produce the major triad (e.g. C–E–G), the foundation of music from the mid-sixteenth to the late nineteenth century.

All musical elements have among themselves secret alliances and elective affinities grounded in natural laws. Those elective affinities, invisibly governing rhythm, melody, and harmony, demand compliance in human music, and they stamp every contradictory connection as arbitrary and unattractive. Although not in the form of scientific awareness, they reside instinctively in every cultivated ear, which by pure contemplation perceives, accordingly, the organic quality, the rationality, or the nonsensical, unnatural quality of a tone group, without a logical concept providing the criterion or *tertium comparationis*.[7]

[81] The tone system's further capability to take on *positive* content of beauty is rooted in this negative, interior rationality, which is inherent in the system through natural laws.

Composing is an operation of the intellect in material of intellectual capacity. As rich as we have deemed this musical material to be, it proves to be as elastic and permeable for artistic imagination. Unlike the architect, artistic imagination does not build out of raw, ponderous stone but rather upon the aftereffect of previously dissipated tones. More intellectual and more subtle in nature than the material of any other art, the tones readily assimilate each and every idea of the composer [*Künstler*]. Because tone combinations, in whose relationships musical beauty resides, are not achieved through a mechanical stringing together [82] but rather through the free creativity of the imagination, the intellectual power and individuality of that particular imagination imprint themselves on the product as *character*. Accordingly, as the creation of a thinking and feeling intellect, a musical work has to a high degree the ability to be itself intellectually

7. "Poetry may freely make use of the ugly (the unbeautiful) to some extent. For because the effect of poetry reaches feeling only through the medium of concepts evoked directly by the poetry, the mental image of purposefulness will temper the impression of ugliness (the unbeautiful) to the extent that, as stimulus and contrast, it even elicits the maximal effect. However, the impression of music is perceived and enjoyed directly through sense. The acceptance by understanding comes too late to balance out the disturbance of the displeasurable quality. Shakespeare may thus go as far as the atrocious; Mozart's limit was the beautiful" (Grillparzer, *Sämtliche Werke*, 10 vols. [Stuttgart, 1872], vol. 9, pp. 141–142).

stimulating and soulful [*gefühlvoll*]. We will require such intellectuality in every musical artwork, but it may not be attributed to any
aspect of it other than to the *tone formations themselves*. Our view
on the seat of the intellect and feeling of a composition relates to
the common opinion [on them] as the concept of *immanence* relates
to *transcendence*. Every art has as goal to externalize an idea that
has come alive in the artist's imagination. In music, this ideational
aspect consists of *tones*, not concepts, which would first have to be
translated into tones. The motivation that is the point of departure
for all of the composer's creative activity is not the intent to musically portray a particular passion but rather the invention of a particular melody. Through that primitive, [83] mysterious power, whose
workshop humankind's eye will now and never penetrate, a theme, a
motive resounds in the mind of the composer.[8] We cannot travel back
behind the origin of this *first* seed; we must accept it as a basic given.
Once it has entered into the artist's imagination, his creative activity
begins that, starting from that main theme and continually referring
to it, pursues the goal of presenting it in all of its relationships. The
beauty of a self-sufficient simple theme announces itself in aesthetic
feeling with a kind of immediacy that allows no explanation other
than the inner functionality [*innere Zweckmäßigkeit*] of the phenomenon, the harmony of its parts, without reference to an external,
third factor. It pleases us in itself, like the arabesque, the column, or
like products of nature's beauty, such as a leaf and a flower.

Nothing could be more fallacious and more prevalent than the
view that differentiates between "beautiful music" with and without
intellectual content. It construes the concept of beauty in music
much too narrowly and conceives the artfully compounded form
[84] as something existing unto itself, conceives the mind poured in
likewise as something self-sufficient, and then systematically divides

---

8. *Translators' note*: Hanslick's terminology is not always as clear-cut as we might
assume. "Musical idea" and "musical thought," for example, appear to be two different
concepts, but Hanslick did not differentiate between the terms. Similarly, also "theme"
and "motive" are used interchangeably throughout the treatise.

compositions into full and empty champagne bottles. However, musical champagne has the characteristic of growing *with* the bottle.

One particular musical idea is clearly intellectually stimulating in itself, another ordinary. One particular concluding cadence sounds dignified, through the alteration of two notes it becomes dull. We quite rightly describe a musical theme as magnificent, graceful, tender, vapid, banal. However, all of those expressions describe the musical *character* of the passage. To characterize that musical expression of a theme we often choose terms from our *psychic life*, like "proud, disgruntled, tender, valiant, yearning." But we can also take the descriptions from other domains of life and call music "fragrant, spring-fresh, hazy, chilly." For the description of musical character, feelings are thus just *phenomena* like others that offer similarities for descriptions. We may use epithets of that sort with awareness of their figurative imagery, [85] indeed we cannot do without them. But we must beware of saying, this music *portrays* pride, and so forth.

However, the close consideration of all musical specifications of a theme convinces us that, with all the inscrutability of the ultimate ontological bases, the intellectual expression of certain music still possesses a precise relationship with a number of accessible causes. Each individual musical element (i.e. each interval, timbre, chord, rhythm, etc.) has its own characteristic physiognomy, its specific manner of operating. The artist is inscrutable, the artwork scrutable.

One and the same theme sounds different placed over a triad than over a sixth chord. A melodic step to the [scalar] seventh has a completely different character than a step to the sixth. The rhythmic accompaniment of a theme, whether loud or soft, of this or that type of [instrumental] sonority, alters its specific color. In short, each individual factor of a musical passage necessarily contributes to its adopting precisely *that* intellectual expression, [86] and affects the listener in that way and no other. What makes *Halévy*'s music bizarre, *Auber*'s graceful, what brings about the distinctiveness by which we immediately recognize *Mendelssohn, Spohr*, can all be traced to purely *musical* determinants, without calling on enigmatic *feeling*.

Why *Mendelssohn*'s frequent six–five chords and scalar themes, *Spohr*'s chromatic and enharmonic practice, *Auber*'s short-breathed binary periodicity, and so on, produce that particular unmistakable impression—of course, neither psychology nor physiology can answer those questions.

However, if we inquire about the *proximate* determining cause—and in art that is what matters primarily—the impassioned effect of a theme does not lie in the composer's ostensible augmented anguish but in the theme's augmented intervals, not in the trembling of his soul but in the tremolo of the kettledrums, not in his yearning but rather in the chromaticism. The *connection* of the two should by no means be ignored, in fact should be presently [87] more closely examined. However, it is to be firmly maintained that only those musical factors lie immutably and objectively open to scientific investigation regarding the effect of a theme, never the presumed mood that filled the composer. If we want to argue from the composer's mood directly to the effect of the work, or to explain the latter from the former, the conclusion can *perhaps* turn out to be correct, but the crucial middle term of the syllogism, namely the *music* itself, was skipped.

The competent composer has a *practical* knowledge of the character of every musical element, whether in a more instinctive or conscious manner. But a *theoretical* knowledge of the aforementioned characters, from their richest combination to the last distinguishable element, is necessary for a scientific explanation of the various musical effects and impressions. The particular impression with which a melody gains power over us is not simply an "enigmatic, cryptic wonder" that we may only "feel and intuit," but rather an inevitable consequence of the musical factors that [88] operate in this particular connection. A more clipped or expansive rhythm, diatonic or chromatic progression—everything has its characteristic physiognomy and special manner of addressing us. A trained musician will therefore get an incomparably clearer mental picture of the expression of a work unknown to him—from that, for example, too many diminished seventh chords and tremolos predominate—than from the poetic description of the emotional crisis that the reviewer experiences.

Research on the nature of every individual musical element, of its association with a specific impression—only of the [empirical] fact, not of the ultimate cause—and finally the derivation of these specific observations from general laws: That would be the "philosophical grounding of music" that so many authors desire, without telling us, in passing, what they actually understand by that. The psychic and somatic effect of every chord, every rhythm, every interval, will never be explained by saying that this one is red, that one green, or this one hope, that one disgruntlement, but rather only [89] by subsuming the specific musical characteristics under general aesthetic categories, and those under a supreme principle. If in that manner the individual factors were explained in isolation, then it would have to be shown, further, how they reciprocally determine and modify one another in the most varied combinations. Most learned musicians have granted *harmony* and *contrapuntal* accompaniment the foremost position in the intellectual *content* of a composition. But in that affirmation they have approached the task much too superficially and atomistically. They designated *melody* as the inspiration of genius, as the bearer of sensuousness and feeling. The Italians received gracious praise in this regard. In *contrast* to melody, *harmony* was specified as the bearer of well-wrought content, as learnable and the result of deliberation. It is curious how long people could be satisfied with such a feeble viewpoint. There is some element of truth in both assertions, but they are not valid in that degree of generality, nor do they occur in such isolation. The intellect is a unity and likewise the musical invention [90] of a composer. Melody and harmony emerge from the head of the composer in a *single* casting. Neither the law of subordination nor of opposition applies to the *nature* of the relationship of harmony to melody. In one instance, both can exert their developmental power simultaneously, in another instance can freely be subordinate to one another. In the one case as in the other, the highest intellect-laden beauty can be achieved. Is it possibly the (entirely lacking) *harmony* in the main themes of Beethoven's *Coriolanus* and Mendelssohn's *Hebrides Overture* that imbues them with the expression of thought-laden profundity? Would we fill *Rossini*'s theme "O Mathilda" or a Neapolitan folksong with more intellect if we provided a basso continuo or a complicated chord progression at places with meager harmony? *This* particular melody must have been conceived simultaneously with this particular harmony, with *this* rhythm and *this* type of [instrumental] sonority. The intellectual content comes about only through the union of *all* of them, and the mutilation of one member damages the expression of the others. The *predominance* of the melody or harmony or [91] rhythm benefits the whole, and finding all intellect in the chords in one instance, in another all triviality in the lack of chords, is sheer pedantry. The camellia appears without fragrance, the lily without color, the rose flaunts for both senses. Nothing can be transferred, and yet each of them is beautiful!

Thus the "philosophical grounding of music" would first have to do research on which necessary intellectual determinants are linked with each musical element and how they are associated with one another. The dual requirement of a rigorous scientific framework and a highly detailed case history make the task into a very difficult but hardly an insurmountable one: unless we wanted to aspire to the idea of an "exact" musical science on the model of chemistry or physiology!

The manner in which the act of creation occurs in the mind of the composer of instrumental music gives us the surest insight into the uniqueness of the principle of musical beauty. A *musical* idea arises primitively in the imagination of the composer. He unfolds it. It generates [92] ever-more crystals until, imperceptibly, the shape of the whole structure stands before him in its main forms, and only the artistic realization must be carried out, checking, gauging, revising. The instrumental composer is not thinking about the representation of a specific content. If he does that, he assumes a mistaken standpoint, more peripheral to music than within it. His composition will be the translation of a *program* into tones, which then remains incomprehensible without that program. We neither deny nor underestimate *Berlioz*'s brilliant talent if we mention his name at this point. *Liszt* followed him with his far weaker "symphonic poems."

Just as out of the same marble one sculptor carves captivating forms, another angular bunglings, so the musical scale is shaped in different hands into a Beethoven overture or into one by Verdi. What distinguishes the two overtures? Possibly that the one represents more elevated feelings, or the same feelings more accurately? No, rather it is that the one constitutes more beautiful tone forms. Only that makes a piece of music good or bad, [93] that one composer deploys an animated theme, the other a mundane one; that the first develops it ever freshly and significantly in all relationships, the second makes his, if anything, ever worse; the harmony of the one unfolds varyingly and inventively, while the other never makes any headway because of creative poverty; here the rhythm is a warm, skipping pulse, there a military drum call.[9]

There is no art that exhausts so many forms and as quickly as does music. Modulations, cadential progressions, intervallic and harmonic progressions wear out in fifty, even thirty years such that the intellectually stimulating composer can no longer employ them and will be constantly pressured to invent new, purely musical features. Without inaccuracy, we can say of a host of compositions that rank high above the norm of their time that they *were* once beautiful. The imagination of the intellectually stimulating composer will discover among the secret primordial relationships of musical elements and their innumerable possible combinations the most refined, most recondite ones. It will [94] fashion tone forms that appear to be invented out of freest caprice, yet at the same time linked to necessity through an invisible, fine thread. Without hesitation, we call such works or their details "intellectually stimulating." With that in mind, *Oulibicheff*'s mistakable view that instrumental music cannot be intellectually stimulating is easily corrected because "for a composer the intellect consists exclusively and solely in a particular *application* of his music to a direct or indirect program." In our view, it would be fully correct to call the famous D-sharp [at m. 3] in

---

9. *Translators' note*: Hanslick's term here is *Zapfenstreich*, a military signal correctly translated as "tattoo" by both Payzant and Cohen. Tattoo, however, is not commonly understood (except as colorful images on the skin), and also lacks the specificity of Hanslick's example. The context of the term is rhythm and the signal would thus be performed by a percussion instrument.

the allegro of the *Don Giovanni* overture, or the descending unison passage therein [mm. 45–48 and analogous places] an intellectually stimulating feature. But the D-sharp has never represented, or ever will (as Oulibicheff holds), "Don Giovanni's hostile attitude toward humanity," nor the unison passages the fathers, spouses, brothers, and lovers of the women seduced by him. If all such interpretations are reprehensible in themselves, they are doubly so with Mozart who, as the most musical personality that history possesses, transformed everything he touched into music. *Oulibicheff* also sees in the [95] G-minor symphony the story of a passionate love accurately expressed in four different phrases. The G-minor symphony is music and nothing further. That is in any case sufficient. We should not seek out the representation of specific psychic processes or events in pieces of music, but rather seek *music* above all, and we will enjoy purely what it fully provides. Where the musically beautiful is lacking, it will never be replaced by imposing a contrived, grand meaning, and the latter is pointless where the former exists. In any case, it leads musical understanding in a completely false direction. The same people who want to claim a prominent place for music among the epiphanies of the human intellect—a place that music does not have and will never attain because it is not capable of conveying *beliefs*—those same people have brought into fashion the expression "intention." In music, there is no "intention" that could substitute for lacking "invention." Whatever is not manifest in music is not there at all, but what has manifested itself has ceased to be mere intention. The expression "He has intentions" [96] is mostly used with the aim of praising. To me it seems more a rebuke that, translated into dry German, would be: the composer would surely like to, but cannot. However, *art* derives [etymologically] from *ability*.[10] Whoever lacks ability has "intentions."

---

10. *Translators' note*: Literally speaking, Hanslick's point here is that the notion of art [*Kunst*] is derived from the notion of ability [*Können*]. Etymologically, they both have the same root: *kunnan* in Old High German. However, the etymology does not hold in English, and we therefore adopted a solution that captures Hanslick's argument without sounding odd to English ears.

Just as the beauty of a piece of music is rooted solely in its musical determinants, so too the laws of its construction follow only those determinants. A host of vacillating, erroneous views flourishes, from which only one will be cited here.

That is the commonly accepted theory of the *sonata* and *symphony* that arose from the feeling perspective. In the individual movements of a sonata, the composer, so goes the theory, is to portray four different *psychic states*, which are, however, interrelated with one another (how?). To justify the undeniable coherence of the movements and to explain their differing effect, the listener is virtually forced to attribute specific feelings to the movements as the content. The interpretation sometimes fits, more often not, never with necessity. But this [97] will always fit with necessity: that four movements are united into a whole that, according to *music*-aesthetic laws, are to contrast with and enhance one another.

We owe thanks to the imaginative painter *M. v. Schwind* for the very appealing illustration of *Beethoven's* Piano Fantasy, op. 80, whose individual movements the artist interpreted and portrayed as the interrelated events of the same main characters. Just as the painter discerns scenes and figures in the tones, so the listener imputes feelings and events. Both interpretations have a certain coherence but neither a *necessary* coherence, and scientific laws deal only with necessary coherence.

People tend to point out often that Beethoven is supposed to have had specific events or psychic states in mind when sketching some of his compositions. Where Beethoven or any other composer followed this process, he used it merely as an aid to facilitate the preservation of musical unity through association with an actual event. If Berlioz, Liszt, *among others*, believed they gained *more* than that from the [98] poetry, from the title or the experience, it is self-deception. The unity of *musical atmosphere* is what earmarks the four movements of a sonata as organically unified, not, however, the connection with the *object* thought of by the composer. Where the composer denied himself such poetic apron strings and created purely musically, we will find there no unity of the parts other than a musical one. Aesthetically it is a matter of indifference whether Beethoven possibly chose specific precompositional ideas in all of his compositions. We do not know them; for the work they are thus nonexistent. Without all commentary, the work itself is what is in evidence, and just as the lawyer feigns out of existence everything that is not in the files, so for aesthetic judgment nothing exists that resides outside of the artwork. If the movements of a composition seem unified to us, then the cohesiveness must have its foundation in *musical* determinants.[11]

[99] We want, finally, to counter a possible misunderstanding by laying down our concept of the "musically beautiful" from three perspectives. [100] The "musically beautiful" in our assumed specific sense is not limited to the "classical" style, nor does it include a preference for that style over the "romantic." It pertains to the one as well as to the other orientation, rules over Bach as well as Beethoven, Mozart as well as Schumann. Our thesis thus does not contain even an indication of partisanship. The [101] entire course of the present investigation does not declare any *Should Be* but rather considers only what *Is*. No particular musical ideal may be deduced

---

11. These lines completely horrified Beethoven soothsayers such as Mr. Lobe, among others. We can answer them no better than with the following explanation, with which we fully concur, in Otto Jahn's essay on Breitkopf and Härtel's new Beethoven edition ("Collected Essays on Music"). Jahn takes up Schindler's well-known report that Beethoven, asked about the meaning of his D-minor and F-minor [piano] sonatas, answered, "Just read Shakespeare's *Tempest*." Presumably, Jahn says, the questioner will pick up from his reading [of the play] the certain belief that Shakespeare's *Tempest* will affect him differently than Beethoven, and does not give rise in him to any D-minor and F-minor sonatas. It is of course not without interest to find out that precisely this drama could stimulate Beethoven to such creations. Attempting to derive an understanding of them from Shakespeare would mean attesting to an incapability of musical comprehension. In the adagio of the F-major quartet (op. 18, no. 1), Beethoven is supposed to have had in mind the tomb scene from *Romeo and Juliet*. Whoever attentively rereads that scene and then, on listening to the adagio, attempts to envision it, will he enhance or disrupt the genuine enjoyment of this piece? Titles and notes, even originating with Beethoven himself, would not assist substantially in penetrating to the meaning and significance of the artwork. Rather, the fear is that they would just as likely cause misunderstandings and perversities as those that Beethoven published. The beautiful sonata in E-flat major (op. 81) bears the title "Les adieux, l'absence, le retour" and is interpreted, accordingly, with certainty, as a reliable example of program music. "We assume," says Marx, leaving open whether or not the lovers are married,

from that standpoint as authentic beauty; rather, it may merely be demonstrated what beauty is in every style in the same way, even in the most opposed ones.

It is not long ago that people began to consider artworks in connection with the ideas and events of the time that produced them. That undeniable connection likely also exists for music. As a manifestation of human intellect, music must also be in a reciprocal relation to intellect's other activities: to the contemporaneous creations of literary and visual art, to the poetic, social, scientific conditions of its time, finally to the individual experiences and beliefs of the composer. Accordingly, the examination and substantiation of this relation based on individual composers and musical works are surely justified and praiseworthy. Yet we must always bear in mind that drawing such parallels between special artistic features and [102] specific historical conditions is an *arthistorical* process, by no means a purely *aesthetic* one. As necessary as the linking of art history with aesthetics seems from the methodological standpoint, each of those two sciences must certainly maintain its own nature in pure form against an inadvertent confounding with the other. Whereas the historian, interpreting an artistic phenomenon by and large, may envisage in *Spontini* the "expression of the French Empire," in *Rossini* the "political restoration," the aesthetician must stick solely to the works of those men in order to investigate what is beautiful about them, and why. Aesthetic inquiry knows nothing, and may know nothing,

"that they are scenes in the life of a loving couple, but the composition also provides the *proof*." Lenz says of the conclusion of the sonata, "The lovers extend their arms as do migratory birds their wings." However, Beethoven wrote on the original of the first section "Farewell on the occasion of the departure of His Imperial Highness Archduke Rudolf, May 4, 1809," and on the second "Arrival of His Imperial Highness Archduke Rudolf, January 30, 1810." How he would have protested that, with regard to the archduke; he is supposed to have portrayed this "in fawning caressings beatified desire" wing-flapping lover! "We can therefore be satisfied," concludes Jahn, "that Beethoven (as a rule) did not utter such words that would only have misled too many to the error that whoever understands the title will also understand the artwork. His *music says everything that he wanted to say*."

of the personal relationships and of the historical environment of the composer. It hears and believes only what the artwork itself articulates. Accordingly, even without knowing the name and biography of the composer, aesthetic inquiry detects in *Beethoven*'s symphonies tumultuousness, struggling, unfulfilled longing, energetic defiance, but that the composer was of a republican mind, unmarried, was deaf, and all of the [103] other traits that the art historian illuminatingly offers up, such inquiry will never extract them from the works and may not invoke them in evaluating the works. Comparing the differences in worldview of *Bach, Mozart, Haydn*, and deriving the contrast of their compositions from those differences may qualify as a highly attractive, meritorious undertaking. But it is infinitely complicated and will be the more prone to false conclusions the more rigorously it attempts to demonstrate the causal nexus. The danger of exaggeration is extraordinarily great in accepting that principle. One can easily present the most tenuous influence of contemporaneousness as an internal necessity, and interpret the eternally untranslatable language of tones in whatever way needed. It depends purely on the nimble minded account of the same paradox: spoken by an intellectually keen person, it seems like wisdom, by a simple person, like nonsense.

In discussing music, *Hegel* also often misled by confounding his predominantly *art-historical* standpoint imperceptibly with the purely aesthetic one, and points out certainties in music [104] that, in themselves, music never possessed. The character of every piece of music has "a connection" with that of its composer—certainly—but that connection is not accessible to the aesthetician. The idea of a necessary connection among *all* phenomena can be exaggerated in its actual demonstration to the point of caricature. Nowadays it requires real heroism to confront this appealing,[12] brilliantly presented trend, and to declare that "historical understanding" and "aesthetic

---

12. *Translators' note*: Hanslick's term here is "piquant." Whereas today's usage of the word in German indicates something provocative, even salacious, Hanslick uses the word in its nineteenth-century meaning of "appealing, pleasing."

judgment" are different things.[13] Objectively certain is, *first*, that the diversity of expression of the various works and schools [of composition] is based on a thoroughly different disposition of *musical* elements, and *second* that what rightly pleases about a composition, be it the strictest *Bach* fugue or the dreamiest nocturne of *Chopin*, is *musically* beautiful.

Even less than with the classical can [105] the "musically beautiful" coincide with the *architectonic*, which the musically beautiful encompasses as a branch. The rigid majesty of superimposed towering figurations, the artful entwining of many voices of which *none* is free and independent because *all* of them are, have their everlasting justification. Yet those magnificently somber vocal pyramids of the old Italians and Netherlanders are just one small province in the domain of musical beauty, as are the many delicately fashioned shapes in the suites and concertos of Sebastian Bach.

Many aestheticians consider musical enjoyment sufficiently explained through delight in *regularity* and *symmetry*, though beauty, moreover musical beauty, never consisted in those. The most banal theme can be constructed perfectly symmetrically. "Symmetry" is indeed only a relational concept and leaves open the question of *what* it is, then, that appears symmetrical. The regular ordering of uninspired [*geistlos*], worn-out fragments will be identified especially in the absolute worst compositions. [106] The musical mind demands ever *new* symmetrical constructions.[14]

[107] *Oersted* has recently developed the Platonic view for music on the example of the circle, for which he claims positive beauty. Has he never experienced for himself the horror of a completely circular composition?

More cautious perhaps than necessary, we add yet finally that musical beauty has nothing to do with *the mathematical aspect*. The

13. If we mention Riehl's *Musikalische Charakterköpfe* here, it is nevertheless with grateful acknowledgment of this intellectually stimulating book.

14. (*Translators' note*: The following footnote was added in the sixth edition. The long passage, taken from one of Hanslick's reviews, underlines his openness to history—a facet of his aesthetic thinking that is often overlooked. For further detail,

idea, which laymen (among them sentimental authors) foster about the role that mathematics plays in musical composition, is a peculiarly vague one. Not [108] satisfied that vibrations of tones, span of intervals, consonance, and dissonance can be traced to mathematical relationships, they are convinced that the *beauty* of a musical work, too, is founded on numbers. The study of harmony and counterpoint is taken for a type of Cabbala that teaches the "calculation" of the composition.

Although mathematics furnishes an indispensable key for researching the physical dimension of music, its significance for the completed musical work should not be overestimated. In a musical composition, be it the most beautiful or the worst, nothing at

---

see our essay on Hanslick's central concepts, pp. xxxvi–xxxvii.) I allow myself to quote here a passage from my book, *The Modern Opera* (Preface, p. vi), by way of explanation:

"The famous axiom that the 'truly beautiful' (who is the judge of this property?) can never lose its enchantment, even after the passage of a long time, is for music little more than a nice turn of phrase. Music operates like nature, which every autumn allows a world full of flowers to decay, from which new blossoms arise. All music is the work of humans, the product of a particular individuality, time, culture, and therefore is constantly suffused with elements of faster and slower mortality. Among the great musical forms, opera is the most complex, most conventional, and thus the most transient. It may sadden that even newer operas of the most noble and brilliant design (Spohr, Spontini) are already beginning to disappear from the theater. However, the fact is irrefutable and the process cannot be stopped by the stereotypical scolding of the wicked 'spirit of the time' in all periods. Time is also a spirit and creates its body. The stage represents the forum for the actual needs of the public, in contrast to the study-chamber for silent score-readers. The stage signifies the life of the *drama*; the struggle for ownership of the stage signifies the struggle for drama's *existence*. In that struggle, a lesser work quite often prevails over its better ancestors if it provides us with the air of the present, the heartbeat of *our* sentiments and desires. The public and artist alike feel a justified impulse for the new in music, and criticism, which only has admiration for the old and not the courage for acknowledging the new as well, undermines [creative] productivity. We must renounce the belief in the immortality of beauty. Every era has proclaimed the timelessness of *their* best operas with the same deluded confidence. Yet Adam Hiller in Leipzig maintained that if *Hasse*'s operas should ever no longer delight, general barbarity must break out. Yet *Schubart*, the aesthetician from Hohenasperg, assured of *Jomelli* that it was unthinkable that this composer could ever fall into oblivion. And what are Hasse and Jomelli to us today?"

all is mathematically calculated. Creations of imagination are not arithmetic problems. All monochord experiments, acoustical figures, intervallic proportions, and the like have no place here. The *aesthetic* domain first begins where the significance of those elementary relationships ends. Mathematics regulates merely the elemental material capable of intellectual treatment, and operates concealed in the simplest relationships. However, the musical idea emerges without it. When *Oersted* asks, "Might the [109] lifetime of several mathematicians suffice to calculate all of the beauties of a *Mozart* symphony?"[15] I confess that I do not understand that. *What* should or can be calculated? Perhaps the vibrational relationship of each tone to the next, or the comparative lengths of the individual sections? What makes music into a work of musical art and elevates it from the rank of physical experiments is the element of freedom, intellect, and is thus incalculable. Mathematics has as small or as large a part in a musical *artwork* as in the products of the other arts. For in the end mathematics must also guide the hand of the painter and sculptor. Mathematics operates in the proportions of lengths of verses and strophes, in the constructions of the architect, in the patterns of the dancer. In every exact body of knowledge, the application of mathematics must have a place as the activity of reason. We just must not grant it a truly positive, creative power, as some musicians, [110] those conservatives of aesthetics, would gladly like. The issue of mathematics [in music] is similar to the one of producing feelings in a listener: It occurs in all arts, but a great racket is made about it only in music.

With *language*, too, there have often been attempts to draw parallels with music, and to institute in music the laws of language. The kinship of *song* with language was close enough if one wanted to keep to the similarity of physiological requirements or to the shared character as externalizing inner life through the human voice. The analogical relationships are too evident for us to take that up here.

---

15. *Geist in der Natur*, vol. 3, trans. Kannegießer, p. 32.

Accordingly, where in music it is really merely a matter of the subjective externalization of an inner impulse, we would simply explicitly grant that the laws regulating someone *speaking* will indeed be decisive to some degree for someone *singing*. The fact that someone who gets worked up into a frenzy raises his voice in pitch whereas the voice of someone calming down falls in pitch; that statements of particular gravity are spoken slowly and inconsequential minor matters quickly: [111] These and similar cases the composer of vocal music may not ignore, especially a composer of *dramatic* vocal music. But people were not satisfied with these circumscribed analogies but *rather* interpreted *music itself* as a (less definite or more subtle) *language,* and now wanted to derive its laws of beauty from the nature of language. Every trait and effect of music was derived from similarities with language. We are of the view that, where it is a matter of the specific properties of an art, its differences from related domains are more important than the similarities. Undeterred by these often tempting analogies that are not at all relevant to the actual nature of music, aesthetic inquiry must unrelentingly forge ahead to the point where language and music irreconcilably part ways. Truly fruitful determinations for music can spring forth only from that point. The essential difference, however, is that in language the *sound* [*Ton*] is only a sign, that is, a *means* to an end for the expression of something completely foreign to that means, while in *music* the *tone* [*Ton*] is an entity, *that is,* occurs *as an end it itself.* [112] The autonomous beauty of tone forms in music and the absolute sovereignty of the idea over the tone as a mere means of expression in language are so exclusively opposed that a blending of the two principles is a logical impossibility.

The focal point in the matter of essence is situated completely differently with language and music, and around that point all other characteristics are arrayed. All specifically *musical* laws will revolve around the autonomous significance and beauty of tones, all *linguistic* laws around the proper application of sound for the purpose of expression.

The most damaging and confusing views have arisen from the effort to interpret music as a type of language. Those views present us daily with the practical consequences. Thus it must have seemed convenient mainly to composers of weaker creative powers to regard for them unattainable autonomous musical beauty as a false, sensuous principle, and instead to raise the banner of the characteristic meaningfulness of music. Completely disregarding Richard Wagner's [113] operas, we often find in the most modest instrumental pieces interruptions of the melodic flow by abrupt cadences, recitative-like passages, and the like that, alienating the listener, behave as though they *signified* something special whereas, in fact, they do not mean anything but unattractiveness. People tend to claim of modern compositions that continually breach large-scale periodicity in order to inject enigmatic interpolations or accumulated contrasts that in them music is striving to breach its narrow boundaries and to elevate itself to a *language*. Such praise has always seemed to us quite equivocal. Music's boundaries are by no means narrow, but are quite exactly and firmly staked out. Music can never be "elevated to a language"—be demeaned we would have to say from the musical standpoint, as music would obviously have to be an *enhanced* language.[16]

[114] That fact is forgotten even by our singers, who in moments of greatest affect, in *speaking*, belt out words, indeed phrases, and [115] believe they have intensified the music to the utmost. They overlook that the transition from singing to speaking is always a lowering, just as the [116] highest tone normal for speaking still sounds lower than even the lower tones sung by the same voice. Just as bad as those practical consequences, indeed worse yet because not instantly refuted by experiment, are *theories* that attempt to impose on music the developmental and constructional laws of language as attempted in former times in part by *Rousseau* and *Rameau*, in more modern times by the disciples of Richard *Wagner*. The true heart of music, the self-contented beauty of form, is thereby impaled and the

16. It may not be suppressed that one of the most inspired and magnificent works of all times has, through its brilliance, contributed to this favorite falsehood of more contemporary music criticism about the "music's inner compulsion for the definiteness of spoken language" and "for the discarding of the fetters of ordered, proportionate harmoniousness." We are speaking of Beethoven's *Ninth*. It is one of those

illusion of "meaning" pursued. An aesthetics of music would have to count among its most important tasks relentlessly laying out the fundamental difference between the nature of music and that of language, and to maintain in all inferences the principle that, in matters of the specifically musical, analogies with language have no application whatsoever.

intellectual watersheds that inserts itself conspicuously and insurmountably between the currents of opposing persuasions.

Musicians for whom the grandness of the "intention" supersedes the intellectual significance of the abstract purpose place the *Ninth Symphony* at the pinnacle of all music, while the small crowd who, clinging to the unsurpassed standpoint of beauty, fight for purely aesthetic demands, put some constraints on their admiration. As can be guessed, it is primarily a matter of the Finale, as scarcely any argument will arise among attentive and prepared listeners about the high level of beauty of the first three movements. In that last movement, we have never been able to see more than the gigantic shadow cast by a giant body. One can understand perfectly and recognize the grandeur of the idea of ultimately bringing a soul isolated unto despair to reconciliation to the joy of all, and yet finding the music of the last movement unattractive (for all of its brilliant distinctiveness). We know quite well the general condemnatory judgment accorded to such a divergent opinion. One of the most brilliant and versatile of Germany's scholars, who in 1853 in the A. *Allgemeine Zeitung* undertook to contest the fundamental formal basis of the Ninth Symphony thus recognized the humorous necessity of declaring himself right on the title page as a "narrow mind." He elucidated the aesthetic monstrousness involved in ending a multimovement instrumental work with a *chorus*, and compares *Beethoven* to a sculptor who fashions legs, body, torso, arms of a figure out of uncolored marble, but colorizes the head. We are to believe that every sensitive listener must be overcome with the same discomfort at the entry of the human voice, "because here the artwork changes its focus with a jolt, and thereby threatens to knock over the listener." Nearly a decade later, we were delighted when the "narrow mind" unmasked himself as *David Strauss*.

By contrast, *Dr. Becher*, who may appear here as a representative of a whole class, in an essay published in 1843 on the Ninth Symphony calls the *fourth movement* "an issue of *Beethoven*'s ingenuity that is entirely incongruous with every other existing musical work with regard to distinctiveness in design as well as grandeur of composition and boldest upsurge of individual ideas," and assures that this work stands for him "with Shakespeare's *King Lear* and perhaps a dozen other emanations of the human intellect in the Himalayan mountains of art as a Dhaulagiri peak in its consummate poetical power, even towering over its equals." Like almost all of his like-minded colleagues Becher provides a detailed *description of the significance* of the "content" of each of the four movements and their deep symbolism, but of the music there is not one syllable. That is highly typical for an entire school of music criticism, which loves to dodge the question of whether some *music* is beautiful with the profound discussion what grand things it *means*.

Chapter 4

Analysis of the Subjective Impression of Music

[117] Although we consider it as a principle and first task of musical aesthetics that it place the usurped sovereignty of feeling under the rightful sovereignty of beauty—because not feeling but imagination, as an activity of pure contemplation, is the agency from and for which all beauty of art originates initially—the affirmative expressions of feeling in practical musical life do assert too noticeable and important a role to be shrugged off through mere subordination.

As much as aesthetic contemplation must focus on the artwork itself, this autonomous artwork in reality proves to be [118] an effective median between two animated forces: its *whence* and *whither*, that is, the composer and listener. In the psychic life of those two, the artistic activity of *imagination* cannot be segregated out down to the pure metal as it exists in the completed, impersonal artwork. Rather, it operates in their psyche in close interrelation with feelings and sensations. Thus *before* and *after* the complete work, initially in the composer, then in the listener, feeling will affirm a significance from which we may not withdraw our attention.

Let us consider the *composer*. During creative activity, an elevated mood will fill him as can scarcely be thought dispensable for liberating beauty from the mine of imagination. Depending on the composer's individuality, that this elevated mood more or less takes on the hue of the emerging artwork; that the mood will flow now powerfully, now more moderately, although never to the point of an overpowering affect that thwarts artistic creation; that throughout, the clear reflection maintains at least equal importance with the rapture—[119] those are familiar determinants that are part of a general theory of art. Regarding what bears on the creative act of the *composer* in particular, it must be kept in mind that it is a continuous *building*, a *shaping* in tone relationships. The sovereignty of feeling, which is so readily attributed to music, seems nowhere worse applied than when it is presupposed of the composer during the creative act, and that act is interpreted as enraptured improvisation. The stepwise process by which a piece of music, conceived initially by the composer only in outline, is chiseled out into a specific shape down to the individual measures, possibly into the delicate, multifaceted form of an orchestral work, [that process] is so calmly reasoned and complicated that someone who has himself never tried his hand at it can scarcely understand it. Not just fugal or contrapuntal pieces, in which we methodically maintain a note-against-note setting, but also the most flowing rondo, the most melodious aria requires, as our language meaningfully calls it, a "working out" in the tiniest detail. The composer's activity is in its manner *graphically vivid* and comparable to that of the visual artist. Just as little as the visual artist, [120] the composer may not be dependently absorbed in his material, for like the visual artist, the composer must of course objectively present his (musical) ideal, shape it into pure form.

Rosenkranz may perhaps have overlooked that when he notes, but leaves unresolved, the contradiction of why *women*, by nature more likely to be dependent on feeling, achieve nothing in composition.[1] Aside from the general conditions that hold women back from intellectual achievement, the reason lies in the graphically vivid aspect of composing, which demands an *externalization* of subjectivity no less than the visual arts, though in a different direction. If strength and liveliness of feeling were really decisive for composing, the entire lack of female composers alongside the so numerous female authors and

---

1. Rosenkranz, *Psychologie*, 2nd ed, p. 60.

painters would be difficult to explain. It is not feeling that composes but rather the particularly musical, artistically trained talent. Hence it sounds delectable when *Friedrich Daniel Schubart* puts forward the [121] "masterful Andantes" of the composer *Stamitz* completely seriously as a natural "consequence of a sensitive heart,"[2] or when Christian *Rolle* assures us that "an affable, tender personality gives us the skill to mold slow movements into masterworks."[3]

Without internal warmth, nothing great or beautiful in life has been achieved. With a composer, as with every poet, richly developed feeling will be present, only it is not the composer's creative factor. Even when he is wholly filled with a strong, specific pathos, it may become the motivation and initiation of many an artwork but—as we know from the nature of music, which has neither the capability nor the role of representing a specific affect—it may never become its subject matter. An interior *singing*, not a mere interior feeling, motivates the musically talented individual to create a piece of music.

[122] We interpreted the activity of composing as a constructing. As such, it is thoroughly *objective*. The composer shapes something autonomously beautiful. The intellectual material of tones, with infinite capacity for expression, allows the subjectivity of the tone constructions to find expression in the manner of his shaping. Because the individual musical elements already possess a characteristic expressiveness, predominant traits of the composer—sentimentality, energy, cheerfulness, and so forth—will express themselves through the consistent preference for certain keys, rhythms, transitions, according to the *general* aspects that music is capable of reproducing. Once absorbed by the artwork, however, those traits are of interest thereupon as musical determinants, as the character of the composition, not of the composer.[4] What the sentimental [123] and what

2. Schubart, *Ideen zu einer Ästhetik der Tonkunst*, 1806.
3. *Neue Wahrnehmungen zur Aufnahme der Musik*, Berlin, 1784, p. 102.
4. The caution necessary with inferences about the human character of the composer based on the compositions and how great the danger is of imagination influencing levelheaded investigation to the disadvantage of truth have been recently demonstrated by, among other things, *A. B. Marx*'s Beethoven biography, whose

the intellectually stimulating composer offers, the charming or the sublime composer, is primarily and above all *music*, objective structure. Their works will differentiate themselves from one another by unmistakable characteristics, and as an overall image will reflect the individuality of their creators. Yet all of the works, the one type as well as the other, were created purely musically and for their own sake as autonomously beautiful.

It is not the actual feeling of the composer, as a mere subjective affection, that awakens the same mood in the listeners. If we grant music such a compelling power, we thereby acknowledge its cause as something objective in the music, for only something objective is *compelling* in all beauty. That objective aspect here is the *musical* specifics of a piece of music. Strictly aesthetically, we can say of any particular theme that it *sounds* proud or sad, not, however, that it is an expression of proud or sad feelings of the composer. Yet more remote from the character of a musical work as such [124] are the social and political circumstances that dominate its time. That *musical* expression of the theme is a necessary consequence of its tone elements, selected just so and not otherwise. That this selection arose from psychological or cultural–historical causes would have to be substantiated in the specific work (not merely from the year or locale of origin), and if substantiated, the connection, however interesting, would from the outset be a solely historical or biographical fact. *Aesthetic* contemplation cannot rely on circumstances that lie outside of the artwork itself.

As certain as the composer's individuality will find symbolic expression in his creations, it would be as erroneous to want to derive from that personal aspect concepts that have their true foundation solely in the objectivity of artistic construction. The concept of *style* belongs in that category.[5]

---

musically biased panegyric believed it was liberated from the facts, and thus has been corrected on many points by *Thayer's* thorough research of the sources.

5. Erroneous is thus *Forkel's* derivation of various musical styles from "differences in thinking," according to which the style of every composer has its basis in the effusive, the pompous, the cold, immature, and pedantic man introducing bombast and

[125] We prefer to have style in music understood from the perspective of its specific *musical* features, as perfected technique as it appears in the expression of creative thought as [an element of] habituation. Realizing the clearly conceived idea, the master verifies "style" by omitting everything fussy, incongruous, trivial, and thus consistently preserves the artistic disposition of the whole in every technical detail. With Vischer (*Ästhetik*, §527) we would use the word *style* in its absolute sense also in music and would say, disregarding historical and individual classifications, this composer *has style* in the sense of how we say that someone has *character*.

With regard to the issue of style, the *architectonic* facet of the musically beautiful enters quite clearly into the foreground. A higher logic than that of mere proportionality, the *style* of a piece of music is violated by a single measure that, irreproachable in itself, does not accord with the expression of the whole. [126] Just as with an incompatible arabesque in an architectural work, we designate as lacking in style a cadence or modulation that stands out from a unified development of the basic idea as inconsistent. That unity is to be understood, naturally, in the wider, higher sense, in which in some cases it includes contrast, an episode, and some freedoms.

Thus in the *composition* of a piece of music, a disclosure of one's own personal affect occurs only insofar as the limits of a predominantly objective, shaping activity allow.

The act in which the direct emanation of feeling in tones can unfold is not the *creation* of a musical work but rather the *reproduction*, the performance of it. Without reference to its performance, the fact that the composed piece of music is, philosophically, the *completed* artwork must not hinder us always to bear in mind the splitting of music into composition and reproduction—one of the most consequential features of our art—in all cases in which it contributes to the explanation of a phenomenon.

unbearable emphasis into the context of the composer's thoughts, or is cool and affected" (*Theorie der Musik*, 1777, p. 23).

[127] That feature asserts itself most especially in the investigation of the subjective impression of music. It is granted to the *performer* to release the feeling that momentarily dominates him directly through his instrument, and to breathe into his performance the wild agitation, the ardent glow, the cheerful power and joy of his inwardness. Even the *corporeal* interiority that, through my fingertips, abruptly presses the internal quivering onto the string or draws the bow or even becomes audible in singing actually makes possible the most intimate outpouring of the mood in playing music. Here subjectivity becomes *audibly* effective directly in tones, not merely silently formative in them. The composer creates slowly, discontinuously, the performer in inexorable flight; the composer creates for permanence, the performer for the fulfilled moment. The musical work is formed, the performance we *experience*. Thus the cathartic and stimulating aspect of music resides in the act of reproduction, which lures the electric spark from obscure secrecy and causes it to leap the gap into the heart of listeners. The player can of course deliver only that [128] which the composition contains, but the latter compels little more than the accuracy of the notes. It is said that "the mind of the *composer* is solely what the performer must guess and reveal." Perhaps, but precisely that appropriation in the moment of the re-creative act is his, the performer's mind. The same piece annoys or enchants according to how it is animated into acoustical reality. It is like the same person construed once in his most transfigured rapture, and another time in discontented daily life. A mechanical music box cannot move the feelings of a listener, but the simplest amateur musician will do it if he is soulfully absorbed in his tune.

The disclosure of a state of mind through music achieves the utmost immediacy in which creation and performance coincide in a single act. That occurs in *free improvisation*. Where improvisation occurs primarily not with formally artistic but with predominantly subjective tendency (pathologically in the higher sense), the expression that the performer coaxes from the keys can become true speech. Whoever has experienced for themselves this uncensored speech, this unfettered self-surrender [129] under the influence of a powerful spell, will know without question how love, jealousy, rapture, and sorrow sweep in from their night, unveiled and yet untraceable, celebrate their feasts, sing their sagas, wage their battles, until the master recalls them, calmed, disquieting.

Through the released motion in the performance, the expression of the music performed is communicated to the *listener*. Let us turn to that individual.

We often see him seized by some music, moved to happiness or melancholy, borne to the core far above merely aesthetic pleasure, or shattered. The existence of these effects is undeniable, actual and genuine, often reaching the highest degree, too familiar, ultimately, to require us to dwell on a description. It is a matter here of just two things: As distinct from other movements of feeling, what might the specific character of this arousal of feeling through *music* consist in, and how much of that effect might be *aesthetic*?

Even if we must attribute to *all* arts, without exception, the capability of affecting feelings, [130] there is yet something specific in the way *music* does it, peculiar only to *it*, that cannot be denied. Music works quicker and more intensively on the state of mind than anything else artistically beautiful. With a few chords, we can be put into a mood that a poem would achieve only through a longer exposition, a painting through sustained contemplation, although poetry and painting, in advantage compared with music, have at their service the entire sphere of mental images upon which our thinking depends for knowledge of the feelings of pleasure and pain. The effect of tones is not only quicker but also more direct and intensive. The other arts persuade us, music invades us. We experience this, music's distinctive power over our psyche, most strongly when we are in a state of greater agitation or dejection.

In psychic states in which neither paintings nor poems, statues nor architectural structures are able any longer to stimulate us to participatory attentiveness, *music* will still have power over us, indeed even more intensively than otherwise. Whoever [131] has to listen to or play music in a painfully agitated mood, for them it throbs like vinegar in a wound. No other art can penetrate as deeply and as acutely into our soul. The form and character of what is heard then completely lose their significance. Whether a gloomy nocturnal adagio or a brightly sparkling waltz, we cannot disentangle ourselves from its sounds. We no longer feel the musical work but rather the tones themselves, the music as an amorphously demonic power as it intensely closes in on the nerves of our whole body.

When in advanced age *Goethe* once again experienced the power of love, a previously unknown receptivity for music awoke in him. He writes to *Zelter* (1823) about those wonderful days at Marienbad. "The tremendous power of music over me in these days! Milder's voice, Szymanowska's sonorous richness, indeed even the public parade of the local infantry open me up as one amicably relaxes a clenched fist. I am fully convinced that I would have to leave the room in the first measure of your choir." Too insightful not to recognize the [132] large share of *nervous* agitation in this symptom, Goethe closes with the words, "You would cure me of pathological excitability, which is surely to be regarded, actually, as the cause of this phenomenon."[6] These observations must certainly make us attentive to the fact that in musical effects on feeling a foreign element, not purely aesthetic, is frequently in play. A purely aesthetic effect addresses itself to the full health of neural life and does not reckon with a pathological more or less in that life.

The more intensive impact of music on our nervous system in fact allows music's claim to an excess of power over the other arts. However, when we investigate the nature of that excess, we recognize that it is a *qualitative one* and that the distinctive quality is based on *physiological* conditions. The sensuous factor, which in all enjoyment of beauty bears the intellectual factor, is greater in music than in the other arts. Music, the most intellectual art owing to its [133] incorporeal material, the most sensuous art from the perspective of its subjectless formal play, illustrates in this mysterious union of two opposites a lively effort to align with the *nerves*—those no less

6. Correspondence between Goethe and Zelter, vol. 3, p. 332.

enigmatic elements of the invisible telegraph service between body and mind.

The intensive effect of music on neural life is fully acknowledged as a fact by psychology as well as by physiology. Unfortunately, an adequate explanation of that effect is still lacking. *Psychology* will never be able to explain the magnetically compelling aspect of the impression that certain chords, timbres, and melodies have on the entire organism of the human being, because that depends primarily on a specific stimulation of the nerves. The triumphantly advancing science of *physiology* has contributed just as little of anything decisive about our problem.

Concerning musical monographs on this hybrid subject, they nearly consistently prefer to present music by laying out brilliant showpieces in an imposing aura [134] of miracles than by tracing in scientific research the connection between music and our neural life to its true and necessary elements. But that alone is what is essential for us, and not the steadfast conviction of a *Doctor Albrecht*, who prescribed music for his patients as a means of inducing perspiration, nor the disbelief of *Oersted*, who explains the howling of a dog at certain tonalities as resulting from rationally applied beatings by means of which the dog had been conditioned.[7]

It may be unfamiliar to some music lovers that we possess an entire literature on the bodily effects of music and its therapeutic applications. Rich in interesting curiosities but unreliable in observations, unscientific in explanations, most of these music doctors seek to prop up a very composite and incidental trait of music to autonomous effectiveness.

From *Pythagoras*, who is supposed to have been the first to carry out miraculous cures through music, down to our [135] day, the theory crops up intermittently again and again, enriched more through new examples than new ideas, that the stimulating or soothing effect of tones can be applied to the bodily organism as

---

7. *Der Geist der Natur*, vol. 3, p. 9.

a remedy against numerous illnesses. Peter *Lichtenthal* reports at length in his *Musical Doctor* how *gout, sciatica, epilepsy, catalepsy, plague, delirium, convulsions, typhoid fever*, indeed even "*stupidity*" [*stupiditas*] are supposed to have been cured by the power of tones.[8]

In light of the *substantiation* of their theory, these authors can be divided into two categories.

Authors in the one category reason from the *body* and base the curative power of music on the physical influence of sound waves, which [136] are supposed to communicate through the auditory nerve with the other nerves, and through such general vibrations are supposed to bring about a salutary response of the ailing organism. These affects, which are simultaneously noticeable, are supposed to be just one consequence of this nervous vibration, as not only do passions elicit certain bodily changes but rather the latter, for their part, are also capable of producing corresponding passions.

According to this theory, to which (following the lead of the Englishman *Webb*) Nikolai, *Schneider, Lichtenthal, J. J. Engel, Sulzer*, among others, adhere, we are moved by music no differently than, say, are our windows and doors, which begin to vibrate with powerful music. As supporting evidence, examples are cited such as *Boyle's* attendant, whose gums began to bleed as soon as he heard a saw being sharpened, or many people who get convulsions at the scratching of a knifepoint on glass.

But that is not music. That music shares the same substratum—sound—with those phenomena that affect the nerves so intensely will [137] become important enough to us for later inferences. Here is only to be stressed that, in contrast to a materialistic view, music first begins where those isolated sonic effects leave off. Incidentally, also melancholy, which an adagio can induce in a listener, cannot be compared at all with the bodily sensation of a shrill discord.

---

8. This theory reached the greatest confusion with the famous doctor *Baptista Porta*, who combined the concepts of medicinal plant and musical instrument and cured edema with a flute made from *hellebore* stems. A musical instrument made from the *poplar* is supposed to cure sciatica, one carved out of a *cinnamon shoot* fainting.

The other half of our authors (among them *Kausch* and most aestheticians) explain the curative effects of music from the *psychological* perspective. Music, so they argue, produces affects and passions in the mind. Affects cause intense movements in the nervous system. Intense movements in the nervous system cause a salutary reaction in an ailing organism. This line of reasoning, whose leaps need not even be pointed out, is defended by the aforementioned idealistic "psychological" school of thought so staunchly against the earlier discussed materialistic school that, in defiance of all physiology, under the authority of the Englishman *Whytt* it denies the connection of the auditory nerve with the other nerves, so that a [138] *corporeal* transfer of the stimulus received by the ear to the organism as a whole of course becomes impossible.

The idea of arousing specific affects in the mind through music, such as love, melancholy, anger, delight, which heal the body through beneficial excitation, does not sound so bad. In that connection, the delectable expert opinion that one of our most famous natural scientists issued about the so-called "*Goldberger* electromagnetic chains" always occurs to us. He said it is not agreed whether electrical current is capable of curing certain illnesses. However, it is agreed that "*Goldberger* electromagnetic chains" are not capable of producing any electrical current.[9] Applied to our tone doctors, that means it is *possible* that certain affects bring about a fortunate turning point in bodily illnesses, but it is not possible through music to evoke at any time just any desired affects.

In that regard, the two theories, the psychological and the physiological, are aligned in that they infer from dubious assumptions yet more dubious deductions, and ultimately derive from them the most dubious [139] *practical* conclusions. A mode of therapy may perhaps

---

9. *Translators' note*: Hanslick refers to an electromagnetic device first promoted in 1850 as a cure for rheumatism. The chains were quickly dismissed as charlatanism. See "Die Goldberger'sche Rheumatismuskette," *Polytechnisches Journal* vol. 116/1850, pp. 244–45; http://dingler.culture.hu-berlin.de/article/pj116/mi116mi03_3.

tolerate logically founded criticisms,[10] but it is disconcerting that up to now no doctor has ever been moved to send his typhus patients to Meyerbeer's *The Prophet* or to pull out a French horn instead of a lancet.

The bodily effect of music is neither so strong in itself nor so certain, nor so independent of psychic and aesthetic presuppositions, nor, finally, is the effect so arbitrarily manipulable that it could be considered an actual therapy.

Any therapy carried out with the assistance of music has the character of an exceptional case whose success was never to be ascribed to music alone, but rather also depended on special, perhaps entirely individual bodily or mental conditions. It is quite remarkable that the only application of music that actually occurs in medicine, namely in the treatment of the mentally ill, reflects mainly on the intellectual facet of musical effects. As is known, modern psychiatry employs music in many cases and with favorable results. [140] However, that outcome is based neither on physical tremors of the nervous system nor on the arousal of passions, but rather on the soothing, exhilarating influence that musical action, half distracting half enthralling, is capable of exercising on a melancholic or overwrought psyche. Although the mental patient listens to the sensuous, not to the artistic aspect of music, if he listens attentively he attains a level of aesthetic comprehension, albeit a subsidiary one.

What, then, do all of these musical–medicinal works contribute to a correct knowledge of music? The confirmation of a long since observed strong physical arousal in the case of all "affects" and "passions" evoked by music. Once it has been established that an integral part of psychic motion produced by music is *physical*, it then follows that this phenomenon, occurring essentially in our neural life, would also have to be researched from this, its corporeal side. Accordingly, the musician can form no scientific opinion on this

---

10. *Translators' note*: Hanslick's term here is *logische Ausstellungen*. *Ausstellung* is an antiquated word for criticism. In modern-day German, it is no longer used in this meaning.

problem without acquainting himself with the results [141] to which the current standpoint of *physiology* holds in investigating the connection of music with feelings.

If we follow the course that a melody must take in order to act on our mood, we find its path from the vibrating instrument to the auditory nerve amply clarified, especially according to the epoch-making advances in that area through *Helmholtz's Lehre von den Tonempfindungen*. Acoustics demonstrates precisely the external conditions under which we hear a tone at all, under which we hear this or that particular tone. With the help of a microscope, anatomy reveals to us the structure of the organ of hearing to the innermost and minutest detail. Physiology, finally, cannot of course conduct any direct experiments on this extremely small and delicate, deeply concealed wondrous structure, but has determined its mode of operation in part with certainty, in part clarified so much through an hypothesis established by Helmholtz that now the entire process of tone sensation is physiologically intelligible. Even beyond that, [142] in the domain where natural science already intersects closely with aesthetics, the investigations of Helmholtz on consonance and the affinities of tones have shed considerable light, where up until just recently considerable darkness prevailed. But with that, we are of course at the end of our knowledge. The most important thing for us is and remains unexplained: the neural process through which the *sensation* of tone becomes *feeling*, becomes a *state of mind*. Physiology knows that what we perceive as tone is a molecular motion in the neural matter, [and] indeed knows at least as well that it is motion in the auditory nerve [*Akustikus*] [11] in the related parts of the central nervous system.[12] It

---

11. *Translators' note: Akusticus* is short for *nervus acusticus*, analogous to *opticus* (optical or visual nerve). Today, what we call the auditory nerve is the *nervus vestibulocochlearis*, which encompasses both the *nervus vestibularis* (*staticus*) and the *nervus cochlearis* (*acusticus*). However, *akusticus* in Hanslick's time was both the *vestibularis* and the *cochlearis*.

12. *Translators' note*: Hanslick's term is *Centralorgane*. *Centralorgane* as a plural term relates to *nervöse Centralorgane*, meaning the central nervous system (already correctly identified in the Payzant translation).

knows that the filaments of the auditory nerve are related to the other nerves, and that the filaments transmit the auditory nerve's stimuli to them, and that hearing in particular is connected with the cerebellum and cerebrum, the larynx, the lungs, and the heart. Unknown to physiology, however, is the specific manner in which music affects those nerves, moreover, the diversity with which specific musical factors—chords, rhythms, instruments—affect different nerves. Is a musical [143] auditory sensation distributed to all nerves connected with the auditory mechanism or only to some of them? With what intensity? By which musical elements is the brain most affected, by which the nerves leading to the heart or to the lungs? It is undeniable that dance music causes a twitching of the body, particularly the feet, in young people, whose natural temperament is not completely restrained by civilization. It would be biased to deny the *physiological* influence of march and dance music and to attempt to reduce it exclusively to a *psychological* association of ideas. What is psychological about it—the awakened memory of the known pleasure of dancing—does not lack an explanation, yet that explanation by no means suffices. It lifts the feet not because it is dance music; rather, it is dance music because it lifts the feet. Whoever looks around a bit at the opera will soon notice how women involuntarily bob their heads back and forth to lively, accessible melodies. However, we will never see that with an adagio, no matter how stirring or melodic. Can we conclude [144] from this that certain musical relationships, in particular rhythmic ones, affect motor nerves, other relationships only sensory nerves? When is the former the case, when the latter?[13] Does the solar plexus, traditionally taken as the primary seat of sensation,

13. It is a very uncertain hypothesis when *Carus* explains the motor stimulus by having the auditory nerve originate in the cerebellum, locates there the seat of volition, and, among others things, derives from both the distinctive effects of auditory impressions on the activities of mind. For the origin of the auditory nerve in the *cerebellum* is not even a scientifically settled fact.

Harless (in Rudolph *Wagner's Handbuch der Physiologie* article "hearing") claims for mere perception of rhythm, without all aural impression, the same motor impulse as for rhythmic music.

undergo a particular affectation through music? Do the "sympathetic nerves" undergo such an affectation (to which *Purkinje* once commented to me that their name is the prettiest aspect of them)? Why one sound seems shrill, repugnant, another pure and harmonious, is explained by way of acoustics through the uniformity and nonuniformity of the [145] successive compressions and rarefactions of air, why several simultaneously sounded tones are consonant or dissonant through their [respectively] undisturbed and regular, or disturbed and irregular flow [of simultaneous sound waves].[14] But these explanations of more-or-less-simple *auditory sensations* cannot satisfy the aesthetician. He demands the explanation of *feeling* and asks how it comes about that one series of harmonious sounding tones gives an impression of grief, a second series of equally harmoniously sounding tones the impression of joy. Whence the opposed moods, often arising with compelling force, that various chords or instruments of equally pure harmonious sound instill in the listener?

As far as our knowledge and judgment reaches, physiology cannot answer any of these questions. And how should it? After all, it does not know how pain produces tears, how joy produces laughter. It does not even know what pain and joy *are*! Thus all should beware [146] of demanding from a science information that it cannot give.[15]

Of course the reason for any feeling elicited by music must lie primarily in a particular manner of affection of the nerves through an aural impression. But how a stimulation of the auditory nerve, which we cannot even trace to its origins, enters into consciousness as a

---

14. Helmholtz, *Lehre von den Tonempfindungen*, 2nd ed., 1870, p. 319.

15. One of our most intellectually gifted physiologists, Lotze, says in his *Medicinische Psychologie* (p. 237), "The contemplation of *melodies* would lead to the admission that *we know nothing at all about the conditions* under which a transition of nerves from one form of stimulation to another offers a physical basis for the powerful aesthetic feelings that follows upon the succession of tones." Further, on the impression of pleasure and displeasure that even a simple tone can make (p. 236), "It is completely impossible for us to provide a physiological reason for these particular simple sensations, since the orientation toward which they alter neural activity is too unknown for us to be capable of deducing from that activity the extent of the benefit or disruption that it undergoes."

specific sensatory quality, how the corporeal impression ultimately becomes a state of mind, the sensation a feeling—that lies on the other side of the obscure bridge that has not been crossed by any researcher. There are a thousandfold [147] roundabout descriptions of the one primordial riddle: of the connection of the body with the mind. That sphinx will never reveal its secrets.[16]

What physiology offers to the science of music is of utmost importance for our understanding of auditory impressions as such. In that regard, some progress can still occur by way of physiology. In the main musical issue, that will scarcely ever be the case.

This result yields for music aesthetics the consideration that those theorists who construct the principle of beauty in music upon the effects of feeling are scientifically lost because they can know nothing about the nature of that interrelation, thus at best are able only to guess or imagine. An artistic or scientific determination of music can never begin from the standpoint of feeling. With the portrayal of subjective motions [148] that overcome the critic on hearing a symphony, he will not be able to substantiate its value and significance, and beginning from affects, he can just as little teach something to an aspiring musician. That last point is important. For were a relation between specific feelings and certain modes of musical expression to be as reliably available as people are inclined to believe, and as that relation would have to exist in order to assert its claimed significance, it would be a simple matter to guide the prospective composer to the heights of the gripping effects of music. People actually wanted that, too. *Mattheson* teaches in the third chapter of his *Der vollkommene Kapellmeister* how pride, humility, and all passions are

16. Du Bois-Reymond's address "On the Limitations of the Knowledge of Nature" at the 1872 conference of natural scientists in Leipzig contains a new, valuable confirmation of this view. *Translators' note*: In the German original, the passage reads "that sphinx will never throw herself off the rock" [*Diese Sphinx wird sich niemals vom Felsen stürzen*]. Hanslick's image refers to the myth of Oedipus. On his way to Thebes, Oedipus was stopped by a sphinx who would let travelers pass only if they solved a riddle. Oedipus was the first one to answer the sphinx's question correctly. The sphinx was outraged and threw herself to her death. The myth is used as an allegory for the limits of human knowledge.

to be composed by saying, for example, the "inventions for *jealousy* must all contain something annoying, fierce, and pitiful." Another master of the last century, *Heinichen*, gives eight pages of musical examples in his *Generalbass* on how music should express "frenzied, quarreling, stately, fretful, or amorous feelings."[17] The only thing we would need [149] is for such prescriptions to begin with the cookbook phrase "Take a . . . ," or would end with the medical abbreviation m.d.s.[18] Such efforts yield the most informative opinion that special rules of art are always both too narrow and too broad.

However, these inherently groundless rules for the musical arousal of specific feelings belong all the less in aesthetics because the targeted effect is not purely aesthetic, but rather an inextricable part of it is *physical*. The *aesthetic* recipe would have to instruct how the composer is supposed to produce beauty in music, not, though, how to produce any chosen affect in the concert hall. The consideration of how magically powerful these rules *would have* to be shows most beautifully how completely impotent they really *are*. For if the emotional effect of every musical element were a necessary and [150] explorable one, then we could play the mind of the hearer like a keyboard. And if we were capable of that, would the purpose of art be thereby resolved? That alone is the rightful question, and it negates itself. *Musical beauty* alone is the true power of the composer. On its shoulders, he strides securely through the raging waves of time, in which the aspect of feeling offers him no straw against drowning.

We see that our two questions—namely, which specific aspect distinguishes the effect of feeling caused by *music* and whether that aspect is of an essentially aesthetic nature—are settled through

17. Delectable is the guidance of Privy Councilor and doctor of philosophy [Franz Friedrich Siegmund August] *von Böcklin*, who on page 34 of his *Fragmente zur höheren Musik* (1811) says, among other things, "Assuming the composer wanted to portray someone who has been *insulted*, full aesthetic warmth after warmth, beat after beat, a *sublime* melody must spring forth most buoyantly in this music, the inner voices race and shuddering jolts terrify the expectant listener."

18. *Translators' note*: m.d.s. is an abbreviation for the Latin phrase misce, da, signa, or mix, give, and write (on the label), used by pharmacists when dispensing prescription medications.

knowledge of one and the same factor: of the intensive impact on the *nervous system*. In comparison with every other art not operating through *tones*, the distinctive intensity and immediacy with which music is able to arouse affects is based on that impact.

However, the stronger an effect of an art occurs as physically, that is, pathologically overpowering, the less is its *aesthetic* share— a proposition that of course cannot be reversed. In [151] musical production and understanding, another element must therefore be highlighted that the unalloyed aesthetic aspect of this art represents, and that, as the opposite of the specific musical arousal of feeling, approaches the general conditions of beauty of the remaining arts. This is *pure contemplation*. In the next chapter, we will examine its particular manifestation in music, as well as the diverse relationships in which, in practice, it engages with the sphere of feeling.

Chapter 5

Aesthetic Compared to Pathological Perception of Music

[152] Nothing has hampered the scientific development of music aesthetics as harmfully as the excessive value attributed to the effects of music on feelings. The more noticeably these effects manifested themselves, the higher they were praised as heralds of musical beauty. To the contrary, we have seen that, from the listener's side, a most potent amount of *corporeal* stimulation is admixed with precisely the most overpowering impressions of music. From music's side, this intense penetration into the nervous system lies not so much in its *artistic* aspect, which of course emanates from and addresses the intellect, as rather in its [153] *material* aspect, which nature has endowed with that imponderable physiological affinity. It is the *elemental* aspect of music, *sound* and *motion*, that puts the defenseless feelings of so many music lovers in chains, with which they so gladly rattle. Far be it from us to attempt to curtail the rights of feeling for music. But this feeling, which in fact is more or less coupled with pure contemplation, can count as artistic only if it remains aware of its aesthetic origin, that is, aware of the joy in exactly this particular *beauty*.

If that awareness is lacking, if the free contemplation of the particular artistic beauty is lacking and the mind feels ensnared by the natural power of the tones, then *art* can take credit for such an impression all the less the more strongly it appears. The number of those who listen to or actually feel music in that manner is very substantial. By allowing the elemental in music to affect them in passive

receptivity, they end up in vague, supersensuously sensuous agitation determined only by the very general character of the piece of
music. [154] Their behavior toward music is not contemplative but
pathological, a constant dozing, feeling, rhapsodizing, fear, and dread
in resounding nothingness. If we have several pieces of, say, a similar exuberantly joyful character played for a musician of feeling, he
will remain under the spell of that impression. His feelings assimilate
only what these pieces share, the motion of exuberant joyfulness,
while the special qualities of each piece, the artistic individuality, escape his understanding. The musical listener will proceed in exactly
the opposite manner. The distinctive artistic designing of a composition, that which marks it as an independent artwork among a dozen
similarly acting ones, will so dominate his attention that he assigns
only minimum weight to the same or different expression of feelings.
For such musical cultivation, the segregated perception of an abstract
feeling-content instead of the concrete art phenomenon is entirely
characteristic. A common analogy to such cultivation would only
be the power of a special illumination of a landscape when it seizes
someone, [155] rendering him incapable of giving any account at all
about the illuminated landscape itself. An unmotivated and thus all
the more penetrating overall impression will be altogether absorbed.[1]

Half awake, nestled into their armchairs, those enthusiasts let
themselves be carried away and rocked by the vibrations of the tones,
instead of contemplating them keenly. The way it swells ever more
loudly, attenuates, jubilates, or quivers away, it transports them into

---

1. The love-struck duke in Shakespeare's *Twelfth Night* is a poetic personification
of such hearing of music. He says,

If music be the food of love, play on.

. . . .

O, it came o'er my ear like the sweet south,
That breathes upon a bank of violets,
Stealing and giving odor!

And later, in act 2, he declares,

Give me some music. . . .
Methought it did relieve my passion much. . . . .

an indefinite state of feeling, which they are naïve enough to consider purely intellectual. They constitute the most "appreciative" audience and the one likely to most assuredly discredit the dignity of music. The aesthetic characteristic of *intellectual* enjoyment is lacking in their hearing. [156] A fine cigar, a spicy delicacy, a warm bath achieves for them, unconsciously, the same thing as a symphony. From those who sit there mindlessly at leisure to others who are deeply enraptured, the principle is the same: pleasure in the *elemental* in music. Incidentally, for listeners who seek only the deposit of feelings in music, without all activity of the intellect, recent times have made a wonderful discovery that outdoes music by far. We mean sulfuric ether and chloroform. These drugs in fact magically induce in us an intoxication that sweet-dreamily pulsates through the entire body, without the baseness of drinking wine, which is also not without musical effect.

For such understanding, works of music fall in line with *products of nature*, whose enjoyment can charm us but cannot compel us to think, compel us to ponder a consciously creative intellect. The sweet fragrance of an acacia tree can be dreamily inhaled even with closed eyes. Products of human intellect prevent that altogether, if they are not to simply sink to the level of sensuous natural stimuli.

[157] In no other art is this possible to such a high degree as in music, whose sensuous side at least allows nonintellectual enjoyment. Although works of the remaining arts *endure*, the very *evanescence* of music resembles, in a dubious formulation, the act of something being consumed.

A picture, a church, a play cannot be guzzled, but an aria certainly can. That is also why the enjoyment of no other art lends itself to such ancillary service. The best compositions can be played as *dinner music* and facilitate the digestion of pheasants. Music is the most intrusive and conversely also the most forbearing art. We have to *hear* the most miserable barrel organ posted in front of our house, but we do not have to *listen* even to a Mendelssohn symphony.

The [here] censured manner of hearing music is, incidentally, not identical with the naïve public's joy, existing in every art, in the merely sensuous aspect of it, whereas the ideal content is recognized only by cultivated understanding. This unartistic conception of a piece of music involves, not the actual sensuous part, [158] the rich diversity in itself of tone successions, but rather its abstract overall idea perceived as mere feeling. The preeminently unique position that the intellectual *substance* [Gehalt] assumes vis-à-vis the categories of *form* and *content* [Inhalt] thereby becomes apparent. People tend, namely, to view the feeling permeating a piece of music as the content [Inhalt], the idea, the intellectual substance [Gehalt] of it; the artistically created, specific *successions of tones*, by contrast, as the mere form, the image, the sensuous guise of the supersensuous. But precisely the "specifically musical" part is the creation of the artistic intellect, with which the contemplating intellect comprehendingly unites. The intellectual substance [Gehalt] of the composition resides in those concrete tone configurations, not in the vague overall impression of an abstracted feeling. The form, simply (the tone structure), as opposed to feeling as the supposed content [Inhalt], is precisely the true *content* [Inhalt] of music, is the music itself, whereas the produced feeling cannot be called either content or form, but rather a de facto effect. Similarly, the supposed material, the representational element, is precisely the structured element produced by the intellect, whereas the ostensibly [159] represented element, the effect of feeling, inheres in the *material* of tone and conforms largely to *physiological* laws.

From the foregoing considerations, the correct assessment of music's so-called *moral effects* emerges readily, which were emphasized by older authors with so much fondness as a splendid counterpart to the aforementioned "physical" effects. Because by those lights music is not enjoyed in the remotest as something beautiful but is perceived, rather, as a raw natural force that urges toward a point of unbridled actions, we then stand in direct opposition to everything aesthetic. Moreover, the commonality between those ostensible "moral" effects and the acknowledged physical ones is obvious.

The insistent creditor who is moved by the tones of his debtor to forgive the entire sum is motivated no differently than someone resting who is suddenly inspired by a waltz melody to dance.[2] The first is moved [160] more by the more intellectual elements, harmony and melody, the second by the more sensuous rhythm. However, neither acts out of free self-determination; neither is overpowered by intellectual predominance or ethical beauty but rather as a consequence of facilitating neural stimuli. Music relaxes the feet of the one or the heart of the other, just as wine does the tongue. Such victories preach only about the weakness of the vanquished. Incurring unmotivated, directionless, and empty affects through a power that has no connection with our volition and thinking is unworthy of human intellect. When people allow themselves to be completely carried away by the elemental aspect of an art to such a high degree that they are no longer in control of their free actions, that seems to us no eminence for the art, and much less yet for the champions themselves.

Music does not at all have that purpose. Its intensive element of feeling alone enables it to be enjoyed with that orientation. This is the point at which the oldest indictments against music have their root: that it enervates, mollycoddles, slackens.

[161] Where music is played as a stimulant for "indefinite affects," as nourishment for "feeling" in itself, there the accusation becomes only too true. *Beethoven* demanded that music should "strike fire in the mind of the listener." *Nota bene* "should." The question, however, is whether fire itself, engendered and nourished by *music*, inhibits strong-willed, intellectual development of the listener.

In any case, this indictment of musical influence seems to us more worthy than its excessive praise. Just as the *physical* effects of music are in direct relation to pathological excitation of the collaborating nervous system, so the *moral* influence of tones increases with the crudeness of intellect and character. The smaller the reverberations of cultivation, the more powerful the intrusion of such force. As is known, music exerts the strongest effect on primitives.

---

2. Told by the Neapolitan singer *Palma* and others (Allatson Burgh, *Anecdotes on Music*, 1814).

That does not deter our music moralists. As if warming up, they begin, preferably, with numerous examples, "how even animals" succumb to the power of music. It is true [162] that the trumpet call fills the horse with courage and battle fervor, the violin inspires the bear to attempts at ballet, the delicate spider and the clumsy elephant hearken and move to favorite sounds. But is it then really so honorable to be a music lover in *such* company?

The human showpieces follow the animal acts. They are mostly according to the taste of Alexander the Great, who at first became enraged at the flute playing of *Timotheus*, and was then soothed by singing. The less-known king of Denmark, *Ericus Bonus*, had a famous musician play in order to convince himself of the lauded power of music, and had all weapons removed in advance. By the choice of his playing, the musician first put all minds into a state of sadness, then happiness. He was able to escalate the latter into frenzy. "Even the king broke down the door, grabbed a sword, and killed *four* of the bystanders" (*Albert Krantzius*, Dan. lib. V., chapter 3). And that was yet the "*good Eric.*"

If such "moral effects" [163] of music were still an order of business today, out of indignation we would probably not even get to the point of speaking out rationally about the bewitching power that, in sovereign extraterritoriality, subdues and confuses the human mind, unconcerned about its thoughts and decisions.

However, the consideration that the most famous of these musical trophies belong to hoary antiquity makes us inclined to derive an historical perspective from the matter.

There is no doubt at all that music had a far more direct effect among ancient peoples than at present, because humanity in its primitive stages of development was more related to and subject to the *elemental* than in later times, when consciousness and self-determination come into their own. The unique status of music in Greek antiquity beneficially accommodated this natural receptivity. It was not an *art* in our sense. *Sound* and *rhythm* functioned in nearly isolated independence and represented in scant prominence the role of the rich, intellect-laden forms that constitute current music. [164]

Everything known about music of those times leads with certainty to the conclusion that it had a merely sensuous impact, but still within that limitation a refined one. Music in the modern, artistic sense did not exist in classical antiquity. Otherwise, it could no more have been lost for later development than have classical poetry, sculpture, and architecture. The Greeks' fondness for a thorough study of their tone relationships, down to the subtlest detail, has, as a purely scientific matter, no place here.

The lack of harmony, the constraint of melody in the narrowest limits of recitative-like expression, finally the inability of the ancient tone system to develop truly musical richness in design rendered impossible an absolute significance of music as an art in the musical sense. It was also almost never autonomous but rather always used in connection with poetry, dance, and theatrical acting, thus as a supplement to other arts. Music had only the role of animating through rhythmic pulses and variety of timbres, ultimately [165] to comment on words and feelings as an intensive heightening of recited *declamation*. Music thus operated chiefly through its *sensuous* and *symbolic* aspects. Constrained to those factors, it had to expand them, through such concentration, to greater, indeed more refined effectiveness. The overrefinement of the melodic material to the use of quarter tones and the "enharmonic genus" is as little featured in today's music as the characteristic special expression of the modes [*Tonarten, tonoi*] and their close adherence to the spoken or sung word.

Moreover, for their narrow compass these heightened tonal [*tonlich*] relationships met with a much broader receptivity in *listeners*. Just as the Greek ear was able to grasp infinitely more subtle intervallic differences than ours, conditioned to tempered tuning, so too was the psychic disposition of those peoples far more receptive and desirous of varying mood changes by means of music than we are, who foster contemplative pleasure in the artistic structuring of music, which paralyzes its elemental [166] influence.[3] Thus a more intensive effect of music in antiquity surely seems comprehensible.

3. *Translators' note*: See Chapter 6, *Translators' note* 2.

A modest portion of the histories that have come down to us about the specific effect in antiquity of the various *modes* report similarly. Their basis of explanation lies in the strict differentiation with which the individual modes were chosen for specific purposes and maintained pure. The ancients used the Dorian mode for serious, especially for religious occasions. With the Phrygian, they inflamed the army. The Lydian signified grief and melancholy, and the Aeolian resounded for merrymaking in love or wine. Through this strict, conscious separation of four main modes for just as many categories of states of mind, as well as through their consistent connection *with only* those poems appropriate *to that mode*, the ear and mind had to instinctively acquire a decided tendency at the sounding of music to immediately reproduce the feeling corresponding to its mode. Based on this biased development, music was thus an indispensable, pliable accompaniment of all [167] the arts, a means for pedagogical, political, and other ends. It was everything, but not an independent *art*. If it required only a few Phrygian strains to send a soldier courageously up against the enemy, and the loyalty of the grass widow was assured through Dorian songs, then the demise of the Greek tone system might be mourned by generals and husbands. But the aesthetician and composer will not wish its return.

We contrast being seized pathologically with *deliberate*, pure contemplation of a musical work. This contemplative manner of hearing is the sole artistic, true one. By contrast, the raw affect of primitives and the gushing affect of music enthusiasts fall into a single category. An enjoying, not a submitting, correlates with the beautiful, as the phrase "enjoyment of art" meaningfully expresses. The emotional enthusiasts of course consider it heresy against the almighty of music if someone retreats from the revolutions and riots of the heart that they encounter in every piece of music and earnestly participate in. One is then obviously "cold," "unfeeling," "cerebral." [168] Nevertheless. Following the creative intellect has an elevated and significant effect as it magically reveals to us a new world of elements, coaxes them into all imaginable relationships with one another, and so builds, tears down, produces, and destroys, ruling over the entire wealth of a domain that ennobles the ear to become the subtlest and most highly developed tool of the senses. It is not an ostensibly portrayed passion that sweeps us along in sympathy. Joyfully, in affect-free yet wholehearted intellectual enjoyment, we watch the artwork passing before us, and celebrate in it what *Schelling* so beautifully calls "the sublime indifference of the beautiful."[4] This joyfulness with intellectual alertness is the worthiest, most wholesome manner of hearing music, and not the easiest.

The most important factor in the psychic process that accompanies the comprehension of a musical work and makes it enjoyable is most frequently overlooked. It is the intellectual gratification that the listener finds in continuously [169] following and anticipating the intentions of the composer, here to have his expectations confirmed, there finding himself pleasantly misled. It goes without saying that this intellectual streaming hither and thither, this continual give and take, unfolds unconsciously and lightning fast. Only such music that evokes and rewards this intellectual tracing—which could actually be called a *reflection of imagination*—will offer full artistic enjoyment. Without intellectual activity, there is no aesthetic enjoyment at all. However, *this* form of intellectual activity is especially characteristic of *music* because its works do not exist unalterably and instantaneously but rather spin out successively in the listener. They thus require of the listener, not a type of *contemplation* that permits optional lingering and interruption, but rather tireless *participation* in keenest alertness. With complex compositions, this participation can escalate to intellectual labor. Like many separate *individuals*, some *nations*, too, can manage such work only with great difficulty. The tuneful tyranny of the treble voice with the Italians has a main cause [170] in the intellectual complacency of that people, for whom sustained [intellectual] penetration is unattainable, whereby the northerner loves to follow an artistic network of harmonic and contrapuntal complexities. Consequently, the enjoyment is *easier*

---

4. *Über das Verhältnis der bildenden Künste zur Natur* [1807].

for listeners whose intellectual activity is minimal, and such music drunkards can consume masses of music, in the face of which the artistic intellect shudders.

The *intellectual* aspect necessary for all enjoyment of art will turn up actively in very different gradations in listeners hearing the same musical work. With sensuous and sentimental natures it can sink to a minimum, in predominantly intellectual personalities it can become the literally decisive element. In our opinion, the true "*happy* medium" here must sooner incline toward the right. To become intoxicated requires only weakness, but true aesthetic *hearing* is an *art*.[5]

[171] Wallowing in feelings is mostly an affair of those listeners who have no education for the artistic understanding of the *musically beautiful*. The layperson "feels" music the most, the cultivated artist the least. The more significant [172] the *aesthetic* aspect in the listener (just as in the artwork), the more levelled out is the merely elemental. Thus the theorists' venerable axiom that "Somber music arouses in us feelings of grief, buoyant music happiness" is to this extent not always correct. If every vacuous requiem, every noisy funeral march, every whimpering adagio is supposed to have the power to

5. It is perfectly appropriate for Wilhelm *Heinse*'s dissolutely gushing temperament to ignore the specific musical beauty in favor of vague impressions of feeling. He goes so far as to say (in *Hildegard von Hohenthal*), "True music . . . everywhere pursues the goal of conveying to the listeners the sense of the words and of the feeling, so lightly and pleasantly that we do not notice it (the music). Such music endures forever. It is simply so natural that we *do not notice it*; rather only the sense of the words is conveyed."

Directly to the contrary, however, an aesthetic perception of music occurs where we fully "*notice*" it, *attend to it*, and are directly aware of all of its beauties. *Heinse*, whose inspired naturalism we do not deny the duty of fitting admiration, is in poetic, yet more in musical regard very overrated. With the poverty of intellectually stimulating writings on music we have accustomed ourselves to treat and quote Heinse as an eminent music aesthetician. Could we really overlook how after a few apposite aperçus mostly a flood of platitudes and obvious errors bursts in so that we are downright shocked at such cultural illiteracy? Moreover, hand in hand with technical ignorance goes Heinse's skewed aesthetic judgment, as illustrated in his analyses of operas by *Gluck, among others, Jomelli, Traetta*, in which we get almost exclusively enthusiastic exclamations instead of artistic guidance.

make us sad, who would want to live that way any longer? If a composition looks at us with clear eyes of beauty, we deeply rejoice in it, even if it had as its subject all the pain of the century. However, the loudest jubilation of a finale by Verdi or a quadrille by Musard did not always make us cheerful.

The lay and sentimental person likes to ask whether a particular music is jolly or sad, the musician whether it is good or bad. This short cast shadow shows clearly what different sides the two parties take against the sun.

When we said that our aesthetic pleasure in a piece of music orients itself to its artistic value, that does not preclude that [173] a simple horn call, a yodeler in the mountains could sometimes evoke greater delight than the most splendid symphony. However, in that case *music joins the ranks of the naturally beautiful*. The aural experience confronts us, not as *this particular structure* in tones, but rather as this particular type of *natural effect*, and can, in accord with the scenic character of the surroundings and personal mood, surpass in power all aesthetic enjoyment. Thus there is a preponderant impression that the elemental can reach beyond the artistic. However, as the doctrine of the artistically beautiful, aesthetics must conceive music exclusively from its *artistic* side, hence must acknowledge of music's effects on pure contemplation only those that it engenders as the product of human intellect through a specific design of those elemental factors.

The most necessary requirement of an aesthetic perception of music is, however, that a piece of music *is heard for its own sake*, whichever that may be, and in whichever conception. As soon as music is used only as a means [174] of promoting a certain mood in us, accessorily, decoratively, it ceases to act as pure art. The *elemental* in music is endlessly confounded with its *artistic* beauty, that is, one component is taken for the whole, thereby causing unimaginable confusion. Hundreds of pronouncements made about "the art of music" apply, not to music, but rather to the sensuous effect of its material.

In Shakespeare, when *Henry IV*, dying, calls for music to be played (Part 2, Act 4, Scene 4), it is not really to hear the piece performed but rather to lull himself, dreamily, in its ethereal element. *Portia* and *Bassanio* (in *The Merchant of Venice*) would have been as little disposed to pay attention to the requested music during the fateful casket scene [Act 2, Scene 7]. *Johann Strauss* set down charming, indeed intellectually stimulating music in his better waltzes, but it ceases to be so as soon as we only want to dance in time to it. In all of these cases, it is a matter of complete indifference *what* music is played so long as it has the [175] requested basic character. However, where indifference goes up against individuality, there *sonic effect* dominates, not *musical art*. Only someone who retains not merely the general aftereffect of feeling but rather the unforgettable, specific contemplative experience of precisely *this* particular piece of music has heard and enjoyed it. Those uplifting impressions on our mind and their high psychic as well as physiological significance may not prevent criticism from distinguishing everywhere what is artistic in a given effect from what is elemental. Aesthetic contemplation should conceive music not so much as cause than as effect, not as producing but as product.

Music's general harmonic nature—moderating and mediating repose and motion, dissonance and concordance—is confused with musical art itself as often as is the elemental effect of music. Given the current status of music and philosophy, in the interest of both we may not allow the ancient Greek extension of the concept of "music" to embrace *all* science and art, as well as the cultivation of all psychic forces. The famous apology for [176] music in *The Merchant of Venice* (Act 5, Scene 1[6]) is based on such a confounding of music itself with the spirit of euphony, of concordance, of proportion that dominate it. Without much change, we could in similar passages replace "music" with "poetry," "art," indeed with "beauty" in general. That *music* in particular tends to be singled out from the arts is due to the equivocal power of its popularity. The very next lines of the previously cited

---

6.
The man that has no music in himself,
Nor is not moved with concord of sweet sounds,
Is fit for treasons, stratagems and spoils.

address [about music] attest to this fact, in which the subduing effect of the tones on beasts is much vaunted, that is, music appearing once again as a tamer of animals.

Bettina's "musical explosions," as Goethe gallantly describes her letters about music, offer the most instructive examples. As the true prototype of all vague rhapsodizing about music, Bettina shows how inappropriately the concept of this art can be extended in order to cozily romp about with it. With the pretension [177] of talking about music itself, she speaks continually about the obscure effect that music has on her psyche, and whose rich, dreamy bliss she intentionally seals off from all probing thought. She always sees an unfathomable product of nature in a composition, not a human artwork, and thus never grasps music other than purely phenomenologically. Bettina calls countless phenomena "music," "musical," that have only one or another element in common with musical art: euphony, rhythm, arousal of feeling. However, it is not at all a matter of those factors but rather of the specific manner in which they appear in artistic design as *music*. It goes without saying that the music-intoxicated lady sees in *Goethe*, indeed in *Christ*, great musicians, even though no one knows of the latter whether he was one, whereas of the former everyone knows that he was not.

We honor the right of historical interpretation and poetic license. We understand why *Aristophanes* calls a finely cultivated intellect "wise and musical" [σοφὸν χαὶ μουσιχόν] in *The Wasps*, and find Count Reinhardt's phrase fitting [178] that [Adam] *Oehlenschläger* has "musical eyes." But scientific considerations may never attribute to, or presuppose for, music any concept other than the *aesthetic*, if all hope of eventually establishing this shaky science is not to be abandoned.

Chapter 6

The Relation of Music to Nature

[179] The relationship to nature is for every entity the first, most venerable and most influential one. Whoever even fleetingly takes the pulse of the current times knows that the dominance of that insight is in the midst of tremendous growth. A trend toward the natural aspect of all phenomena runs so strongly through modern research that even the most abstract investigations gravitate noticeably toward the method of the natural sciences. *Aesthetics*, too, if it is not to lead a mere pseudo-life, must know of the gnarly root as well as the delicate filament by which each individual art is connected to the natural foundation. And for music aesthetics in particular, the relationship of music to nature makes the most important [180] conclusions accessible. The disposition of its most complicated issues, the solution of its most controversial questions, depends on the proper appreciation of this connection.

The arts—considered initially as receiving, not yet as reacting— stand in a dual relation to surrounding nature, first through the raw, physical material from which they create, second through the beautiful content available to them for artistic treatment. Nature relates to the arts in both cases as the maternal benefactor of the first and most important endowment. We now attempt to cursorily review this endowment in the interest of music aesthetics, and to scrutinize what this rationally and thus [among the arts] unequally endowing nature has done for music.

If we investigate the extent to which nature might provide *material* [*Stoff*] for music, the outcome is that nature does so only in the sense of raw material, which humankind compels to resound in tones. The silent ore of the mountains, the wood of the forest, the skin and gut of animals are all that we find for preparing the actual building material [181] for music, *pure* tone. We thus initially receive [raw] material for [musical] material, the latter of which is pure tone, determined in height and depth, that is, measurable tone. It is the primary and inescapable prerequisite of all music, which fashions tone into *melody* and *harmony*, the two chief factors in music. Neither occurs in nature; they are creations of human intellect.

We do not hear in nature the ordered succession of measurable tones that we call *melody*, even in the most meager beginnings. Nature's successive sonic manifestations lack intelligible proportion and elude reduction to our scale. Melody, though, is the "crux of the matter," the life, the first artistic shape in the realm of tone. Every additional determination, all realization of content, is linked to it.

Nature, that magnificent harmony of all phenomena, knows as little of melody as of *harmony* in the musical sense, as the joint resounding of particular tones. Has anyone heard a triad in nature, a sixth or a seventh chord? Like melody, so too was [182] harmony a product of human intellect (only in a much slower evolution).

The Greeks knew no harmony. Rather, they sang at the octave or in unison, as those Asiatic peoples still do nowadays where singing is encountered. The use of *dissonances* (among which [for the Greeks] were the *third* and *sixth*) began gradually from the twelfth century onward, and up into the fifteenth century dissonances were restricted to progressions ending on the octave. Each of the intervals that our harmony now uses had to be achieved individually, and often even a century was not enough for such a small accomplishment. The most artistically cultivated people of antiquity, like the most learned composers of the early Middle Ages, could not do what our shepherdesses in the remotest Alps can do, singing in thirds. However, through harmony not only did a new light come about for music, but rather for the first time there was daylight. "The entire musical creation first originates from that time forward" (Nägeli).

Harmony and melody are thus lacking in nature. Only a third element in music, [183] the one by which the first two are supported, exists prior and external to humankind: *rhythm*. In the gallop of the horse, the clatter of a mill, the song of the blackbird and quail, a unity is expressed into which successive segments of time assemble and form an intuitively accessible whole. Not all but many manifestations of sound in nature are rhythmic. In particular, the law of *bipartite* rhythm, as arsis and thesis, antecedent run-up and consequent run-out predominate in nature. What distinguishes this natural rhythm from human music must be readily apparent. In *music*, there is no isolated rhythm as such, but rather only melody and harmony that manifest themselves rhythmically. By contrast, rhythm in nature bears no melody or harmony but only immeasurable air vibrations. Rhythm, the sole primordial musical element in nature, is also the first to awaken in humankind, the earliest to develop in children, in primeval humans. When South Sea islanders clatter rhythmically with pieces of metal and wooden sticks, and along with it bellow out an unintelligible howling, that is *natural* music, for it [184] is *not music* at all. However, what we hear a Tirolean peasant singing, to which apparently no trace of art has penetrated, is definitely *artifactual [künstliche] music*.[1] The man of course thinks he is just singing as it comes naturally to him. But in order for that to be possible, the seed had to grow over the centuries.

We have thus considered the necessary elemental components of our music and have found that humankind did not learn to make music from the natural world surrounding him. The history of music teaches the manner and sequence in which our current tone

---

1. *Translators' note*: Hanslick uses the German word *künstlich* here, which is an antonym to *natürlich* [natural]. In English, the most obvious antonym to "natural" would be "artificial," but "artificial" does not fit the context, and "artificial music" sounds odd to English ears. Payzant's translation of *künstlich* as "artistic" does not capture the meaning of the German original. In German, "artistic" is *künstlerisch*. Both words, *künstlich* and *künstlerisch*, have *Kunst* [art] as the root word, but whereas *künstlerisch* refers to artistic activity, *künstlich* refers to something manmade as opposed to something occurring in nature. The latter meaning is crucial here. See our essay on Hanslick's central concepts, p. xxxv.

system evolved. We have to presuppose the evidence and must only keep in mind the outcome that melody and harmony, that our intervallic relationships and scale, the division of major and minor according to the positioning of semitones, that tempered tuning, finally—without which our (European–Occidental) music would be impossible—are creations of the human intellect that arose slowly and gradually.[2] Nature has endowed humankind only with the organs and the desire to sing, additionally with the ability to gradually construct a tone system based on [185] the simplest relationships. Only these simplest relationships (triad, [numerical] harmonic series) will endure as unalterable fundamental pillars of every prospective further construction.[3] We should beware of the confusion as *though this* (present) *tone system itself* necessarily lies in nature. The experience that nowadays even naturalists deal unconsciously and casually with musical relationships as inborn powers that are self-evident by no means brands the prevailing musical laws as natural laws. This is already a consequence of the endlessly disseminated musical culture. *Hand* notes quite correctly that for this reason even our children in the cradle can already sing better than adult primitives. "If the succession of tones in music were readily available in nature, every person would always sing in tune."[4]

2. *Translators' note*: Hanslick's reference to *schwebende Temperatur* [literally beating temperament]—a form of tuning—is ambiguous. We would have expected him to specify equal [*gleichschwebend*] or unequal [*ungleichschwebend*] temperament, not just beating temperament. Every tempered tuning necessarily involves deliberately mistuning intervals, creating beats, in which each tuned interval (fourths/fifths, thirds/sixths) is slightly widened or narrowed, such that all resulting semitones are the same size (equal temperament) or varying sizes (unequal temperament). As forms of temperament, both equal and unequal temperaments were well known and used in nineteenth-century Europe (and centuries before). In stating that Western European music would be impossible without tempered tuning, Hanslick may have had equal temperament in mind. Aesthetically acceptable performance of nineteenth-century chromatic practices is not feasible without some kind of temperament, and equal temperament would have represented an ideal—though at the expense of unique characteristics of the various major and minor keys that unequal temperaments feature.

3. *Translators' note*: See p. 44, note 6, on the harmonic series, in Chapter 3.

4. Hand, *Ästhetik der Tonkunst*, vol. 1, p. 50. In the same passage, it is fittingly noted that the Gaels in Scotland share with the tribes in India the lack of the [scalar]

[186] When our tone system is called "artifactual," that word is not used in the sophisticated sense of an arbitrary conventional invention. It merely designates something evolved as opposed to something created.

Hauptmann overlooks that when he calls the concept of an artifactual tone system "completely invalid," "because musicians can as little have determined the intervals and invented a tone system as linguists can have invented words of language and syntax."[5] Language in particular is an artifactual product in the same sense as is music in that neither is modeled in surrounding nature, but rather evolved gradually and must be learned. Nations, not linguists, construct their language according to their character, and continually modify it toward perfection. In that way, too, [187] the "learned musicians" have not "erected" our music but rather have simply secured and substantiated what the general, musically enabled intellect had unconsciously conceived with rationality but not with necessity.[6] It follows from this process that our tone system, too, will undergo enrichments and modifications in the course of time. Yet such manifold and expansive developments are still possible within the current laws that a change in the *nature* of the system may seem very remote. If, for example, the enrichment were to consist in the "emancipation of quarter tones," of which a contemporary author believes to have found hints in *Chopin*,[7] theory, training in composition, and aesthetics of music would be completely different. For

---

fourth and seventh, so that the succession of their tones runs c–d–e–g–a–c. Among the physically very well-developed Patagonians in South America, there is no trace of music or singing. The development of our musical system has recently been thoroughly presented, completely agreeing in results with what has been previously said, by *Helmholtz* (*Lehre von den Tonempfindungen*).

5. Moritz Hauptmann, *Die Natur der Harmonik und der Metrik*, 1853, p. 7.

6. Our view agrees with the investigations of *Jacob Grimm*, who indicates, among other things, "Whoever has come to the opinion that language was a free invention of humankind will also not doubt the source of poetry and *music*." *Über den Ursprung der Sprache*, 1852.

7. Johanna Kinkel, *Acht Briefe über Klavierunterricht*. Cotta, 1852.

the present, then, the music theorist can scarcely [188] allow for the prospect of that future other than through the simple acknowledgment of its possibility.

People will object to our claim that there is no music in nature by pointing out the wealth of manifold voices that so wonderfully animate nature. Should the babbling of the brook, the splash of ocean waves, the thunder of avalanches, the raging of a cyclone not have been the occasion and model for human music? Did all of the whispering, whistling, crashing sounds have nothing to do with our musical life? We must in fact answer in the negative. All of these manifestations of nature are just *noise* and *sound*, that is, successive irregular vibrations of air. Very seldom, and then only in isolated instances, does nature produce a *tone*, that is, a sound of a specific, measurable height and depth.[8] However, tones are the foundational conditions of all music. No matter how powerfully or delightfully these manifestations of sound in music may stimulate the mind, they are not a step toward human music but rather merely rudimentary indications of such, although they later frequently offer very powerful stimulations for developed human [189] music. Even the purest manifestation in the sonorous world of nature, birdsong, has no relation to human music because it cannot be aligned with our scale. The phenomenon of the harmony of nature [*Naturharmonie*, i.e. overtone series]—in any case the sole and incontrovertible natural foundation upon which the chief relationships of our music are based—must also be traced to its proper significance. The harmonic series arises of its own accord on the unison-tuned Aeolian harp, is thus founded on a natural law. But we do not hear the phenomenon itself directly produced anywhere by nature. When no specific, measurable fundamental tone is played on a musical instrument,

---

8. *Translators' note*: In the German original, this passage reads "Klang von bestimmter, meßbarer Höhe and Tiefe." Payzant's translation, "sound of determinate, measurable pitch, high or low," is a bit imprecise as it lacks the idea of a continuity central to Hanslick's definition. "Measurable" refers to determinable vibration rates. See our essay on Hanslick's central concepts, p. xl.

no sympathetically vibrating subsidiary tones appear, no harmonic series.[9] The human being must thus ask so that nature can give an answer. The phenomenon of an echo is explained even more easily. It is curious how even the most competent authors cannot rid themselves of the idea of an actual "music" in nature. Even *Hand*, from whom we earlier intentionally cited examples that illustrate his insight into the incommensurable [190] character of natural sonic phenomena, unsuitable for art, includes a separate chapter titled "On the Music of Nature," whose sonic phenomena must "to some extent" also be called music. Likewise Krüger.[10] However, where questions of principle are at issue, there is no "to some extent." What we perceive in nature either *is* music or it is *not* music. The decisive factor can be located only in the measurability of tones. *Hand* emphasizes everywhere the "intellectual animation," "the expression of inner life, inner feeling," "the power of spontaneity, through which something internal achieves external expression." According to that principle, birdsong would have to be called music, the mechanical music box, by contrast, would not, when precisely the opposite is true.

The "music" of nature and the music of humankind are two different domains. The transition from the first to the second is by way of *mathematics*. An important [191] proposition, rich in consequences. Of course we cannot think of that proposition as though humankind had organized its tones according to intentionally applied calculations. That occurred, rather, through the unconscious application of primordial conceptions of magnitude and relationship, through a concealed measuring and counting, whose systematic regularities science verified only later.

Because in music everything must be commensurable, but in the sounds of nature nothing is commensurable, these two realms of

9. *Translators' note*: See also Chapter 3, note 6. Although the "primordial law of the harmonic series" is essentially a mathematical concept, Hanslick here appears to have the overtone series in mind, as a musical manifestation of the abstract mathematical relation.

10. *Beiträge für Leben und Wissenschaft der Tonkunst*, p. 149ff.

sound exist almost unreconciled side-by-side. Nature does not give us the artistic material of a completed, preconstructed tone system, but rather only the raw material of the physical masses that we make serviceable for music. Not the voices of animals but their gut is important to us, and the animal to which music owes the most is not the nightingale but the sheep.

After this inquiry, which for the case of the musically beautiful was only a substructure, though a necessary one, we advance a step higher, to the aesthetic domain.

The measurable tone and the organized tone system [192] are initially that *with which* the composer creates, not *what* he creates. Just as wood and ore are only "material" for tone, so is tone only "material" for music. There is yet a third and higher meaning of "material," material in the sense of the subject matter dealt with, the represented idea, the topic. From where does the composer take *that* material? From where does the content of a particular composition emerge, the subject matter that marks it as something individual and distinguishes it from others?

Poetry, painting, sculpture have their inexhaustible sources of material in surrounding nature. The artist finds himself stimulated by something naturally beautiful; it becomes for him material for his own creation.

Nature's precreation is most noticeable in the *visual* arts. The painter could draw no tree, no flower, if they were not prefigured in external nature, the sculptor no statue without knowing and taking the actual human figure as a pattern. The same goes for invented materials. In the strict sense, they can never be "invented." [193] Is the "ideal" landscape not composed of rocks, trees, water, and cloud shapes, all things that are prefigured in nature? The painter cannot paint anything that he has not *seen* and precisely observed, no matter whether he paints a landscape or creates a genre painting or history painting. If contemporaries paint for us a "Huß," a "Luther," an "Egmont," they have never actually seen their subject, but for every element of each they must have derived the model exactly from nature. The painter need not have seen *this* [particular] man, but he must have seen many men, how they move, stand, walk, are illuminated, throw shadows. The most brusque rebuke would certainly be the impossibility or unnaturalness of his figures.

The same holds for *poetry*, which has a yet much larger scope of beautiful models in nature. People and their actions, feelings, fates, as they are presented to us through personal awareness or through tradition (for tradition, too, is among preexisting things, things presented to the poet) are material for the poem, the tragedy, the novel. The poet can describe no [194] sunrise, no snowfield, cannot portray any state of feeling, cannot put on stage any peasant, soldier, miser, no one love-struck if he has not seen and studied the models in nature or has not animated in his imagination through accurate traditions such that they replace direct experience.

If we now counterpose *music* to those arts, we recognize that music nowhere finds a model, material for its works.

For music, there is nothing naturally beautiful.[11]

This distinction between music and the other arts is profound and has weighty consequences (only *architecture* likewise has no model in nature).

The creative work of the painter, the poet, is a constant (internal and actual) retracing, copying. There is nothing in nature for *music-making to copy*. Nature knows no sonata, no overture, no rondo, but it does know landscapes, genre images, idylls, tragedies. The Aristotelian proposition about imitation of nature in art—still commonplace among philosophers [195] of the previous century, is long since corrected and, already beaten to death—necessitates no further discussion here. Art should not slavishly imitate nature, it should *transform* it. That phrase already shows that, *before* art can occur, something had to be there to be transformed. This is precisely the model presented by nature, the naturally beautiful. The painter, on encountering a charming landscape, a group of people, a poem,

---

11. *Translators' note*: See our essay on Hanslick's central concepts, p. xxxv, for his notion of the beautiful in art vis-à-vis the beautiful in nature.

the poet a historical event, an experience, is motivated to an artistic portrayal. However, with what observation in nature could the *composer* ever exclaim: that is a splendid model for an overture, a symphony! The composer cannot *transform* anything, he has to *newly create* everything. Through the concentration of his inner being, the composer must develop what the painter, the poet encounter in observing the naturally beautiful. He must wait for the propitious moment when something begins to sing and resound within him. Then he will immerse himself and create something from within that has no equivalent in nature and, hence, unlike [196] the other arts, is also literally not of this world.

It is by no means because of partisan definition that we counted *human beings* among the "naturally beautiful" for the painter and poet, for the composer, by contrast, were silent on the artful song that springs from the human heart. The singing shepherd is not the object but already the subject of art. If his song consists of measurable, organized yet so simple tone successions, it is a product of human intellect whether a young shepherd composed it or Beethoven.

Accordingly, if a composer employs actual national melodies, that is not something naturally beautiful, for one would have to trace back to the one who invented them. From where did he get them? Did *he* find a model in nature for them? That is the rightful question. The answer can only be in the negative. The folksong is not something preexisting, not something naturally beautiful, but rather the first stage of genuine art: *naïve art*. It is for music no more a model produced by nature than flowers and soldiers scrawled with charcoal in guardhouses and [197] granaries are natural models for painting. Both are manmade products of art. Models in nature can be demonstrated for the charcoal drawings, but not for the folksong. We cannot get *behind* it.

We end up in a very familiar state of confusion if we take the concept of "material" in music in an applied, higher sense and point out that Beethoven actually wrote an overture to *Egmont* or—so that the little word "to" does not remind us of dramatic purposes—wrote a musical work *Egmont*, Berlioz a *King Lear*, Mendelssohn a *Melusina*. Did these stories, one asks, not supply the composer with material just as they did for the poet? By no means. For the poet, these figures are actual models that he transforms; for the composer, they provide merely a *stimulus*, more precisely a *poetic* stimulus. For the composer, the naturally beautiful would have to be something *audible*, as for the painter it is something visible, for the sculptor something tangible. The content [198] of Beethoven's overture is not the figure Egmont, not his deeds, experiences, attitudes, as is the case in the *portrait Egmont*, in the *play Egmont*. The content of the overture is *successions of tones*, which the composer created entirely freely from within himself according to musical laws of thought. For aesthetic contemplation, the tone successions are autonomous and completely independent of the mental image "Egmont," which only the poetic imagination of the composer has associated with the tone successions, whether in some unfathomable manner that mental image planted the seed for the invention of those tone successions or whether the composer retrospectively found the image appropriate for his precompositional idea. That association is so loose and arbitrary that someone listening to the piece would never figure out its supposed subject matter if the composer had not imposed the specific orientation on our imagination from the outset through the *explicit designation*. Berlioz's somber overture to *King Lear* is, in itself, no more connected with the mental image of the title character than a Strauss waltz. We cannot express this explicitly enough because the most erroneous views on this matter are common. The Strauss [199] waltz seems contradictory to, conversely the Berlioz overture appropriate to, the mental image of King Lear only at the moment when we *compare* those musical works with that mental image. However, there is no inherent cause for this comparison, rather only express coercion from the composer. We are compelled by a certain title to a comparison of a piece of music with an object external to it. We have to gauge it according to a certain criterion that *is not musical*.

We may perhaps say, then, Beethoven's *Prometheus* overture could be not grand enough for that precompositional idea. However, we cannot arrive at that opinion from any internal evidence in the overture, cannot anywhere demonstrate a musical breach or deficiency. It is perfect because it realizes its *musical* content completely. Realizing its *poetic* theme analogously is a second, wholly different requirement. That requirement arises and vanishes with the title. Moreover, such a requirement imposed on a musical work with a specific title can refer to only certain characteristic traits such as that music sound exalted or dainty, somber or cheerful, [200] or that it evolve from a straightforward exposition to a sorrowful conclusion, and so forth. The material imposes on poetry or painting the requirement of a specific, concrete *individuality*, not mere traits. For that reason it would certainly be conceivable that Beethoven's overture to *Egmont* could also be titled *William Tell* or *Joan of Arc*. The *play* Egmont, the *portrait of* Egmont allow at most the mix-up that it is a different individual in the same circumstances, but not that it is completely different circumstances.

We see how closely the relationship of music to the naturally beautiful is connected to the whole question of music's *content*.

One might bring up another objection from the musical repertoire to claim that music can be naturally beautiful. Examples, namely, that composers have taken from nature, not merely the poetic motivation (as in the aforementioned histories), but have directly imitated actually audible expressions of nature's sonic life: the rooster call in Haydn's *The Seasons*, the cuckoo, nightingale, and quail calls in Spohr's *Consecration of Tones* and [201] in Beethoven's *Pastoral Symphony*. But when we *hear* even this imitation, and hear it in a *musical* artwork, they have in it no musical but rather poetic significance. The rooster's call should then be presented to us not as *beautiful* music, or as music at all. Rather, only the impression that is associated with that natural phenomenon is supposed to be recalled. "I have practically seen Haydn's *Creation*," *Jean Paul* writes to *Thieriot* after a performance of that work. It is generally familiar keywords, quotations, that remind us that it is early morning, mild summer's night, spring. Without that merely descriptive tendency [in music], a composer has never been able to utilize sounds of nature directly for actual musical purposes. All of the sounds of nature on earth together cannot produce a *theme* precisely because they are *not music*,[12] and it seems significant [202] that music can make use of nature only when it dabbles superficially in painting.

12. From this misapprehension of directly importing natural sounds literally into the artwork—which, as Otto Jahn aptly notes, can be conceded only in rare cases in jest—it is surely wholly different, and should actually not be called painting, when through their rhythmic or harmonic character certain quasi-musically functioning elements existing in nature are not exactly "imitated" by composers—as contained in rustling and splashing of water, birdsong, wind and weather, the whizzing of arrows, the whirring of the spinning wheel, and the like—but rather offer composers impulses for themes of autonomous beauty, which they artistically freely conceive and elaborate. "The poet invokes this right in language as in rhythm. In music, however, it extends much further because many of the musical elements are scattered throughout the whole of nature," and wonderful examples from our classical no less than from our contemporary composers (who operate incomparably more refined than the classicists) are for everyone abundantly present to mind.

Chapter 7

The Concepts "Content"
and "Form" in Music

[203] *Does music have a content?*

Since people began to reflect on our art, that has been its most heatedly debated issue. It has been decided pro and con. Weighty opinions assert the lack of content in music. They are almost all *philosophers: Rousseau, Kant, Hegel, Herbart,*[1] *Kahlert,* among others. Of the numerous physiologists who support these convictions, the most important for us [204] are *Lotze* and *Helmholtz*, thinkers outstanding for their musical erudition. The incomparably more numerous contenders argue for the *content* of music! Those are the actual *musicians* among the authors, and the majority of general opinion stands with them.

It may seem almost strange that precisely those who are conversant with the technical determinants of music cannot break free from the error of a view that contradicts those [technical] conditions, a view for which we could more easily excuse the abstract philosophers. That is because on this point it is for many authors on music more a matter of the putative honor of their art than of truth. They combat the doctrine of the lack of content in music, not as opinion against opinion, but as heresy against dogma. The opposing view seems to them an unworthy misapprehension, a crude, outrageous

---

1. In his *Allgemeine Ästhetik als Formwissenschaft* (Vienna, 1865), Robert Zimmermann has most recently developed in rigorous ramifications the formal principle for all arts, thus also for music, on a *Herbartian* foundation.

materialism. "What, the art that elevates and inspires us, to which so many noble minds have dedicated their lives, which can serve the loftiest ideas: that art is supposed to be freighted with the curse of lacking content, mere mechanical workings [205] of the senses, empty tinkling!?" With that kind of oft-heard exclamations, as they usually let fly in pairs even though one sentence does not follow from the other, nothing is refuted or proved. It is not a matter here of a point of honor, of partisanship, but simply of the recognition of truth, and to attain that, one must above all be clear about the concepts that one contests.

It is the confounding of the concepts of *content* [*Inhalt*], *subject matter* [*Gegenstand*], and *material* [*Stoff*] that has caused and continues to cause such a lack of clarity on the issue, as everyone uses a different term for the same concept, or links different ideas with the same word. "*Content*," in the original and actual sense, is what something *contains*, holds within itself. In that meaning, the *tones* that constitute a piece of music, which as its components form a whole, are the content. No one is likely to be satisfied with that answer, dismissing it as something entirely self-evident, because we commonly confound "content" and "subject matter." [206] On the issue of "content" [*Inhalt*] in music, people have in mind the notion of a "*subject matter*" [*Gegenstand*] (material, topic), which as the idea, as the abstract ideal, they almost contrapose to the tones as "material constituents." In fact, music does not have a content [*Inhalt*] in that definition, a *material* [*Stoff*] in the sense of the subject matter [*Gegenstand*] treated. With justification, *Kahlert* emphatically buttresses his argument that music does not allow for providing a "verbal description," as does painting (*Aesthetics*, p. 380), although his additional assumption is erroneous that such a verbal description could ever offer a "remedy for the lacking enjoyment of art." However, it can provide a clarificatory understanding of what is at issue. The question of the "What" of musical content would necessarily have to allow for a verbal answer if the piece of music really had a "content" [*Inhalt*] (a *subject matter* [*Gegenstand*]). For an "indefinite content," which everyone can conceive differently, which allows itself only to be felt, not reproduced in words, is precisely not a content in the aforementioned definition.

Music consists of tone successions, tone forms; [207] these have no content other than themselves. They remind us once again of architecture and dance, which likewise present us with beautiful relationships without a specific content. However each person, according to his individuality, may speak of and designate the effect of a piece of music, its *content* is nothing but just the heard tone forms. For music speaks not merely *through* tones, its speaks *only* tones.

Krüger, probably the most knowledgeable defender of musical "content" against Hegel and Kahlert, claims that music gives merely a different *facet* of the same content that is due the other arts, for example, painting. "Every graphically vivid form," he says (*Beiträge*, p. 131), "is inert. It conveys, not the action, but the past action or the state of being [*das Seiende*]. Thus the painting does not state that Apollo conquers but rather shows the conqueror, the furious warrior," and so forth. On the contrary, "music furnishes the verb, the action, the inner surging, for that stationary, vivid noun. And if with painting we have recognized raging, loving as the true inert content, then with music we recognize [208] no less the true impelling content: [it] rages, loves, rustles, surges, storms." The latter claim is only half correct. Music can "rustle," "surge," and "storm," but it cannot "rage" and "love." Those are empathically projected passions. Here we must refer back to our second chapter. *Krüger* continues to set the determination of *musically performed* content side by side with that of *painted* content. He says, "The *visual artist* represents Orestes pursued by the Furies. On the exterior of his body, in eye, mouth, forehead, and posture, there appears the expression of someone fleeing, somber, despairing, beside him the figures of the curse that rule over him in commanding, frightful grandeur, likewise externally in frozen outlines, facial features, postures. The *composer* presents the pursued Orestes, not in static outline, but from the perspective that the visual artist lacks. He sings of the horror and trembling of his soul, of the fighting impulse in flight," and so forth. This is in my opinion completely wrong. The composer can represent *Orestes* neither so nor so; he cannot represent him *at all*.

[209] One ought not to argue that the visual arts are in fact also incapable of giving us the specific historical personage and that we would not recognize the painted figure as *that* individual if we did not bring to it the knowledge of the historically factual circumstances. Of course it is not *Orestes*, the man with *these* experiences and specific biographical factors. That Orestes only the *poet* can represent because only he is able to narrate. Yet the *image* "Orestes" surely shows us unmistakably a youth with noble features, in Greek attire, fear and anguish in his countenances and movements. It shows us the frightful figures of the goddesses of vengeance pursuing and tormenting him. That is all clear, indubitable, visibly narratable, whether the man is named Orestes or otherwise. Only the themes—that the youth has committed matricide, and so forth—are not expressible. In response to that visible content of the painting (abstracted from the historical circumstances), what can music offer in specificity? Diminished seventh chords, minor-mode themes, surging basses and the like, in short, musical forms that could just as well signify a woman instead of a [210] young man, someone pursued by henchmen instead of by Furies, someone jealous, vengeful, someone tormented by physical pain—in short, could mean anything imaginable if we really want to have the piece of music mean something.

There is probably no need to refer to the earlier established proposition that, in speaking about the content and the representational capability of music, it is necessary to proceed only from pure *instrumental music* as a starting point. No one will forget that to the point of countering us, for example, with Orestes in Gluck's *Iphigenia*. Of course the *composer* does not provide that "Orestes." The poet's words, performer's figure and facial expressions, costuming, and the painter's scenery—these are what create the complete Orestes. What the composer adds to that is perhaps the *most beautiful element* of all, but it is precisely the only element that has nothing to do with the actual Orestes: singing.

Lessing has explained with wonderful clarity what the poet and what the visual artist are able to make out of the story of Laocoön. Through language, the poet [211] presents the individualized specific, historic Laocoön, the painter and sculptor, by contrast, an aged man with two boys (of a particular age, appearance, dress, etc.), entwined by the dreadful serpents, expressing the agony of impending death through mien, posture, and gesture. Lessing says nothing about the *composer*. Fully understandable, for there is indeed nothing for a composer to make of Laocoön.

We have already indicated how closely the issue of the *content* of music is connected with its status vis-à-vis the *naturally beautiful*. The composer nowhere finds a model [in nature] for his art, which in the other arts ensure the specificity and recognizability of their content. An art that lacks the naturally beautiful prefigured will be, in the actual sense, incorporeal. Nowhere do we encounter the primordial image of its manifestation, and it is therefore lacking in the sphere of our accumulated concepts. The image reproduces no already familiar, named subject matter. For our thinking, conceived in definite concepts, music therefore has no nameable content.

We can really speak of the *content* of an artwork only when we juxtapose that content [212] to a *form*. The concepts "content" and "form" mutually depend on and complement one another. Where for thought a form does not seem separable from a content, there exists no autonomous content. However, in music we see content and form, material and design, image and idea fused in an obscure, indivisible unity. This uniqueness of music in possessing form and content indivisibly contrasts sharply with literary and visual arts, which can represent the same idea, the same event in different forms. *Florian* created a historical novel from the story of William Tell, *Schiller* a play, *Goethe* began to work on it as an epic. The content is the same in all cases, to be resolved into prose, narratable, recognizable, [although] the form is different. Aphrodite rising from the ocean is the same content in innumerable painted and sculpted artworks, which are not confused with one another because of the different forms. With music, there is no content opposed to form, because it has no form outside of the content. Let us consider this more closely.

[213] In every composition, the independent unit of musical thought, aesthetically not capable of further division, is the *theme*. The primitive designations that people ascribe to *music* as such must always be demonstrable in the *theme*, the musical microcosm. Let us listen to any main theme, for example to Beethoven's B-flat major symphony. What is its content, its form? Where does the latter begin and the former end? We hope to have demonstrated, and it will seem only ever more evident in this and in every other concrete instance, that a specific feeling could not be the content of the movement. What, then, will we call the *content*? The tones themselves? Certainly. But they are already formed. What will we call the *form*? Again, the tones themselves. But they are already *fulfilled* form.

Every attempt in practice to try to separate form from content in a theme leads to contradiction or caprice. For example, does a theme that is repeated by a different instrument or in a higher octave change its content or its form? If we assert the latter, as usually occurs, there would remain as *content* [214] of the theme merely the series of intervals as such, as a pattern of note heads as they present themselves to the eye in the score. However, that is not *musical* specificity but something abstract. It is similar to colored glass windows of a pavilion through which we can view the same scene in red, blue, yellow. The scene changes thereby neither its *content* or its *form* but merely the *coloring*. Such countless changes in color of the same forms, from the most glaring contrast to the most subtle shadings, is highly typical for music, and constitutes one of the richest and most developed facets of its effectiveness.

A melody designed for piano that someone later orchestrates likewise obtains thereby a *new* form, but not *form* for the first time. It is already a formed idea. Less yet would we attempt to claim that, through transposition, a theme would alter its *content* and retain the form, as in that view the contradictions are doubled. The listener must presently reply that he recognizes a content familiar to him, but "it sounds changed."

[215] With entire compositions, especially of larger scope, we of course tend to speak of their form and content. But then we are not using those concepts in their original logical sense but rather in a specifically *musical* meaning. We call the "form" of a symphony, overture, sonata, aria, a chorus, and so forth, the architectonic of the joined individual components and groups of which the piece of music consists, more precisely, the symmetry of those components in their succession, contrast, recurrence, and development. We then understand the content to be the *themes* worked into such an architectonic. Thus there is no more talk here of a content as "subject matter" but solely of a musical content. Accordingly, in the case of whole pieces, "content and "form" are used in an artistically applied definition, not in the purely logical one. If we want to apply *that* purely logical definition to the concept of music, we must concern ourselves, not with a whole and therefore composite artwork, but with its ultimate core, which is aesthetically not capable of further division. That is the *theme* or themes. With them, form and [216] content cannot be separated in any sense. If we want to identify the "content" of the theme for someone, we have to *play the theme itself* for him. The content of a musical work can therefore never be understood concretely but rather only musically, namely as that which actually resounds in each piece of music. Because the composition follows formal laws of beauty, its course is not improvised in capricious, aimless rambling but rather develops in an organically, clearly organized, gradual manner, like luxuriant blossoms from a single bud.

This bud is the *main theme*, the true material and content (subject matter) of the entire tone structure. Everything in that structure is a spontaneous consequence and impact of the theme, conditioned and shaped by it, dominated and fulfilled by it. It is the autonomous axiom that satisfies in the moment, but that our intellect wants to see contested and developed, as then occurs in the musical elaboration, analogous to a logical chain of reasoning. Like the principal character of a novel, the composer places the theme into the most diverse contexts and environments, into the most varying outcomes and moods. Everything else, [217] no matter how contrasting, is conceived and shaped with reference to it.

Accordingly, we will for instance call *"contentless"* that most impromptu preludizing in which the performer, more relaxing than actively creating, indulges in chords, arpeggios, modulatory sequences, without allowing an autonomous tone configuration to emerge distinctly. Such impromptu preludes are not recognizable or distinguishable as individualized compositions. We might say they have no content (in the broader sense) because they have no theme.

The theme, or themes, of a piece of music is therefore its essential content.

Aesthetics and criticism have fallen far short of placing the proper emphasis on the *main theme* of the composition. The main theme alone already reveals the mind that created the entire work. When a Beethoven begins the overture to *Lenore* or a Mendelssohn the overture to *Fingal's Cave* in a particular way, every musician, without knowing, sensing, a note of the further elaboration, will know before what palace he is standing. But when we are confronted with the theme like that of Donizetti's *Fausta* Overture or [218] Verdi's *Luisa Miller*, no further probing into the interior is necessary in order to convince us that we are in a tavern. In Germany, theory and practice place a preponderant value on musical elaboration as opposed to thematic substance [*Gehalt*]. But whatever does not reside in the theme (overtly or covertly) cannot subsequently be organically developed, and it is perhaps less a matter of the art of development than of the symphonic potency and fecundity of the *themes* that our day has no more Beethovenian orchestral works to show.

With the issue of the *content* of music, we must be particularly careful of taking the word in a laudatory sense. It does not follow from the fact that music has no content [*Inhalt*] (subject matter [*Gegenstand*]) that it is devoid of *substance* [*Gehalt*]. Those who campaign with partisan zeal for the "content" of music apparently mean "intellectual substance." We must refer here to what was said in chapter 3. Music is [a kind of] playing [*Spiel*] but not playing around [*Spielerei*]. Thoughts and feelings flow like blood in the arteries of the harmoniously [219] beautiful body of sound. They are not the *body*, are also not *visible*, but they animate it. The composer *poetizes* and *thinks*. However, he poetizes and thinks in *tones*, removed from all concrete reality. That triviality must still be expressly repeated here because it is all-too-often denied and breached in its consequences, even by those who acknowledge it in principle. They think of composing as the translation of a conceived content [*Stoff*] into tones, when in fact the tones themselves are the untranslatable primordial language. The lack of content in music follows from the fact that the composer is forced to think in tones, as every conceptual content would have to be able to be conceived in *words*.

Although in the investigation of *content* [*Inhalt*] we had to strictly exclude all music on specified texts as contradictory to the pure concept of music, the masterworks of vocal music are nevertheless indispensable in the appreciation of the *substance* [*Gehalt*] of music. From basic song up to richly appointed opera and the venerable religious ceremony by means of church music, music [220] never ceased to accompany and thus indirectly to glorify the most cherished and important activities of the human mind.

Along with our claim for intellectual *substance* [*Gehalt*], a second result must be emphatically highlighted. The subjectless formal beauty of music does not prevent it from being able to mark its creations with *individuality*. The manner of artistic treatment, as well as the invention of a particular theme, is in any case so unique that it can never dissolve into a higher generality, but rather exists as something *individual*. A melody by Mozart or Beethoven stands as firmly and unalloyed on its own feet as a verse of *Goethe*, an adage of *Lessing*, a statue of *Thorwaldsen*, a painting of *Overbeck*. Autonomous musical ideas (themes) have the certitude of a quotation and the vividness of a painting. They are individualized, personal, eternal.

If we thus cannot share *Hegel*'s view of the lack of substance in music, it seems to us yet more erroneous that he assigns to that art only the communication of the "unindividualized [221] interior." Even from *Hegel*'s musical standpoint, which overlooks the essentially formative, objective activity of the composer—conceiving music as a spontaneous externalizing of *subjectivity*—the "lack of individuality" of that subjectivity does not follow, because the subjectively creative intellect appears essentially as individualized.

In chapter 3, we touched on how individuality imprints itself in the choice and treatment of the different musical elements. Countering the *charge* of a lack of content, therefore, music does have a content, but musical content, which is no less a spark of divine fire than the beautiful in every other art. However, only by unrelentingly denying every other kind of "content" [*Inhalt*] for music can we rescue its "substance" [*Gehalt*]. For an intellectual significance for music cannot be derived from indefinite feeling, to which that content can, at best, be traced, but can very well be derived from the definite beautiful tone configuration as the spontaneous creation of the intellect out of material of intellectual capacity [cf. chapter 3, p. 45].[2]

2. *Translators' note*: This is how Hanslick ended the text from the third edition onward. In Mark Evan Bonds's words, Hanslick "amputated" most of the book's original ending in the second edition and, finally, the remaining part in the third. For the missing passage and the context of Hanslick's deletion, see our Appendix.

APPENDIX

A.1 CHAPTER 1 (FIRST EDITION), OPENING PARAGRAPHS

[1] The time is past of aesthetic systems that considered the beautiful only in reference to the "sensations" [*Empfindungen*] it evokes.[1] The urgency for objective knowledge of things, insofar as it is granted to human investigation, had to topple a method that begins with subjective sensation in order to end up back at sensation after a stroll across the entire fringe of the investigated phenomenon. No path leads to the heart of the matters, yet every path must be directed there. The courage and the ability to penetrate to the matters themselves—to investigate what their permanent, objective, unchangingly valid aspect might be, detached from the thousandfold shifting impressions that they wield on a human—that courage and ability characterize modern science in its various branches.

This objective approach could not fail straightaway to inform research of *the beautiful*. The philosophical treatment of aesthetics, which attempts to approach the nature of the beautiful by way of metaphysics and to reveal its ultimate elements, is an achievement of more recent times.

All the same, in the treatment of aesthetic issues, should a reversal in scholarship be under way that, in place of a metaphysical principle, were to promote to powerful influence and, at least, to temporary predominance a

1. Eduard Hanslick, *Vom Musikalisch-Schönen: Ein Beitrag zur Revision der Aesthetik der Tonkunst* (Leipzig: Rudolph Weigel, 1854), pp. 1–2.

perspective allied with the method of inductive science, meanwhile the latest leaders of our scholarly community are still present and remembered, and [2] for all time merit credit for having annihilated the sovereignty of the unscientific aesthetics of sensations, and for having thoroughly researched the beautiful in its native, pure elements.

If at one point the elements of the beautiful were evident in their generality, it was the province of the experts to investigate the specific manner in which those elements manifest themselves in and determine the individual arts.

The aesthetic principles of painting, architecture, music had to be determined and *aesthetics specialized* for the individual arts developed. Those genre-specific aesthetics are of course to be substantiated in a wholly different manner than through a mere adaptation of the general concept of beauty because that concept involves a series of new differentiations in each art. Every art must be known in its technical determinants, demands to be understood and evaluated from within itself. The genre-specific aesthetics, as well as their practical derivatives, the art critics, must in all differences of their viewpoints nevertheless unite in the one inalienable conviction, that in aesthetic investigations the beautiful object is primarily to be researched, and not the perceiving subject. They must break with the older manner of contemplation, which undertook the investigation solely in consideration of—almost *out* of consideration for—the feelings evoked by the object, and raised the philosophy of the *beautiful* from baptism as a daughter of *sensation* [άισθησις].

Objective contemplation is today no longer a merely scientific attainment but rather has quite generally penetrated into artistic consciousness. Modern poets or painters hardly persuade themselves to have accounted for the beautiful in their art by investigating what "feelings" this landscape painting, that comedy, conjures up in the public. Rather, they seek to find in the characteristic nature of the artwork itself those elements that mark it as something beautiful, and precisely that particular type of the beautiful. For them, the mere fact of awakened delight does not suffice. They will trace the compelling power behind *why* the work pleases.

A.2 COMMENTARY

Our excerpt from the first edition of chapter one, just provided, is limited to the initial contiguous passages of *On the Musically Beautiful* (*OMB*) as it appeared in 1854. It shows how Hanslick originally organized the opening section of the book. From the second edition of 1858 onward, *OMB* starts with the tenth-edition text that we translated. In the remaining sections of chapter one, Hanslick reorganized and expanded parts of the text and added footnotes. In the sixth edition (1881), he undertook more substantial changes, among them, notably, a long footnote presenting and criticizing Herbart's remarks on music aesthetics (Chapter 1, pp. 10–11 of our translation). Further, for the sixth edition he also cut a long passage on the relation of feelings and beauty and replaced it with a passage that lacks some of the general remarks on the separation of aesthetics and psychology. Instead, Hanslick offers an elaborated account of the historical relativity of musical tastes and ideals. The passage (Chapter 1, pp. 8–9) is consistent with the newly added footnote in chapter three, where Hanslick also emphasizes the historical dimension of musical beauty (Chapter 3, pp. 57–58, note 14).

The most significant emendation with respect to all editions is the new beginning of chapter one, the most significant deletion the "amputated ending" of chapter seven. Both passages appear in this Appendix. Although it is not our goal to give a comprehensive overview of all changes in the ten editions of the book published during Hanslick's lifetime, some of the changes provide useful information about his aesthetics: the way it was originally conceived and the way it evolved over the decades.

Awareness of the different versions of *OMB* and their importance for a full understanding of Hanslick's aesthetics has increased in recent years, helping to prevent misinterpretations, though not entirely. Gordon Epperson, for instance, mistakenly maintained in 1967 that Hanslick's aesthetics never allowed "an opening for 'something more,'" meaning the possibility of extramusical content.[2] It was precisely this "something more" that Hanslick addressed at the end of the first edition, but that he deleted in subsequent ones.[3] In a recent article, Mark Evan Bonds provides a comprehensive analysis of this "amputated" ending, as he calls it.[4] Peter Kivy, still asserting that *OMB* remained "substantially unchanged throughout the numerous editions," shares Bonds's view of the amputated passages.[5] However, although the changes that Hanslick made at the end of the book (and in a few other related passages) are well documented and vividly

---

2. Gordon Epperson, *The Musical Symbol: An Exploration in Aesthetics* (Ames: Iowa State University Press, 1967), p. 121.

3. Bojan Bujić comments on the deletions in "Delicate Metaphors," *The Musical Times* 138 (1997), pp. 16–22, 19.

4. Mark Evan Bonds, "Aesthetic Amputations: Absolute Music and the Deleted Endings of Hanslick's *Vom musikalisch-Schönen*," *19th-Century Music* 36, no. 1 (2012), pp. 3–23.

5. Peter Kivy, *Antithetical Arts: On the Ancient Quarrel Between Literature and Music* (Oxford: Clarendon, 2009), pp. 66–67.

debated today, the heavily reworked opening section of chapter one that we translated—by far the most extensive alteration in the second and all later editions—has attracted relatively little attention. It is plausible that both the deleted ending of chapter seven and the reworked opening of chapter one are reactions to Zimmermann's review of *OMB*, though Anglo-American scholarship has barely examined and discussed the reasons and motivations for the new beginning.[6]

Whereas the new beginning of *OMB*, with a few pages completely rewritten for the second edition, went almost unnoticed even by the scholarly community, the relatively short amputated ending of the treatise stirred quite a bit of controversy.[7] As Zimmermann observed in his review, the original ending does not quite align with the rest of the treatise. It is only in those closing passages that Hanslick allowed for an extramusical and, so to speak, deeper significance of music. Here is the passage in its original, first-edition wording (1854):

> In the psyche of the listener, furthermore, this intellectual substance [*Gehalt*] unites the beautiful in music with all other grand and beautiful ideas. Music affects the psyche not merely and absolutely by means of its own particular beauty, but rather simultaneously as a sounding reflection of the great motions of the cosmos. Through profound and covert relationships to nature, the significance of tones increases far above themselves, and allows us at the same time always to feel the infinite in the work of human talent. Because the elements of music—sound, tone, rhythm, forcefulness, gentleness—exist in the entire universe, so does man rediscover the entire universe in music.[8]

Hanslick first amputated the opening sentence of the original ending in the second edition ("In the psyche . . . beautiful ideas"), but then decided to excise the whole passage in revisions for the third edition (1865). As Bonds observes, the deletion is related to a similar passage in chapter three, where Hanslick removes a remark on music's ability to "possess symbolic significance reflecting the great cosmic laws."[9]

---

6. Robert Zimmermann, "Vom Musikalisch-Schönen," *Studien und Kritiken*, vol. 2 (Vienna: Wilhelm Braumüller, 1870), pp. 239–53.

7. Christoph Landerer and Nick Zangwill, "Hanslick's Deleted Ending," *British Journal of Aesthetics* 57, no.1 (2017), pp. 85–95.

8. Hanslick, *Vom Musikalisch-Schönen*, 1st ed., p. 104.

9. Hanslick, *Vom Musikalisch-Schönen*, 1st ed., p. 32.

Apart from the unexplained amputation of the original ending and related passages, and from the new beginning of chapter one, textual changes in the various other editions of *OMB* are typically less noteworthy. Hanslick corrected errors, expanded a few passages, and cut others. He updated references to scientific findings and incorporated more material relating to the latest scientific developments.[10] However, there are two developments in the text that are crucial for understanding how his aesthetics is rooted in contemporary philosophical and musical discourses and how Hanslick's position changed over time. Compared with the first edition of *OMB*, Hanslick downplayed the relevance of Friedrich Theodor Vischer by cutting several references and adding references to Herbart, including some critical observations.[11] He also added and sharpened remarks on Wagner and Liszt, though his growing resistance to the "music of the future" is confined chiefly to the different versions of the Preface. Remarkably little of that appears in the main text. At the same time, Hanslick did change his views about preclassical music, at least to some degree. While he polemicized more vigorously against the latest musical developments of his time, his attitude toward Bach became more nuanced—and more tolerant. Despite all the unreconciliatory polemics against the "music of the future," however, Hanslick's opposition to Wagner ultimately softened, though not in *OMB*. In a public letter on Wagner's *Parsifal*, written from Bayreuth in 1882, Hanslick called Wagner "the single German composer since Weber and Meyerbeer who cannot be excluded from the history of dramatic music" without leaving a gap.[12] The late Hanslick, it seems, had more receptive ears both for the old masters and for the "Meister" of Bayreuth.

10. See the introductory essay on the book and its history.
11. See the introductory essay on Hanslick's philosophical background.
12. Hanslick, "Briefe aus Bayreuth über Wagner's *Parsifal* IV," *Neue Freie Presse* 6441, 2. August 1882, p. 3.

GLOSSARY

Affect: Belongs to the emotive vocabulary that Hanslick employs. The term is not well defined, and can be both "sentiment" and "feeling" (see the entries for those two words).

Architectonic, the: Denotes an overarching, integrated structure built upon "the joined individual components and groups of which the piece of music consists" (Chapter 7, p. 113). See also "Large-scale rhythm."

Beauty/the beautiful: For both the beautiful conceived as a beautiful object (i.e., a piece of music) and beauty as an abstract trait or group of properties, Hanslick uses the German word *das Schöne* (or *Schönheit*, beauty, when clearly referring to the abstract concept of beauty). This a major source of confusion, though one that often goes unnoticed to the German reader. We have tried to avoid constructions sounding too awkward to the Anglophone ear but have kept Hanslick's usage of "the beautiful" as referring to a beautiful object in a number of cases in which a smoother solution would have led to misunderstanding.

Contemplation: An act or attitude that, in the reception of an artwork, enables the viewer or listener to systematically set aside every aspect that is not of specifically aesthetic nature or relevance. Hanslick describes contemplation as an "act of attentive listening" (Chapter 1, p. 6). He uses *Anschauung* and *Betrachtung* more or less interchangeably. We translate both terms as "contemplation."

Content: Hanslick distinguishes between music's "content" and its "substance." Music has no content [*Inhalt*] other than the tones of a musical piece, that is, its "sonically moved forms."

Elemental: Apart from purely aesthetic aspects, music also possesses an "elemental" or "pathological" side, founded in bodily reactions of listeners and the nervous system. "Pathological" and "aesthetic" listening are two opposed poles of receptive behavior, as Hanslick clearly states: "The more significant the *aesthetic* aspect in the listener (just as in the artwork), the more levelled out is the merely elemental" (Chapter 5, p. 90).

Feeling: This is at the center of Hanslick's emotive vocabulary. It is important to note that "feeling," as Hanslick uses the term in *OMB*, has a cognitive component. Feelings "are dependent on physiological and pathological conditions, are conditioned by mental images, judgments, in short by the entire range of intelligible and rational thought to which people so willingly juxtapose feeling as something opposite" (Chapter 2, p. 15).

Form/forms: Hanslick's aesthetic approach is generally seen as "formalist," but the very term "form," or "forms," is not easy to determine. Contrary to the classical tradition, where "form" refers to the "architectonic" of a piece (see the entry for the word "architectonic"), the constituents of Hanslick's "forms" are the smallest musical units, that is, the individual tones.

Idea (musical idea): The theme or melody (see also "Motive") is at the hub of Hanslick's aesthetics. It is often addressed as "idea" or "thought" (usually translated as "idea" in our translation). Hanslick has a cognitive conception of the theme (as opposed to an emotive one): It is the product of a thought process, but that thought process is a specifically musical one. It is in this sense that Hanslick calls the theme a "formed idea" (Chapter 7, p. 112).

Imagination: Similar to *Geist* (see "intellect") in that it constitutes a connecting link between performer and recipient: "A musical piece emerges from the imagination of the artist for the imagination of the listener" (Chapter 1, p. 5). Imagination is the psychological capacity that enables the composer or listener to act on music in an intellectually meaningful way.

Intellect: *Geist* is one of most central terms of *OMB* and virtually untranslatable. We maintain what we consider the core meaning of *Geist* in Hanslick's aesthetics, which is centered around "intellect," as opposed to "spirituality" or "ideality," used in many instances in the translations by Cohen and Payzant. A detailed discussion of Hanslick's concept of *Geist* appears in our essay on Hanslick's central concepts. *Geist* is present on all levels of musical creation and reception: on the side of the artist, the performer, the listener, and even in the musical material itself that Hanslick determines as *geistfähig* ("material of intellectual capacity" in our translation).

Large-scale rhythm: Similar to the "architectonic" in that Hanslick refers to the overarching structure or "rhythm" of a piece, "the consistency of a symmetrical structure" (Chapter 3, p. 40).

Material: Hanslick not only differentiates music's content from its substance, he also distinguishes between music's "material" [*Stoff*] and its "subject matter" [*Gegenstand*]. Music has a specific material, but one that is confined to tones.

Mind: The English term "mind" usually designates a broader spectrum of psychic states than the German word *Geist*. German *Geist* terms are tricky, and "mind" in our translation generally equates to "intellect."

Motive: See *Theme*.

Musically beautiful, the: Hanslick advocates for a genre-specific aesthetic, as opposed to an understanding of musical aesthetics as expressing general laws of beauty derived from a general philosophy of art. The "musically beautiful" [*Musikalisch-Schönes*] refers to beautiful–aesthetic features that are specific to music as an artistic genre.

Naturally beautiful, the: Contrary to the "musically beautiful" as a manmade artifact, the "naturally beautiful" is not the product of human intellect and hence also not relevant for musical aesthetics: "For music, there is nothing naturally beautiful" (Chapter 6, p. 102).

Pathological: See *Elemental*. Both terms refer to music's bodily effect, its impact on the nervous system.

Psychic disposition/psyche [Gemüt]: The term *Gemüt* is not easy to translate. English lacks a term with a similar meaning and generality. *Gemüt* comprises both the emotional and the cognitive aspects of the human mind. We use "psyche" or "psychic disposition," except for a few instances in which "mind" seemed more idiomatic (see the entry for the word "mind").

Sensation: Whereas "feeling" designates the complex end product of an emotive process, "sensation" is at the start of this process. "Sensation is the perception of a specific sensory quality, a tone, a color. Feeling is the awareness of a furthering or an inhibiting of our psychic state" (Chapter 1, p. 4).

Sentiment: Apart from "sensation," Hanslick uses the German term *Empfindung* also in a second meaning, one that refers to schematic emotional states (affects) that were linked to music–rhetorical figures by eighteenth-century theorists [*Affektenlehre*]. In that connotation, we use the term "sentiment."

Sonically moved forms: This famous phrase (Chapter 3, p. 41) is again virtually untranslatable. In the phrase, and in the paragraphs that follow it, Hanslick gives an explanation of the central components of what he considers the content of music: form, motion, and sound. We offer a new rendering that differs from Payzant's and Cohen's. Our essay on Hanslick's central concepts explains in detail our translation of this Hanslickian music-aesthetic motto.

Specifically musical, the: The "specifically musical" is one of the most central and yet most elusive concepts of Hanslick's aesthetics. Specifically musical beauty is "independent and not in need of an external content, something that resides solely in the tones and their artistic connection" (Chapter 3, p. 40). However, as Hanslick admits, defining the specifically musical is "extraordinarily difficult." He only gives an approximation *ex negativo* by differentiating the concept from architecture, symmetry, mathematics, and language.

Subject matter: Because music has no content other than its tones, it can have no "subject matter" in the sense of a topic, realized through musical means. Both content and subject matter are categories external to music and therefore contradict Hanslick's strictly internalist approach.

Substance: Whereas music has no content other than the tones of the piece, its "substance" [*Gehalt*] is of an intellectual nature and defines its aesthetic significance.

Theme: As the centerpiece of Hanslick's aesthetic conception, the theme or melody is the "fundamental form of musical beauty" (Chapter 3, p. 40). The theme and its development are thus also the main factors that determine the aesthetic significance of a musical work. Hanslick does not distinguish between "theme" and "motive" and uses both terms interchangeably, theme being the more prevalent term.

Tone: The concept of a tone is the most basic one in Hanslick's musical terminology. In German, *Ton* serves as a root word for a broad variety of collocations and word combinations such as *Tonleiter* [scale], *Tonhöhe* [pitch], and *Tonart* [key]. Tones are "the foundational conditions of all music" (Chapter 6, p. 99). In Hanslick's aesthetics, a tone is distinctly defined as "a sound of specific, measurable height and depth" (Chapter 6, p. 99).

SELECTED BIBLIOGRAPHY
IN ENGLISH

Alperson, Philip. "The Philosophy of Music: Formalism and Beyond." In *The Blackwell Guide to Aesthetics*, ed. Peter Kivy. Oxford: Blackwell, 2004, 254–75.

Anderson, Robert. "Polemics or Philosophy? Music Pathology in Eduard Hanslick's 'Vom Musikalisch-Schönen.'" *The Musical Times* 154 (2013), 65–76.

Appelqvist, Hanne. "Form and Freedom: The Kantian Ethos of Musical Formalism." *The Nordic Journal of Aesthetics* 40–41 (2011), 75–88.

Bonds, Mark Evan. *Absolute Music: The History of an Idea*. New York: Oxford University Press, 2014.

Bonds, Mark Evan. "Aesthetic Amputations: Absolute Music and the Deleted Endings of Hanslick's 'Vom Musikalisch-Schönen.'" *19th-Century Music* 36.1 (2012), 3–23.

Bonds, Mark Evan. "Idealism and the Aesthetics of Instrumental Music at the Turn of the Nineteenth Century." *Journal of the American Musicological Society* 50.2–3 (1997), 387–420.

Bowman, Wayne. "The Values of Musical 'Formalism.'" *Journal of Aesthetic Education* 25.3 (1991), 41–59.

Budd, Malcolm. "Hanslick, Eduard." In *A Companion to Aesthetics*, 2nd ed., ed. David Cooper, Stephen Davies, Kathleen Higgins, Robert Hopkins, and Robert Stecker. Oxford: Blackwell Reference, 2009, 314–15.

Budd, Malcolm. "The Repudiation of Emotion: Hanslick on Music." In *Music and the Emotions: The Philosophical Theories*. New York: Routledge, 1985, 16–36.

Bujić, Bojan, ed. *Music in European Thought 1851–1912*. Cambridge: Cambridge University Press, 1988, 7–39.

Burford, Mark. "Hanslick's Idealist Materialism." *19th-Century Music* 30.2 (2006), 166–81.

Carpenter, Patricia. "Musical Form and Musical Idea: Reflections on a Theme of Schoenberg, Hanslick and Kant." In *Music and Civilization: Essays in Honor of Paul Henry Lang*, ed. Christopher Hatch, Maria Maniates, and Edmond Strainshamps. New York: Norton, 1984, 394–427.

Dahlhaus, Carl. *Esthetics of Music*, trans. William Austin. Cambridge: Cambridge University Press, 1982, 52–57.

Dahlhaus, Carl. *The Idea of Absolute Music*, trans. Roger Lustig. Chicago: University of Chicago Press, 1989, 26–29, 108–13.

Davies, Stephen. *Musical Meaning and Expression*. Ithaca, NY: Cornell University Press 1997, chapter 5.

Deas, Stewart. *In Defence of Hanslick*, 2nd ed. Farnborough, UK: Gregg International Publishers, 1972.

Epperson, Gordon. *The Musical Symbol: An Exploration in Aesthetics*. Ames: Iowa State University Press, 1967, chapter 5.

Gay, Peter. "For Beckmesser: Eduard Hanslick, Victim and Prophet." In *From Parnassus: Essays in Honor of Jacques Barzun*, ed. William Keylor and Dora Weiner. New York: Harper & Row, 1976, 42–54; rep. in *Freud, Jews, and Other Germans: Masters and Victims in Modernist Culture*. New York: Oxford University Press, 1978, 255–77.

Goehr, Lydia. "'Doppelbewegung': The Musical Movement of Philosophy and the Philosophical Movement of Music." In *Sound Figures of Modernity: German Music and Philosophy*, ed. Jost Hermann and Gerhard Richter. Madison: University of Wisconsin Press, 2006, 19–63; rep. in *Elective Affinities: Musical Essays on the History of Aesthetic Theory*. New York: Columbia University Press, 2008, 1–44.

Goehr, Lydia. *The Quest for Voice: On Music, Politics, and the Limits of Philosophy. The 1997 Ernest Bloch Lectures*. New York: Oxford University Press, 1998, chapters 2.3 and 3.2.

Grey, Thomas. "Hanslick." In *The Routledge Companion to Philosophy and Music*, ed. Theodore Gracyk and Andrew Kania. New York: Routledge, 2011, 360–70.

Grey, Thomas. *Wagner's Musical Prose: Text and Contexts*. Cambridge: Cambridge University Press, 1995, chapter 1.

Grimes, Nicole, Donovan, Siobhán, and Marx, Wolfgang, eds. *Rethinking Hanslick: Music, Formalism, and Expression*. Rochester, NY: University of Rochester Press, 2013.

Hamilton, Andy. *Aesthetics and Music*. New York: Continuum Books, 2007, chapter 3.

Hirt, Katherine. *When Machines Play Chopin: Musical Spirit and Automation in Nineteenth-Century German Literature.* New York: de Gruyter, 2010, chapter 3.

Karnes, Kevin. *Music, Criticism, and the Challenge of History: Shaping Modern Musical Thought in Late Nineteenth-Century Vienna.* New York: Oxford University Press, 2008, chapter 1.

Kivy, Peter. *Antithetical Arts: On the Ancient Quarrel Between Literature and Music.* Oxford: Clarendon, 2009, chapter 3.

Kivy, Peter. *Introduction to a Philosophy of Music.* Oxford: Clarendon, 2002, chapters 2 and 4.

Kivy, Peter. "On Hanslick's Inconsistency." In *New Essays on Musical Understanding.* Oxford: Clarendon, 2001, 39–43.

Kivy, Peter. "Something I've Always Wanted to Know About Hanslick." *Journal of Aesthetics and Art Criticism* 46.3 (1988), 413–17; rep. in *The Fine Art of Repetition: Essays in the Philosophy of Music.* Cambridge: Cambridge University Press, 1993, 265–75.

Kivy, Peter. "What Was Hanslick Denying?" *Journal of Musicology* 8.1 (1990), 3–18, rep. in *The Fine Art of Repetition: Essays in the Philosophy of Music.* Cambridge: Cambridge University Press, 1993, 276–95.

Lippman, Edward. *A History of Western Musical Aesthetics.* Lincoln: University of Nebraska Press, 1992, chapter 4.

Maus, Fred Everett. "Hanslick's Animism." *Journal of Musicology* 10.3 (1992), 273–92.

Nattiez, Jean-Jacques. "Hanslick: The Contradictions of Immanence." In *The Battle of Chronos and Orpheus: Essays in Applied Musical Semiology,* trans. Jonathan Dunsby. New York: Oxford University Press, 2004, 105–26.

Paddison, Max. "Mimesis and the Aesthetics of Musical Expression." *Music Analysis* 29.3 (2010), 126–48.

Paddison, Max. "Music as Ideal: The Aesthetics of Autonomy." In *The Cambridge History of Nineteenth-Century Music,* ed. Jim Samson. Cambridge: Cambridge University Press, 2002, 318–42.

Payzant, Geoffrey. "Eduard Hanslick and Bernhard Gutt." *The Music Review* 50 (1989), 124–33.

Payzant, Geoffrey. "Eduard Hanslick and the 'geistreich' Dr. Alfred Julius Becher." *The Music Review* 44 (1983), 104–15.

Payzant, Geoffrey. *Eduard Hanslick and Ritter Berlioz in Prague: A Documentary Narrative.* Calgary, Canada: University of Calgary Press, 1991.

Payzant, Geoffrey. "Eduard Hanslick's 'Vom Musikalisch-Schönen': A Pre-Publication Excerpt." *The Music Review* 46 (1985), 179–85.

Payzant, Geoffrey. "Hanslick, Heinse and the 'Moral' Effects of Music." *The Music Review* 49.2 (1988), 126–33; rep. in *The Romantic Tradition: German*

Literature and Music in the Nineteenth Century, ed. Gerald Chapple, Frederick Hall, and Hans Schulte. New York: University Press of America 1992, 79–92.

Payzant, Geoffrey. "Hanslick on Music as Product of Feeling." *Journal of Musicological Research* 9.2–3 (1989), 133–45.

Payzant, Geoffrey. *Hanslick on the Musically Beautiful: Sixteen Lectures on the Musical Aesthetics of Eduard Hanslick*. Christchurch, New Zealand: Cybereditions, 2002.

Payzant, Geoffrey. "Hanslick, Sams, Gay, and 'Tönend Bewegte Formen.'" *Journal of Aesthetics and Art Criticism* 40.1 (1981), 41–48.

Pederson, Sanna. "Defining the Term 'Absolute Music' Historically." *Music & Letters* 90.2 (2009), 240–62.

Rothfarb, Lee. "Hermeneutics and Energetics: Analytical Alternatives in the Early 1900s." *Journal of Music Theory* 36.1 (1992), 43–68.

Rothfarb, Lee. "Nineteenth-Century Fortunes of Musical Formalism." *Journal of Music Theory* 55.2 (2011), 167–220.

Sams, Eric. "Eduard Hanslick, 1825–1904: The Perfect Anti-Wagnerite." *The Musical Times* 116 (1975), 867–868.

Sharpe, Robert. *Philosophy of Music: An Introduction*. Chesham, UK: Acumen Publishing 2004, chapter 1.

Srećković, Sanja. "Eduard Hanslick's Formalism and His Most Influential Contemporary Critics." *Belgrade Philosophical Annual* 28 (2014), 113–34.

Supičić, Ivo. "Expression and Meaning in Music." *International Review of the Aesthetics and Sociology of Music* 2.2 (1971), 193–212.

Titus, Barbara. "The Quest for Spiritualized Form: (Re)positioning Eduard Hanslick." *Acta Musicologica* 80.1 (2008), 67–98.

Yanal, Robert. "Hanslick's Third Thesis." *British Journal of Aesthetics* 46.3 (2006), 259–66.

Yoshida, Hiroshi. "Eduard Hanslick and the Idea of 'Public' in Musical Culture: Towards a Socio-Political Context of Formalistic Aesthetics." *International Review of the Aesthetics and Sociology of Music* 32.2 (2001), 179–99.

Zangwill, Nick. "Against Emotion: Hanslick Was Right About Music." *British Journal of Aesthetics* 44.1 (2004), 29–43.

Zangwill, Nick. *Music and Aesthetic Reality: Formalism and the Limits of Description*. New York: Routledge, 2015.

Zangwill, Nick. "Re-Centering Musicology and the Philosophy of Music." *Journal of Aesthetics and Phenomenology* 1.2 (2014), 231–40.

INDEX

absolute music, 24
aesthetics, xxxi, xxxiv
  of autonomy and heteronomy,
    xxxiii–xxxiv
  and beauty, xxxv, lxxxvi
  and enjoyment, as a product of
    intellectual activity, 89
  and formalism, lvi
  and nature, 94
  perception, 91
  and physiology, xlix
  psychology of, xlix
  "specifically musical," the, lxxxv
  theory, xliii, xliv (see also *Geist*)
affect, xlix–l
André, Anton, 12
architectonic, 57, 67, 113
architecture, and music, 7, 42
  and nature, 102
Aristophanes, 93
Arnaud, Abbé François, 35
art criticism, 2–3
art, diversity of content and
    embodiment of beauty, 14
  philosophy of, xxxi–xxxii
artifactual music, xxxv, 96, 98
Auber, Daniel, 23, 47–48
Austria, Carinthia, xv, xvi
  Klagenfurt, xv, xvi, xix, lxi

revolution, lviii, lxiii
state philosophy and high school
  curriculum, lx, lxii–lxiv
Autodidaktus, Amadeus, 13

Bach, J. S., xxxviii, xxxix, 24n9, 33,
  54, 56, 57
  Christmas Oratorio, 29
  Well-Tempered Clavier, 22–23
Baumgarten, Alexander, xxxi
Bayreuth, xxiii
beauty, xxxvi–xxxvii, 1–4. *See also*
  aesthetics
  artifactual, xxxv
  natural, xxxv, 91, 101, 102, 103, 104,
    105, 111
Becher, Alfred Julius, lxiii, 62n16
Beethoven, Ludwig van, xxxviii, 8, 9, 23,
  54, 85, 115
  incidental music, *Egmont*, Op. 84,
    103–105
  overtures, 51
  overture no. 3 in C major, Op. 72b,
    Leonore, 114
  overture, *Coriolanus*, Op. 62, 49
  Piano Fantasy, Op. 80, 53
  piano sonata no. 26 in E-flat major,
    Op. 81, 54n11
  Prometheus, Op. 43, 20–22, 105

Beethoven, Ludwig van (*cont.*)
  quartet in F major Op.18 no. 1, 54n11
  symphonies, 56, 61n16, 105
  symphony no. 4 in B-flat major,
    Op. 60, 112
Bellini, Fermo, 13
Bellini, Vincenzo, *La sonnambula*, 28
Berlioz, Hector, 50, 53
  King Lear, 104
birdsong, as music, 99–100
Blaukopf, Kurt, lxviii
Böcklin, Franz Friedrich Siegmund
    August von, *Fragmente zur
    höheren Musik*, 79n17
Böhm, Johann Wilhelm, 12
Bolzano, Bernard, lxv–lxxii
Brahms, Johannes, xxxviii
Breakspeare, Eustace, xxvi

Caroline of Hannover, Princess-Elect, 29
Chopin, Frédéric, 23, 57, 98
Cohen, Gustav, xxv, xxxv, xli, xliii, xlviii
color and form in music, 42, 112
composer, the, xlv–xlvi, lviii, 17, 34, 48,
    50, 55, 63–66, 79, 103, 110, 115
composition
  changing appreciation of, lx
  emotive elements in, xlvi, xlvii, xlviii
  and imagination, 43
  nature of melody and harmony in, 49
  regularity and symmetry of, 57
  style in, 66
  women and, 64–65

Dahlhaus, Carl, xviin9
dance, 34
Deaville, James, xxv, xxvii
Dommer, Arrey von, 13
Donizetti, Domenico Gaetano, 23, 28
  Fausta Overture, 114
Du Bois-Reymond, Emil, 78
Dwight's Journal of Music, xxv, xxvi, xxvii

Eitelberger, Rudolf von, lxivn26
emotional effect, mutability of, 9
Engel, Johann Jakob, 12, 72

English analytic tradition, xlviii
Euripides, *Orestes*, 109–110

feelings (*Empfindung*), lvii, 1, 4–5, 7–8,
    9, 30–31, 81–82
  diversity of, in music, 14
  as effect, 84
  as neural stimuli, 85
  properties of, 18
  specific feelings in music, 15–16
Florian, Jean Pierre Claris de, *William
    Tell*, 111
Flotow, Friedrich, 23
folksong, 103
Forkel, Johann Nikolaus, 11, 66n4

Geibel, Emanuel, lxxxv
Geist, lix, xlv, lxix–lxx
Gerhardus, Dietfried, lxix
German Idealism, liv, lxi, lxiii, lxv
German Romanticism, lvi
Gervinus, Georg Gottfried, 24n9
Gluck, Christoph Willibald, 35–36
  Alceste, 25n10
  Armida, 29
  Iphegenia in Tauris, 36, 110
  Orfeo ed Euridice, 26–27
Goethe, Johann Wolfgang von, 20, 70,
    93, 111
Gracyk, Theodore, xxxvi
Greek antiquity, music in, 86–88, 95
Grillparzer, Franz, lxxxiv, 37,
    38n19, 45n7
Grimm, Jacob, 98n6

Habsburg Empire, lvi
Halévy, Fromental, 47
Hand, Ferdinand, lvi, 13, 100
Händel, George Frideric, *Messiah*, 28–29
Hanslick, Eduard, xv, xvi
  Austrian background, lxi
  contradictions in his aesthetic
    theories, lv
  habilitation petition, lxii
  in the Ministry of Education, lxi
  On the Musically Beautiful, xv, xvi

editions, xxiii, xxiv, xxxvii, lxxxiii
organization, xviii
pre-publications, xvi–xvii
title, translation of, xxxv–xxxvi
translations, xxv
role in history of aesthetics of music, liii–liv
Hanslik, Joseph Adolph (father of Eduard Hanslick), xv
harmony, as product of human intellect, 95, 97
Harpe, Jean-François de la, 35–36
Hauptmann, Moritz, 37, 38n19, 98
Haydn, Joseph, 9, 23, 56
  The Creation, 105
  The Seasons, 105
hearing, as distinct from listening, l, 82–83
Hegel, Georg Wilhelm Friedrich, lv, lvii, lix, lxvii, lxxii, lxxxii, 5, 42, 56, 107, 109, 115
Heinse, Wilhelm, 12, 90n5
Helmholtz, Hermann von, 75, 107
Herbart, Johann Friedrich, lx–lxxii, 107
  Encyclopedia, 10–11
Hiller, Ferdinand, 24n9
Hiller, Johann Adam, 58n14
Hummel, Johann Nepomuk, 7
Huron, David, liv

imagination, 6–7, 43, 45, 63. *See also* composition
Italian (race or nation), sense of melody, 89

Jahn, Otto, 54n11, 106n12
Jomelli, Nicolò, 58n14

kaleidoscope, Hanslick's comparison of music to, xlii, 41–42
Kant, Immanuel, lv–lvii, lxi, lxiii, 107
Karnes, Kevin, lxii, lxv
Kirnberger, Johann Philipp, 12
Kivy, Peter, xxxvi
Koch, Heinrich Christoph, 12

language, relationship to music, xxxiv, 44, 56, 59–62
Laocoön, 111
Lawson, Walter, *Aesthetics of Musical Art*, xxvi
Lenz, Wilhelm von, 55n11
Leppert, Richard, xxxiii
Lessing, Gotthold Ephraim, 111, 115
Lichtenthal, Peter, 72
Liszt, Franz, 50, 53
Lobe, Johann Christian, 54n11
Lotze, Rudolph Hermann, *Medicinische Psychologie*, 77n15, 107

Marienbad, 70
Marmontel, Jean-François, 35
Marpurg, Friedrich Wilhelm, 11
Marx, Adolph Bernhard, 54n11
mathematics, relationship to music and the arts, xxxiv, 57–59, 100
Mattheson, Johann, 11
  Der Vollkommene Kapellmeister, 31n13, 78
McClary, Susan, xxxiii
McColl, Sandra, xxxvii
melody, absent from nature, 95
  in composition, xlvi
  fundamental form of musical beauty, 40–41
Mendelssohn, Felix, 23, 47–48
  Die schöne Melusina, Op. 32, 104
  Hebrides Overture, Op. 26, 49, 114
Meyerbeer, Giacomo, 28
Michaelis, Christian Friedrich, lv, 11
Mosel, Ignaz Franz von, 11
motion, as unique to music, 19
Mozart, Wolfgang Amadeus, xxxviii, 7, 8, 9, 23, 24n9, 34n15, 37n19, 54, 56, 115
  Don Giovanni, overture, 51–52
  The Magic Flute, 28
music, aesthetic strength versus physical impact, 80
  as art with ability to evoke affect, 6
  contemplative response to, 82
  content and substance, 108, 114, 116

music, aesthetic strength versus
physical impact (*cont.*)
versus form, 111–113
distinct from isolated sonic effects, 72
as immediate stimulus, 69
as intellectual art, 46, 70
and intention, 52
as language, 61–62
as median between composer and
listener, 63
pleasure in music, 44–45, 51
primal element of, 40
representing abstract concepts, 18–19
rhythm in, 40–41
scientific development of, 81
subject matter, 108
and text, 32–34
therapy, 71–76, 78

nature, relation of arts to, 94, 100
Neidhardt, Johann Georg, 11
northern races, intellectual appreciation
of complexity, 89

Oehlenschläger, Adam, 93
Oersted, Hans Christian, 57, 59, 71
Oulibicheff, Alexander, 51–52

painting, 101, 108
Pall Mall Gazette, xxvi
passive receptivity to music, 81
Payzant, Geoffrey, xvii, xxiv, xxviii, xxxv,
xxxix, xli, xlii, xliv, lv, lix, lxvii,
2n1, 3n3, 24n8
performance, as mechanism to express
or destroy beauty, 68–69
Piccini, Cristiano, 35
Pierer, Heinrich August, 12
Pleasants, Henry, xxxvi
Poetry, 2, 14–15, 18, 25n10, 25–26,
45n7, 101–102, 111
Pole, William, xxvii
Popper, Karl, lxix–lxx
Porta, Baptista, 72n8
Prague, lxi, lxv, lxxi
Proch, Heinrich, *Alphorn*, Op. 18, 28

Purkinje, Jan Evangelista, 77
Püttlingen, Vesque von, xvi
Pythagoras, 71–72

Rameau, Jean-Philippe, 61
recitative, and psychic states, 33
rhythm, 41, 47, 49, 50, 85, 86
large and small-scale, 40
in nature, 96
Riehl, Wilhelm Heinrich, 57n13
Rochlitz, Johann Friedrich, 9n9
Rolle, Christian, 65
Rosenkranz, Karl, *Aesthetics of the
Ugly*, xxxii
Rossini, Gioachino, lix, 28, 37n19, 55
"O Mathilda," 49
Rousseau, Jean-Jacques, 26, 61, 107

Schäfke, Rudolf, lv, lxxin43
Schelling, Friedrich Wilhelm Joseph
von, 89
Schiller, Friedrich, *William Tell*, 111
Schilling, Gustav, 12
Schindler, Anton, 54n11
Schopenhauer, Arthur, lv
Schubart, Christian Friedrich Daniel, 20,
58n14, 65
Schumann, Robert, xxxviii, 2n2, 23, 54
Schwind, Moritz von, 53
science, Hanslick and, li
sculpture, and nature, 101
Seidl, Arthur, *On the Musically
Sublime*, xxxii
sensuous factor in music, 70
Shakespeare, William, tragedy, 7
Henry IV, 91–92
King Lear, 62n16
The Merchant of Venice, 92
Romeo and Juliet, 54n11
The Tempest, 54n11
Twelfth Night, 82
sonata form, xxxviii, 53
Spitta, Philipp, 23n7
Spohr, Louis, 47–48, 58n14
Consecration of Tones, 105
Spontini, Gaspare, lviii, 55, 58n14

Stamitz, Johann, 65
Strauß, David Friedrich, 42, 62n16
Strauß, Dietmar, xvi, xvii, xix, xlvii
Strauss, Johann, 92
Suard, Jean-Baptiste-Antoine, 35
Sulzer, Johann Georg, xlix, 12, 72
    significance in music, 20
    symphony, form and psychic states, 53
symmetry, symmetrical, xxxiv, 21, 40,
    43, 57, 113
Szymanowska, Maria, 70

Thayer, Alexander Wheelock, 66n4
theme, xxxviii, xxxix, xlvi, 46, 47, 48, 51,
    57, 106, 113, 115
    as musical microcosm, 112, 114
Thiersch, Friedrich, 13
Thun-Hohenstein, Leopold, lxi–lxii,
    lxivn26
Tieck, Ludwig, 28
title, translation of, xxxv–xxxvi
Tonarten, 87
Tonbildungen, xl
tone/Ton, xl, xxix, xxxix, 60
tone system, origin of, 98
    and color 19 (see also color and form
        in music)
    as found in nature, 99
    power of, 72
    succession and movement of, 84
tönend, xl–xliii, xlv, lxvi
Tonformen, Tonreihen (Hanslick's
    terminology), xl

Tonkunst, 24, 24n8
tonlich, 87
tuning, tempered, 87, 97

Uhland, Johann Ludwig, 7

Verdi, Giuseppe, 28, 51, 91
    Louise Miller, 114
Vienna, xv, xvi, lxi, 28
    Ministry of Finance, xvi
    Oesterreichische Blätter für Literatur
        und Kunst, xvi, xvii
    Wiener Zeitung, xvi
Vischer, Friedrich Theodor, xvi, lvii,
    lix, lx, lxv, lxvi, lxxi–lxxii,
    lxxxiii, 67
visual arts, 2, 14–15, 18, 41, 101, 111
vocal music, 24, 115

Wagner, Richard, xxiii, xxxii, xxxix, 13,
    24n8, 25n10, 37, 38, 61
    Lohengrin, xxiiin17
    Meistersinger, xxiii
    Tristan and Isolde, 35n15
Weber, Gottfried, 12
Weber, Carl Maria von, 8
    sonata in A-flat major, Op. 39, 9n9
Winterfeld, Carl von, 28
women as composers. See
    composition: women and

Zimmermann, Robert, xxii, lxiii,
    lxv–lxxii, 107n1